MEDITATIONS

MEDITATIONS

THE ANNOTATED EDITION

MARCUS AURELIUS

Translated, Introduced, and Edited by

ROBIN WATERFIELD

BASIC BOOKS

New York

Basic Books
Hachette Book Group
1290 Avenue of the Americas, New York, NY 10104
www.basicbooks.com

Printed in the United States of America

First Edition: April 2021

Published by Basic Books, an imprint of Perseus Books, LLC, a subsidiary of Hachette Book Group, Inc. The Basic Books name and logo is a trademark of the Hachette Book Group.

The Hachette Speakers Bureau provides a wide range of authors for speaking events. To find out more, go to www.hachettespeakersbureau.com or call (866) 376-6591.

The publisher is not responsible for websites (or their content) that are not owned by the publisher.

Print book interior design by Jeff Williams.

Library of Congress Cataloging-in-Publication Data

Names: Marcus Aurelius, Emperor of Rome, 121–180, author. | Waterfield, Robin, 1952– translator.
Title: Meditations / Marcus Aurelius; translated, introduced and edited by Robin Waterfield.
Other titles: Meditations. English
Description: Annotated edition. | New York: Basic Books, [2021] | Includes bibliographical references.
Identifiers: LCCN 2020046877 | ISBN 9781541673854 (hardcover) | ISBN 9781541675605 (ebook)
Subjects: LCSH: Ethics. | Stoics. | Life.
Classification: LCC B580 .H3 M3713 2021 | DDC 188—dc23

LC record available at https://lccn.loc.gov/2020046877

ISBNs: 978-1-5416-7385-4 (hardcover), 978-1-5416-7560-5 (ebook)

LSC-H

Printing 5, 2021

FOR JULIAN AND KATHERINE

CONTENTS

PREFACE

Marcus Aurelius's *Meditations* is high on the list of the most famous and widely read works of philosophy in the world. It has often been translated into English, but the Greek in which Marcus wrote is frequently so difficult that there is always room for another version. The justification of this book, however, is not just an improved translation but an increased degree of annotation. The intention of the Introduction and the notes is that they should deepen anyone's understanding of Marcus's work while falling short of hardcore philosophical commentary. The Introduction covers general issues that illuminate the book as a whole, and I wrote notes wherever I felt that Marcus's meaning would not be immediately clear to at least some readers. So the notes serve, as it were, the short-term function of explaining passages as they are read, whereas the Introduction has a more general purpose.

Stoicism, an ancient philosophical system, has been rediscovered in recent years, and many thousands of people around the world consider themselves Stoics and try to put it into practice. My acquaintance with this Modern Stoicism is minimal, and I have deliberately kept it so because I want to try to understand Marcus on his own terms and in his own day. But *Meditations* is a core text for Modern Stoics, and in a sense they are exactly the kind of reader for whom the book is intended.

I would like to thank James Romm for launching me on this project, and, at Basic Books, Dan Gerstle for commissioning the book, Claire Potter for seeing it through, and Alex Colston and Christina Palaia for their thorough and very helpful editorial work. David Fideler (stoicinsights.com) was supportive in various ways, not least by sharing some of his knowledge of Seneca with me. John Sellars graciously sent me a prepublication copy of his *Marcus Aurelius*. Above all I am grateful to friends new and old: my wife, Kathryn, was as usual my first reader, and then Brad Inwood and John Sellars, two of the world's leading interpreters of Stoicism, commented on the finished typescript. I took note of all their suggestions for improvement.

INTRODUCTION

The famous Aurelian Column, a hundred feet high and still standing in Rome, was erected not long after the death of Marcus Aurelius to commemorate his military victories on the Danube in the early 170s. A frieze of relief sculptures spirals up its outer face, divisible into 116 scenes that reflect the chronological order of the so-called Marcomannic Wars the Romans fought against a number of Germanic peoples, including the Marcomanni. Marcus can be seen in about half of the scenes. Two sections depict famous "miracles." On one occasion, a heavy downpour of rain confounded the enemy, while a battalion of surrounded Roman soldiers was refreshed and able to escape; on another, a Roman fortress was under siege, but the soldiers were saved when lightning destroyed one of the enemy's siege engines.

Many sections of the frieze are taken up with gruesome scenes, not just of murderous battles but of actions that would today be classified as war crimes: prisoners being decapitated,

Marcus receiving severed heads, the massacre of civilians and unarmed opponents, the abduction of women, the devastation of villages, an unarmed woman being stabbed by a Roman soldier. These scenes undoubtedly reflect the ferocity of the war, and the historian Cassius Dio, writing early in the third century, informs us that Marcus himself aimed to annihilate at least one of the enemy peoples and that he offered a generous bounty to anyone who would bring him one of their leaders, or his head.[1]

Yet the Marcus of *Meditations* is regarded as a man of peace, a thoughtful philosopher offering sage advice for daily living and self-improvement. The moral to be drawn from this contrast is the one Marcus frequently stresses in his writing: everyone, even or especially an emperor, has to play the hand he has been dealt. As his friend and teacher Marcus Cornelius Fronto warned him early in his reign: "Even if you succeed in attaining the wisdom of Cleanthes or Zeno, yet against your will you must put on the purple cloak, not the philosopher's tunic of coarse wool."[2] And the emperor's purple cloak often had to be exchanged for armor. Marcus might have preferred to be a private individual with time for reading and making progress on the Stoic path rather than an emperor, but as a Stoic, he had to accept and make the best use of the lot that fate had handed him.

Marcus is famous for the conjunction of imperial power and philosophy and has even been called a philosopher-king, the kind of enlightened ruler that Plato famously held out as

---

1. Cassius Dio, *Roman History* 72.13–14.

2. Fronto, *De eloquentia* 1.12 (Haines II.65).

an ideal.[3] But this is wrong on two counts. First, as is clear from *Meditations*, Marcus felt that he fell short of being a philosopher (see entries 30 and 37 in Notebook 4 [4.30, 4.37] and entry 1 in Notebook 8 [8.1]), and second, it turns out to be a futile exercise to survey what we know of his acts as emperor and interpret them as influenced by his philosophy. No doubt Marcus tried to be guided in his enactments by philosophy—he says as much at 9.29—but on the whole the decisions he made are better seen as a continuation of the work of his predecessors than as attempts to branch out in a new, philosophically inspired direction.[4] More recent leaders such as Bill Clinton have admired Marcus not so much as a philosopher-king but simply as a man who recognized that he had to do his duty as emperor without letting it go to his head and without becoming a tyrant (6.30).[5] He was by far the wealthiest and most powerful man in the world, but self-discipline and philosophy kept him from abusing his position.

Meditations reveals a man who longed to do good and to love all humanity, while the Aurelian Column shows how his status as emperor impeded his attainment of these goals. Hence, at the beginning of entry 10.9 Marcus seems to acknowledge that

---

3. A recent advocate of this view is W. Desmond, *Philosopher-Kings of Antiquity* (Continuum, 2011).

4. He "restored the old laws rather than introduced new ones" (*Historia Augusta: Marcus* 12.1). See G. Stanton, "Marcus Aurelius, Emperor and Philosopher," *Historia* 18 (1969): 570–587.

5. See G. Wills, "Bill and the Emperor," *New York Review of Books*, October 8, 1998.

war was an impediment to the realization of his less worldly hopes. By the same token, the tone of *Meditations* is that of an aspirant, someone who urgently wants to do better and to live as a philosopher, but who is constantly thwarted by events and by his own weakness. But this is why *Meditations* is still so widely read, because no one is perfect and we recognize ourselves in Marcus's flaws and aspirations.

MARCUS'S ROUTE
TO THE IMPERIAL THRONE

Marcus Aurelius Antoninus, emperor of Rome from March 7, 161, until his death on March 17, 180, was born Marcus Annius Verus in Rome on April 26, 121, during the reign of the emperor Hadrian.[6] His parents were extremely wealthy and were close to the imperial court. His father died when Marcus was still a child, and Marcus was brought up by his grandfather, an intimate of the emperor. He received the typical education of a well-born young Roman, and his privileged further education, under no fewer than eighteen tutors, consisted largely of rhetoric and

---

6. The historical sources for Marcus's reign are poor. They are chiefly two: the surviving excerpts and epitomes of Cassius Dio, *Roman History* 71–72 (with occasional references in nearby books), written in the early third century; and the Lives of Marcus, Lucius Verus, and Avidius Cassius in the *Historia Augusta*, a second-rate biographical summary written perhaps late in the fourth century. Other historians, such as the Greek Herodian (writing c. 230), add further snippets of information.

philosophy. Some of the correspondence between him and one of his teachers of rhetoric, Fronto, has survived, and the letters show Marcus to have been an intense, open-hearted, bookish young man. Rhetoric was an inevitable topic of study for someone destined for public life, but philosophy was his personal choice, and he was attracted to it from an early age (1.6).

As a child, he became a favorite of Hadrian. Indicating that he was destined for a brilliant future, the emperor arranged Marcus's betrothal at the age of fifteen to the daughter of his adopted son, Lucius Aelius Caesar, the heir to the throne. Then a couple of years later, after Aelius's death from tuberculosis, Hadrian ordered his second heir, Titus Aurelius Fulvus Boionius Arrius Antoninus, the future emperor known as Antoninus Pius (whose wife was Marcus's aunt), to adopt both Marcus and Aelius's son, Lucius. Hadrian probably intended Lucius to be emperor, reserving Marcus as backup in case of Lucius's early death, but after Hadrian's death it was Marcus that Antoninus promoted over Lucius. This does not seem to have troubled Lucius, who was more devoted to partying than to administration.

The early Antonine emperors were all childless, perhaps as a matter of policy to avoid interfamilial strife; they chose their heirs by adoption instead. Antoninus Pius was emperor from 138 to 161, but he was already over fifty when he gained the throne, and it may be that Hadrian had not expected him to live long and saw him as a kind of temporary filler before Lucius (or Marcus) took up the post. As things turned out, however, the brothers-by-adoption were the heirs apparent for twenty-three years. On the night of his adoption by Antoninus, Marcus is said to have dreamed that he had shoulders of ivory, strong enough to bear the weight of his new responsibilities.[7]

Hadrian had died before Marcus's marriage to Aelius Caesar's daughter could take place, and in 145 Marcus married instead Antoninus Pius's daughter (Marcus's cousin) Annia Galeria Faustina, so that he was thoroughly embedded in the imperial household. There are wicked stories about Faustina's many affairs, but such rumors often arose about members of the imperial household, and they are probably false or exaggerated; at any rate, they clash with Marcus's brief tribute to her in 1.17. She bore him thirteen or fourteen children (including two sets of twins), though many died young, as was normal in those days, even in imperial households. On Marcus's death, five daughters remained, but only one son, the future emperor Commodus (joint emperor, 177–180; sole emperor, 180–192).

Under Hadrian and then Antoninus, Marcus was rapidly promoted through the ranks of the political hierarchy, learning the skills required to administer the city of Rome and its empire, and he succeeded Antoninus on the emperor's death of old age on March 7, 161. He shed the name "Verus"—or rather passed it on to Lucius, who became Lucius Aurelius Verus—and took "Antoninus" instead, so that he was Marcus Aurelius Antoninus. His official name was therefore Imperator Caesar Marcus Aurelius Antoninus Augustus, the sixteenth emperor of Rome. His first move was to make his brother joint emperor, and so Lucius remained until his death left Marcus as sole emperor for

---

7. *Historia Augusta: Marcus* 5.2.

the final eleven years of his reign. This was the first time there had been two emperors, but Marcus made it clear that he was senior (as Antoninus had intended), not least by having Lucius become his son-in-law by marrying his daughter Lucilla.

Marcus occupied the imperial throne for nineteen years. We know little about many aspects of his reign. He expanded the system of child support for poor families in Italy, and revived a system whereby not all court cases generated within Italy had to be heard in Rome itself. He created a new civil service department to deal especially with correspondence with the Greek east of the empire, which matched an existing department that dealt with all correspondence in Latin. He increased the juridical powers of the Senate and in general kept the senators on his side by listening to their advice and delegating some of his powers to them. He was remembered as a hard-working ruler; in Rome, he sometimes presided over the same trial for eleven or twelve days before reaching a decision. During his reign, the "soldiers' religion," the worship of Mithras, entered its heyday, but the persecution of Christians continued unabated. The followers of the "crucified sophist"[8] kept their rites secret, which always attracts rumors of malign practices, such as cannibalism and incest. Marcus revived a law whereby the fomenting of superstition was illegal, forcing Christians further underground and leading, in Lyon in 177, to the worst massacre the new religion had so far experienced.

Christians, then, had good reasons to dislike Marcus, but otherwise he was considered a good emperor. His philosophical

---

8. Lucian, *Peregrinus* 13.

aspirations were widely known, and his courtiers affected hairstyles and dress that signified a greater austerity than was to be found in, for example, Lucius's court. For much of his reign, however, Marcus's court was located not in Rome but in central Europe. For an extended period, the empire was not governed from the imperial city, because what chiefly marked Marcus's reign was warfare and pestilence.

WARFARE, PLAGUE, AND DEATH

Marcus's reign was beset by challenges. Cities flattened by earthquakes in the eastern provinces had to be rebuilt; not long after his accession, the Tiber, the river of Rome, massively overflowed its banks, causing widespread destruction of livestock, crops, and property, and spreading disease. But Marcus's main preoccupation, and the main drain on his finances, was warfare.

On Antoninus's death, trouble had erupted on the borders of the empire, and warfare against the British, some Germanic tribes in central Europe, and the Parthians in the east absorbed much of Marcus's reign. The British rebellion was quickly put down, but the Parthians were another matter. Lucius, as inexperienced in military matters as Marcus,[9] was sent east to manage the crisis. He had good advisers and generals under him, but it took several

---

9. Neither of them received the training in generalship that prospective emperors expected and needed, partly because Pius's reign had been largely peaceful and partly, perhaps, because neither of them had a strong constitution.

years, from 161 until 166, for the Parthians to be driven back from the eastern Roman provinces.

Yet the east still made trouble for Marcus. The eastern army had become so weakened by a plague (probably smallpox) that they were unable to capitalize on their victory and crush the Parthians, the perennial enemies of Rome. And then soldiers returning from the Parthian war brought the sickness back with them, and before long it had become a true pandemic, ravaging the city, the Italian countryside, and the Roman provincial armies. Marcus was forced to shelve plans to travel with Lucius to the Danube, the northern frontier of the empire, where, after many years of peace, the Marcomanni and their allies, under pressure from other Germanic peoples farther north, were crossing the Danube in large numbers, and were barely being contained by the Roman forces on the spot.

When Marcus and Lucius did finally set out, they got no farther than northeastern Italy. Their arrival there was enough to cause the Germanic tribes to pull back, but the plague—the Antonine Plague, as it is known—that was ravaging their army forced the emperors to return to Rome. On their way back in January 169, Lucius, still under forty years old, died, apparently of a stroke. His death left Marcus as sole emperor. The treasury was short of money, due in large part to the plague, and Marcus auctioned off palace treasures rather than raise taxes. By the end of the year, he had at last reached the Danube; he would not see Rome again for many years.

We can only guess what steps were taken to contain the plague. So little was known about the transmission of illness that treatment would have focused more on prayer and herbal medicine than what we today would consider effective. In some quarters, the disease was held to be divine retribution for the destruction of a temple of Apollo during the Parthian war. The crowded conditions of towns, cities, and army camps made measures such as social distancing impossible. In Rome

> corpses were carried away on carts and wagons.... The emperors enacted very strict laws on burying the dead and on tombs: building tombs at country villas was made illegal.... The plague carried off many thousands, including many eminent people. Marcus erected statues to the most prominent of them, and such was his kindness that he ordered funeral ceremonies for the common people to be held at public expense.... Marcus summoned priests from everywhere, performed foreign religious rites, and purified the city in every way.[10]

Christians were blamed for attracting the wrath of the gods to the city, and some of their leaders in Rome were executed by the city prefect, a teacher and close friend of Marcus, Junius Rusticus (1.7). No measures were effective, and the disease was basically left to run its course, causing untold misery over many years. And as I write, in the early 2020s, we are in a good position to guess at the longer-term social and economic consequences on Rome of the Antonine Plague.

---

10. *Historia Augusta: Marcus* 13.1–5.

On the Danube, the Marcomannic Wars (or the separate phases of a single war) lasted for thirteen years, from 167 to 180. This was a serious crisis for Marcus and the empire as a whole. At one point, the Marcomanni got as far as northern Italy, and other tribes took advantage of the Romans' distraction to invade the Balkan provinces, while Moors from North Africa raided Spain. But Roman forces contained these secondary invasions, leaving Marcus free to concentrate on the three main hostile peoples, the Marcomanni, the Quadi, and the Sarmatian Jazyges, a Scythian people who allied themselves with the Germanic tribes in order to attack the Romans. He was based first at Carnuntum (in modern Austria), between 169 and 172, and then at Sirmium and Viminacium (in modern Serbia).[11] It was a hard-fought war, and the first phase of it was brought to an end in 175 not by victory but by treaty, albeit one that was favorable to Rome.

The treaty was needed because Marcus was faced with a serious internal rebellion in the east, where Gaius Avidius Cassius, one of the heroes of the Parthian war and Marcus's governor of Syria, had been proclaimed emperor by the Roman forces in Syria and Egypt. Each of the provinces—the frontier provinces especially—was a center of power in its own right, because substantial armies were posted there, and Cassius's bid

---

11. All three places were in either Upper or Lower Pannonia, as the Romans called their provinces in this part of Europe.

was not unprecedented among provincial governors.[12] Marcus prepared to march east to deal with this new threat, but Cassius was assassinated by some of his senior officers before he got there. Nevertheless, Marcus carried on, taking his son, Commodus, with him, knowing that his presence in the eastern provinces, and especially the distribution of largesse, would help to calm further thoughts of rebellion.

On his way back to Rome in 176, he visited Athens, where, among other measures, he established chairs of philosophy for the four major schools: Stoics, Epicureans, Aristotelians, and Platonists. Back in Rome at the end of 176 for the first time in seven years, he celebrated his victory in the Germanic war,[13] but the situation on the Danube was deteriorating—in fact, there had never really been peace—and Marcus felt he had to return. So in 178 Marcus and Commodus, who had been formally made co-emperor in the previous year, left once again for the Danube frontier.

Marcus died, probably at Sirmium, in 180, just a few weeks short of his fifty-ninth birthday. His health had never been strong;[14] he was probably consumptive (1.17 end) and had perhaps

---

12. Cassius had a foundation of local support because he was originally from Syria. Later, Marcus had a law passed that no governor of a province should have originated in that province.

13. It was probably then that the Aurelian Column was commissioned.

14. Cassius Dio (*Roman History* 71.1.2, 71.6.3–4, 71.24.4, 71.36.3, 72.24.4, 72.36.2) mentions his physical frailties, including pains in the chest, and Marcus's extant letters to Fronto often touch on his health.

been weakened by the plague that was still ravaging the empire. But by the time of his death, the Romans were in a commanding position in the war, and one of Commodus's first acts as emperor was to bring it to a peaceful end. The settlement, which restored the Danube as the frontier, was probably not in keeping with his father's wishes, since Marcus had established a number of semipermanent camps on the far side of the river, presumably with the intention of expanding the empire in that direction, just as he would have overseen the expansion of the empire in the east if the plague had not thwarted him.[15] But little that Commodus did as emperor would have pleased his father.[16] He seems to have been as unpleasant and unstable a character as he was portrayed in the 2000 film *Gladiator*.[17] His reign was brought to an end by assassination in 192.

---

15. If imperialist expansionism seems odd in the man who wrote *Meditations*, it is worth noting Marcus's belief that the lesser are made to serve the greater (e.g., 5.30, 7.55). As a Roman, he would have tended to see any people that had not been civilized by Rome as barbarian and lesser.

16. Edward Gibbon began his world-famous, six-volume *The History of the Decline and Fall of the Roman Empire* (1776–1788) with the reign of Commodus. Cassius Dio ended his account of Marcus's reign with the remark: "Our history now descends from a kingdom of gold to one of iron and rust" (*Roman History* 72.36.4). Commodus brought to an end the previous run of five "good emperors" (as Machiavelli first called them): Nerva, Trajan, Hadrian, Antoninus Pius, Marcus Aurelius.

17. But there is no evidence for the film's notion that Commodus killed his father.

WHAT KIND OF BOOK IS *MEDITATIONS*?

The book you are holding in your hands is unique; there are no other books like it in ancient Greek or any other language. But this is not to say that it was not watered and fertilized by streams of earlier literature. There are Greek precedents for soliloquy, moral encouragement, sermons, and aphorisms, though not at book length, and Marcus was not thinking of these precedents as he wrote. The main influence on him was the Stoic practice of critical self-examination and exhortation to do better. However, if any other Stoic ever kept this kind of journal, it has not survived. This might be due to the fact that Marcus was an emperor, so that his work was considered more valuable and unusual, but we may also doubt that anyone else ever wrote such a thorough journal.

The book is unique also in that it is deeply personal. If it consisted just of philosophical reflections, it might be comparable to, for instance, Nietzsche's *Thus Spake Zarathustra*, Wittgenstein's *Notebooks*, Pascal's *Pensées*, or Gibran's *The Prophet*. Kierkegaard's journals perhaps come closest: many of the entries are as personal, reflective, and self-advisory as are Marcus's notebook entries. Marcus saw philosophy as a path of self-improvement and is concerned more or less exclusively with its impact on him personally. The book is about the divine order of the world and the part in it that human beings should play, but particularly Marcus's own role. He sometimes talks about himself in the first person, but often in the second, and the "you" he admonishes and advises is always himself. About 300 of the 488 entries refer explicitly or implicitly to him in this way, and the rest enunciate general principles or rules of life, still for himself alone. He is not telling anyone else what to do or how to live, nor is he writing a philosophical textbook. In fact, there are many indications that the book was not intended for publication, especially when he refers to people and events that no one but him could know about. Communication was not his aim in writing, and since his only audience was himself, there was no point in dissimulation. The book is utterly sincere.

Leaving aside Notebook 1, which is different in kind,[18] *Meditations* contains no references to datable events, no allusions to any of his experiences (except perhaps one, at 10.10), no mentions of scenery or places or private moments that were important to him. The things of the world are invariably mentioned in passing and with contempt. The book is focused almost entirely on his inner life, and this gives it a remarkable intensity.

Does the fact that *Meditations* was written in Greek, whereas Latin was Marcus's native and daily language, suggest that it was intended for publication? He was more or less bilingual, as all well-educated Romans were, but surely, one might think, if Marcus was talking just to himself, he would have spoken in Latin. Why, then, did he choose Greek when he came to write down his thoughts? This is less of a puzzle than it appears: Greek was still the language of philosophy, and Stoicism employed quite a few technical terms that were difficult to translate into Latin. Very few philosophers were writing in Latin. One of Marcus's

---

18. See the note at the beginning of the first notebook.

great predecessors, the Stoic Seneca the Younger (writing a little over a hundred years earlier), was a notable exception. But Marcus's chief influences were all Greek, from the early Stoics to Epictetus, the former slave who became the foremost teacher of Stoicism in the generation before him—the former slave who influenced the emperor of Rome!

But if *Meditations* as we have it was not intended for publication, might Marcus not have planned one day to polish it up, eliminate or explain the obscurities, and offer it to the general public? Many of the entries in the notebooks were written down in note form, but quite a few are more literate, and in some cases the prose flows very nicely. Are these not signs that Marcus was taking care over his writing, and what would be the point of his doing that if he did not intend others to see it?

In my opinion, the answer to these questions is a firm no. Marcus was an intelligent man and exceptionally well educated. Anyone who has written anything knows that some sentences just naturally come out well the first time. That, I am sure, is sufficient explanation for the more elegant passages of the book. Besides, what Marcus says is altogether too revealing of personal issues, such as his struggle with anger and bitterness; he also occasionally savages others, those around him in his court: they are "liars and crooks," for example (6.47). No one, and especially an emperor, whose position depended to a large extent on others' perception of him, would have shown this side of himself to other people. The book is exactly as it appears to be, an intensely private journal written for the purposes of self-analysis and self-improvement.

HOW *MEDITATIONS* REACHED
US AND GOT ITS NAME

A number of factors indicate that the notebooks were written in the last decade of Marcus's life—above all, the epigraphs that head the second and third notebooks, and Marcus's frequent anticipation of his death. Greater precision is impossible. The scholarly consensus is that the notebooks as a whole were written between 172 and 180, when Marcus died; that Notebook 1 was written between 176 and 180; and that Notebooks 2 and 3 were written between 170 and 175. At any rate, when Marcus died in 180, while out on campaign in central Europe, the notebooks were there with him.

Given the personal and private nature of the work, it is a considerable mystery how and when it became accessible to others. It might well not have survived.[19] I think we have the complete set of these notebooks (though notebooks of other kinds have been lost: 3.14), because the last entry of the final book is such a perfect ending, set down by one who knows he is about to die. The entries were probably written on parchment or vellum and sewn together into book form. Someone close to Marcus—someone who was out on campaign with him—must have preserved the notebooks on his death, by accident

---

19. Ironically, the book's survival has confounded one of Marcus's recurrent expectations. At 7.21, for instance, he says: "Soon you'll have forgotten everything; soon everyone will have forgotten you." Fortunately, the second clause was wrong.

or design, but we have no idea what happened to them over the following centuries. References to the book by authors over subsequent centuries are few and uncertain. It was being read and transcribed—for instance, someone added the reference to the Christians at 11.3—but we cannot track its fortunes. The first absolutely certain reference is when Arethas of Caesarea, a Christian bishop of the late ninth–early tenth century, discussed the book in a letter and mentioned that he had arranged for the transcribing of the old copy he had in his possession. This transcription seems to have given the book a new lease on life.

None of the earliest references to the book give it a proper title; after all, it was just a bundle of notebooks Marcus had written for himself, and he had no need to call it anything. Arethas called it "an ethical work written to and for himself," and *To Himself* is still preferred by some as a title, because that is exactly what happens: Marcus writes to and for himself. But the title *Meditations* has become canonized in the English-speaking world since its invention by Meric Casaubon when he published the first English translation in 1634.

THE STYLE OF *MEDITATIONS*

Some thoughts are developed as mini-essays, but the writing is often concise, occasionally even to the point of being no more than notes and jottings, which may be ungrammatical, carelessly phrased, or compressed to the point of obscurity. Marcus knew what he meant, but it is not always easy for us to decipher his meaning.[20] Some entries are no more than quotations or aphorisms that Marcus appreciated. Nevertheless, the writing is frequently vivid. Metaphor and imagery abound: life, for instance, is variously likened to a play, a battlefield, a journey, a torrent; the rational faculty is a refuge, a citadel, a headland standing against waves, a light that illuminates what it surveys, and even a perfect sphere; praise is "the clapping of tongues" (6.16). But humor is largely lacking; life was a serious business for Marcus. The overall tone can be melancholy, on the border between profundity and sadness, and sometimes Marcus can be jaundiced and downright

---

20. One important consequence of the occasional difficulty in detecting Marcus's train of thought is that it is not always easy to be sure how exactly to divide the entries. If two or more consecutive entries cover much the same ground, should we really be reading them as a single entry? A few entries contain disconnected thoughts: should they perhaps be separate entries? Look at 7.51, for instance, or 9.28. The early editors who divided up the entries cannot always have been true to Marcus's intentions. For the purposes of this translation, however, I have been conservative in that I have not attempted to reorganize or renumber any of the entries, but have followed the divisions found in the standard editions of Marcus's Greek, which are essentially those of Thomas Gataker in his edition of 1652.

caustic about the world and its inhabitants, though he reaches at times for a lofty irony (e.g., 11.14).[21]

A certain degree of repetition and even inconsistency is inevitable in such a work, as ideas were jotted down in no particular order. It is not necessarily the kind of book that one reads from start to finish; some prefer to dip into it, and then put it down and ponder.[22] It raises issues that strike chords with all readers—the inevitability of death, the purpose and meaning of one's existence on earth. It communicates with considerable effectiveness what it means to try to live a life based sincerely on Stoic principles. In his postface to *The Kreutzer Sonata*, Tolstoy described ideals as a light at the end of a long pole carried by oneself—never reachable, but always leading one on. Marcus's *Meditations* shows us a man striving in just such a way.

In the text as we have it, then, there are many rapid changes of topic from one entry to another, and sometimes within single entries. There is some clustering of ideas, when Marcus was preoccupied with particular issues, but the overall impression is one of randomness. Extended development of ideas is rare,

---

21. One feature of Marcus's writing that has been lost in translation is his use of diminutives. Quite often, when he refers to his body or his soul, for instance, he employs words that mean "little body" and "little soul," as a way of disparaging them and seeing them as unimportant when viewed against a universal background. This rarely works in English.

22. This has led to a certain degree of repetition in the notes I have written. A reader who chooses to start by dipping into Notebook 5, say, will have missed the earlier notes, but still needs guidance.

since, to repeat, Marcus was writing for himself alone and had no need to convince himself of what he already believed. But these features, puzzling as they occasionally may be to the reader, are precisely those that can reassure us that we are reading the notebooks more or less as Marcus left them. An editor would no doubt have imposed more order on it.[23]

The repetitiousness of the text—the way that Marcus comes back again and again to the same core topics—is not just a result of Marcus's jotting ideas down as they occurred to him over the course of many years. It is also an essential feature of this kind of writing. Writing things down is always a good way to fix them in your mind, and that is what Marcus was doing. Writing them down again and again, a practice encouraged within Stoicism, fixes them even better.[24] In an exercise he learned from Epictetus, Marcus frequently urges himself to have his core precepts

---

23. The attempt has been made, more than once, to reorganize the text according to topic.

24. In fact, at *Discourses* 2.1.32–33, Epictetus projects the practice back onto Socrates. Marcus's self-admonishment is truly Stoic because one of the most famous Stoic paradoxes was that one was either a sage, whose every action was virtuous, or as imperfect as the worst criminal. Although an aspirant to sagehood could make progress, until actually achieving enlightenment that person was not virtuous. The Roman Stoics of the imperial era were less severe on themselves than this and allowed degrees of goodness and badness in people, but they still felt, as Seneca memorably put it: "I am far from being even a tolerable human being, let alone a perfect one" (*Letters* 57.3). So Marcus urges himself to make progress toward sagehood, to stop being one of the *phauloi*, as the Stoics called them, the "base" or "iniquitous" people.

readily available for consultation, and to keep them pithy and memorable, so that they can strike his mind with their original force. The single-sentence entries in *Meditations*, such as 6.54, 7.29, 9.7, and 9.20, are good examples.

This is what really explains the stylistic details of *Meditations*: the great majority of entries, especially the brief ones, are, above all, Marcus's way of "dyeing his mind" (5.16) with the ideas and teachings that could help him be a better person and a better emperor. The entries are fragments of a kind of dialogue between teacher and pupil, where Marcus simultaneously plays both parts. For Marcus, the notebooks and their entries had a therapeutic aim: to reinforce and revive, if necessary, the moral precepts he had come to accept as true, as a way of helping him put them into practice. Each entry is, as it were, a dose of therapeutic medicine.

MARCUS AND STOICISM

Stoicism is named after the Painted Stoa of Athens—a large colonnade in the Agora where, at the end of the fourth and beginning of the third century BCE, the founder of the school, Zeno of Citium (in Cyprus, modern Larnaka), used to meet his students and discourse on philosophy. A couple of centuries later, Stoicism was taken up by members of the educated and ruling classes of Rome from the end of the Republic and into the imperial era. Many preferred its rival, Epicureanism, but the toughness of Stoic moral discipline appealed to the robust and militaristic Roman ethos, and it allowed and even encouraged a man to pursue a public career, as many upper-class Romans expected to. A Stoic had, above all, a duty to himself to make himself a man of virtue, but an aspect of that was being good to others, and this might well entail a public career.[25]

This was certainly one reason why Marcus was attracted to Stoicism: it allowed him to try to reconcile his twin aims of being a good man and a good emperor. But he was not drawn to it because he was emperor any more than Epictetus was drawn to it because he was a slave. In both cases, it would be closer to the mark to say they found Stoicism *despite* their statuses. It was Stoicism that had the potential to answer their most personal and profound questions; for them, it was Stoicism, just as for others it is Christianity, Tibetan Buddhism, humanism, or whatever. Slaves and emperors are equal if they can both accept the roles destiny has assigned them and do the best they can within those roles, especially toward their fellow men.

However, in Marcus's time, there was no Stoic school as such—no particular teacher recognized as the head of the school, and no particular city where one went to study this brand of philosophy—so his education in Stoicism was somewhat haphazard. His commitment to Stoic principles is clear, but he was

---

25. Other schools also tolerated a public career, but Epicureanism counseled withdrawal from the hubbub of the world: "Live unknown" was its motto. Stoics saw a person's responsibilities in terms of ever-increasing concentric circles: from preservation of the self to care for family, for extended family, for fellow citizens, for fellow countrymen, and finally for the whole human race.

an amateur philosopher.[26] He was introduced to it in his youth by Rusticus and others (1.6–1.9), but when his formal education was over, although he was able to attend occasional lectures,[27] he had to rely largely on reading[28] and regularly checking that he was on what he considered the true path. As I have said, this habit of self-checking and self-admonishment helps to explain the nature of many of the entries in *Meditations*.

Although the Stoic school was not united on every point of philosophy, there was enough of a common core to legitimate talk of orthodoxy and heterodoxy. Marcus was basically an orthodox Stoic,[29] and it is impossible to understand where he is

---

26. See J.-B. Gourinat, "Was Marcus Aurelius a Philosopher?" in *Meditations and Representations: The Philosopher and Emperor Marcus Aurelius in an Interdisciplinary Light*, ed. M. van Ackeren and J. Opsomer (Reichert, 2012), 65–85.

27. Philostratus, *Lives of the Sophists* 557.

28. All the works of the early Stoics are lost to us (the first complete texts are by Seneca, writing in the first century CE), but they were presumably available to Marcus. We now have only fragmentary remains.

29. The considerable scholarly debate about the degree of Marcus's borrowings from other schools of thought can be followed up by means of works listed in the Recommended Reading section at the back of this book.

coming from without some knowledge of Stoicism.[30] This is not to deny that many readers profit from the book without knowing much about Stoicism because Marcus addresses general life issues that strike chords with any reader. But Marcus's own mindset and frame of reference were basically Stoic, and the book takes Stoic principles for granted on every page. He is sometimes charged with holding a Platonic dualism between mind and body (see, e.g., 3.6, 3.17, 5.26, 6.32, 10.1, 11.3), but in fact this too is fully Stoic, since for the Stoics air and fire, the constituents of the soul, are active elements, and water and earth, the constituents of the body, are passive elements. The Platonic distinction depends on the difference between physical matter and an immaterial soul, but, as far as we can tell, Marcus never thinks of the soul as immaterial.

The Stoics divided philosophy into three branches: logic, physics, and ethics. Logic covered not only the rules of correct argumentation, but also grammar, linguistics, rhetorical theory, epistemology, and all the tools that might be needed to discover the truth of any matter. Physics was concerned with the nature of the world and the laws that govern it, and so included ontology and theology as well as what we would recognize as physics, astronomy, and cosmology. Ethics was concerned with how to

---

30. Nevertheless, some readers might like to start with Notebook 5, which is on the whole perfectly accessible without any prior knowledge of Stoicism. In Notebook 1, he recognizes his debt to his family and teachers for everyday moral lessons as well as specifically Stoic ones, but none of the everyday lessons is incompatible with Stoicism.

achieve happiness, or how to live a fulfilled and flourishing life as a human being. A Stoic sage was supposed to be fully expert in all three aspects.

Some Stoics held that the three branches were of equal importance, but others, while acknowledging their inter-dependence, held that logic and physics were subordinate to ethics. They came up with nice images to express this.[31] If logic is the wall and physics the orchard protected by the wall, ethics is the fruit. Or, if logic is the human skeleton and muscles and physics the flesh and blood, ethics is the soul. It is clear that Marcus belonged to this latter group. He confesses to being no expert at logic and physics (1.17 end, 8.1)[32] but regarded that as no impediment to being a good person (7.67). The whole tone of *Meditations* is ethical in that it displays Marcus's personal quest for virtue.

Marcus was certainly familiar with aspects of physics and logic, enough to ground and give a Stoic flavor to his ethics,[33] but it is also clear that he was not very interested in them in themselves. He was more interested in their implications for the daily practice of self-improvement. There are no extended

---

31. Diogenes Laertius, *Lives of the Eminent Philosophers* 7.40.

32. Early in 9.9 he essays a physical explanation of inflammability, but it is rather clumsy.

33. See Gill, *Meditations 1–6*, Introduction; Sellars, *Marcus Aurelius*. So, for instance, Marcus frequently remarks on how the four elements recognized by Stoicism (earth, water, air, fire) are constantly being recycled by the death and disintegration of things.

discussions of logical or physical matters in *Meditations*, as there occasionally are of ethical matters. You can believe in the perfection of the universe, say, and the importance of that for you personally, without holding a theory about how exactly it came to be so. You trust the greater intellects that have handed down the idea. At 10.16, he scorns philosophizing even about ethical matters. The notebooks include no extended discussions even of Stoic moral psychology, although that was closer to Marcus's immediate interests.

It is important to be aware of another general feature of the kind of philosophy that attracted Marcus. Ancient philosophy was considerably different from its modern cousin. Modern philosophy is pursued in classrooms, in seminars, and through the written word, and much of it consists of analyzing abstract concepts and arguments, but much ancient philosophy, and especially Marcus's kind of Stoicism, was philosophy to live by and practice daily. It was supposed to purge your base attachments and make you a better person, and the ideal was to be a master of this art, a Stoic sage.[34] The therapeutic purpose of philosophy attracted Marcus.[35] He describes philosophy as a

---

34. On the Stoic sage, see Sellars, *Stoicism*, 36–41, and for a book-length treatment, R. Brouwer, *The Stoic Sage: The Early Stoics on Wisdom, Sagehood and Socrates* (Cambridge University Press, 2014).

35. On philosophy as therapy, see Hadot, *What Is Ancient Philosophy?*, and Nussbaum, *Therapy*. The therapeutic aspect constituted mainstream Stoicism in the imperial period, and all Marcus's immediate predecessors—Musonius Rufus, Seneca, and Epictetus—were on the same page in this respect.

safe escort and a haven (2.17, 4.3), and as therapy and a source of personal relief (3.13, 5.9, 6.12).

Over the centuries before Marcus's time, philosophy had in effect gone in two directions. High philosophy, as we may call it, was the impersonal presentation of often very subtle ideas and arguments; some of the work of the Stoics, for instance, on logic and epistemology is as challenging as high philosophical work of any era. Low philosophy, on the other hand, was the attempt to make philosophy practical and accessible to the common man and woman. Hence professional philosophers generally presented a public image that stressed poverty, or at least frugality, as a way of advertising the success of their teaching: they had moved beyond the superficial values of the world, and they could teach others to do so as well. The pupils they wanted were those who already felt somewhat at odds with the world.[36] To judge by Marcus's frequent complaints in *Meditations* about the world and the people around him, he was a perfect candidate.

Marcus was drawn to Stoicism by its austerity (1.6) and by the quality he perceived in those who professed themselves Stoics (1.6–1.9), but an aspect of Stoicism to which he frequently returns, especially when contrasting it with Epicureanism, is the orderliness of its universe. Not only does everything have its place in the hierarchical order of things, but also the whole

---

36. As Epictetus put it: "The starting point of philosophy . . . is an awareness of one's own weakness and impotence in matters of essential importance" (*Discourses* 2.11.1).

world has been created by a benign deity and is maintained by the providential care of that deity. Every one of a person's experiences, therefore, has been specifically designed for that individual alone; the world is thus full of meaning. The Epicureans, by contrast, saw the world as a randomly generated conglomeration of atoms, indivisible lumps of matter; they denied the existence of gods, except as special formations of atoms, which in their view exercised no care for human beings or any other aspect of the world. And they denied that it was natural for human beings to care for others.

Although there was plenty of common ground between Stoics and Epicureans—their thoroughgoing materialism, the dominance of reason in the human soul, the search for tranquility—it was clearly Marcus's view that the Epicureans had built the wrong kind of edifice on these foundations. He preferred Stoic asceticism and self-discipline to their notion that pleasure, in some form, constituted the human good; the virtues promoted by Stoicism seemed to him closer to traditional Roman virtues. He could see no point in living in a world without gods, and whereas the Epicureans believed that peace of mind could come only by withdrawing from the world, the Stoics believed that it came from engaging with the world in the right way, and especially from recognizing that all the thoughts and feelings that disrupt tranquility are generated by one's own mind and can therefore be dispelled by one's own mind.

STOICISM: A SKETCH

Marcus begins the second notebook, which is the effective start of the book, with a statement of a fundamental Stoic tenet: the only thing that is good is moral virtue and the only thing that is bad is moral vice or imperfection.[37] Everything else falls into the class of "indifferents," and it is careless talk to describe an indifferent as good or bad. This is a radical thought, since it accuses almost all of us, along with our laws and institutions, of being misguided in our assessment of good and bad.

However, many indifferents can be rated on a scale of value, even if they cannot be rated as good or bad.[38] Their value depends on whether they aid an aspirant's progress toward virtue, and so consideration of the value of things allows us to draw distinctions within the infinite class of indifferents such that some of them are "preferred indifferents," while the rest are "dispreferred." For

---

37. What follows in this section is a general survey of aspects of Stoicism that aid in understanding *Meditations*. It should be supplemented by books listed in Recommended Reading. Some details are also covered in the notes to help readers understand particular entries, but here I contextualize and explain the thinking behind the entries as a whole.

38. This does not apply to all indifferents, some of which are completely and utterly indifferent, such as whether the number of hairs on my head is even or odd. Not everything has value, but many things do. For a thorough study of indifferents, see J. Klein, "Making Sense of Stoic Indifferents," *Oxford Studies in Ancient Philosophy* 49 (2015): 227–281. The contempt Marcus often expresses for the things of this world is a forceful way of reminding himself that they have or should have no value for him.

example, strictly speaking health is neither good nor bad, since it is neither virtue nor vice. But health is still to be preferred over sickness because in obvious ways ill health can impede a person's path toward virtue.[39]

Preferred indifferents and the appropriate actions to take in relation to them are in accord with our nature; it is perfectly natural to prefer health to sickness, a moderate degree of wealth to poverty, and so on. So why not just call them good? Chiefly because they are not reliably good: they can be used for bad purposes and they are not always good for us. But, more subtly, another reason is that we want things that are good, but we should not want an indifferent, though we may "select" it. That leads to a further thought: if we want something, we feel pleasure when we get it, but pleasure is generally to be avoided, and it is certainly an inappropriate response to something that is indifferent. Pleasure is itself an indifferent. If we find pleasure in anything that is not a genuine good, we are further mired in our attachment to the things of this world. Acting with virtue is pleasant in a way, the Stoics acknowledged, but one's focus should be entirely on the virtuous act, not on the incidental concomitant pleasure.

---

39. Marcus quite often employs the technical term "indifferent," and he also spells that out as "morally neutral" (2.11, 3.11, 5.36), as "neither consonant nor dissonant with nature" (4.39), as external to us (i.e., not "up to us"), and as "not proper to a person qua human" (5.15). But he does not explicitly distinguish indifferents as preferred or dispreferred.

Following Socrates's lead, the Stoics held that virtue was knowledge.[40] They recognized four primary virtues—prudential wisdom, courage, moderation, and justice—and analyzed each of them as a kind of knowledge. Wisdom is knowledge of good and bad; courage is knowledge of what to fear and what not to fear; moderation is knowledge of what to pursue and what to avoid; justice is knowledge of what to give or what not to give others.[41] Virtue is the goal, virtue is rational knowledge, and rationality is the only fundamentally human quality, which we share with no other creatures but only with the gods.[42] So a rational, virtuous person is one who has fulfilled his or her potential as a human being, and such fulfillment is, or is the essential prerequisite for, happiness, which, as all the schools of

---

40. For the influence of Socrates on Stoicism in general, see A. A. Long, "Socrates in Hellenistic Philosophy," in *Stoic Studies* (Cambridge University Press, 1996), 1–34, and E. Brown, "Socrates and the Stoa," in *A Companion to Socrates*, ed. S. Ahbel-Rappe and R. Kamtekar (Blackwell, 2006), 275–284. For Marcus in particular, see J. Sellars, "Socratic Themes in the *Meditations* of Marcus Aurelius," in *Brill's Companion to the Reception of Socrates*, ed. C. Moore (Brill, 2019), 293–310.

41. All four of these virtues, along with honesty and sincerity, feature prominently in *Meditations*. The Stoics classified other virtues as species of one or another of the primary four.

42. Mature, rational human beings occupy the apex of a *scala naturae*, and Marcus sometimes deploys the image that all rational beings, humans and gods, are citizens of a Great City, a *cosmopolis* (2.16, 3.11, 4.4, 6.44, 9.9, 10.15, 12.36): see Sellars, *Marcus Aurelius*, chap. 9.

philosophy agreed, is the goal of life.[43] Progress in Stoicism is not acquiring new faculties or powers but learning to trust and depend on your rational faculty.

Because virtue is knowledge and rationality is the essential human capacity, irrational behavior is a sure way to stray from the path of virtue. So, minute by minute, faced as always in life with a host of indifferents, one should use reason to choose among them, to select those that are preferred and deselect those that are dispreferred. Epictetus nicely likened this process to gaming: "The counters are indifferent and the dice are indifferent: how do I know which way they will fall? But to use the throw carefully and skillfully, that is my job."[44]

If virtue is knowledge, it follows that behaving nonvirtuously is a product of ignorance. This is how the argument goes, and Marcus frequently alludes to it (4.8, 5.19, 7.22, 7.62, 7.64, 8.14, 8.55, 9.4, 12.12). All people want what is good for themselves; the Stoics claimed that this was obvious from birth and was the fundamental human motivation, shared with animals. So even people who behave nonvirtuously think that what they are doing is good for themselves, and it is just that they are objectively wrong because what they are doing will not fulfill them as human beings (that is, make them happy). They are denying their

---

43. The Greek word *eudaimonia* implies "having one's inner being in a good state" and is usually (but not entirely happily) translated "happiness." Greek philosophers generally agreed that happiness was the goal in life, but differed over what constituted it.

44. *Discourses* 2.5.3.

potential because they have a mistaken belief. Since all actions thus depend on beliefs, it is critical to get one's belief-set right. Hence, to repeat, the way that in *Meditations* Marcus drums core Stoic beliefs into himself by repetition.

What is more, reason, according to the Stoics, is the spark or splinter of divinity in us.[45] Not only are the gods rational beings, but also reason is the God who guides the whole universe. The Stoics, again following Socrates, employed an argument from design to demonstrate this: the orderliness of the universe, and especially the fact that in many ways it seems to have been made for the good of humankind, shows that it was created and is maintained by a cosmic Reason. For instance, as Marcus insists (e.g., 5.16, 5.30, 7.55),[46] the world has been given a hierarchical structure, from inanimate objects, such as stones, to plants, to animals, to human beings as rational creatures, and each lower level has been made to serve the higher ones. If the world is running on a program, there must have been a programmer.

---

45. In terms of Stoic physics, rationality is a quality of the *pneuma*, spirit, that pervades all things but is found in its least bound form in human beings. The exaltation of reason and its occasional description in tones of religious fervor will strike some readers as strange. It is important to be clear that Marcus was indeed exalting human reason, because it counters a tendency to turn him into some kind of mystic. The history of Greek philosophy as a whole is to a large extent the history of the discovery of the capacities of the human mind rather than the attempt to transcend it.

46. More often, Marcus simply alludes to this *scala naturae*, for example, at 3.6, 6.16, 8.41, and 8.46.

It was a Stoic custom, followed by Marcus throughout *Meditations* (e.g., 1.9, 1.17, 2.9, 3.4, 7.56, 9.1, 10.15, 12.1), to describe the goal of life as "living in accord with nature."[47] The final word is deliberately ambiguous between "Nature" (that is, Nature at large) and "nature" (that is, human nature), because they come to the same thing (5.3). Since universal nature is rational, and since the core of one's human nature is rational, living in accord with one's human nature is at the same time living in accord with Nature. If you observe and understand correctly, Nature/nature dictates the appropriate stepping-stones to virtue and happiness.

What makes an act virtuous is just whether it is in accord with nature. Thus, all self-regarding actions, such as self-preservation, are also moral, according to Stoicism, as long as they are in accord with nature. But it is also in our nature to look out for other people: witness, at its most primitive, the way a mother takes care of her offspring. Traditional Stoicism stressed self-reliance and becoming an independent moral agent. So did Marcus (vividly describing dependence as beggary at 4.29), but the Roman Stoics, and especially Marcus as emperor, also insisted that humans are social creatures (e.g., 7.55, 8.12), that we are all kin (e.g., 3.4, 3.11, 7.13, 7.22, 9.22), and that it is natural and beneficial for us to do good to others like us and to serve one another (5.16, 7.55). So Marcus repeatedly stresses other-regarding virtues such as kindness, leniency, and benevolence.

---

47. For a thorough study, see G. Striker, "Following Nature," in *Essays on Hellenistic Epistemology and Ethics* (Cambridge University Press, 1996), 221–280.

All the virtues arise out of natural human tendencies. We are inherently good. Why, then, are there so many bad people in the world? Because of their upbringing, according to the Stoics: they never grew out of the infantile trap of judging things in terms of pleasure and pain, and so seeking pleasure and avoiding pain became their aims in life. Although it is a natural human tendency to want what is good for oneself, most people mistakenly think that what is good for themselves is pleasure, and that leads them to nonvirtuous behavior. They assent to the wrong propositions.

The Stoics were determinists, and as Marcus's frequent references to providence and fate make clear, he was orthodox in this respect. The rational mind of God, or Nature, or Reason (all terms for the same thing) has a plan for the universe and is seeing it through. A virtuous person—every little virtuous act, in fact—is an assistant in the plan. Everything that happens is a link in endless networks of causes, "variable beyond counting" (5.23), with one event triggering the next (4.10, 5.8, 9.1, 9.29, 10.5). Determinism is, of course, a contentious doctrine. What scope does it leave us for freedom of action? What is the point of trying to behave as rational moral agents when we appear not to be free agents at all? In the short passage from Epictetus that I recently quoted, he talks of skillful use of our lives, but what sense does that make if all our lives are predetermined? Does not determinism encourage laziness, on the grounds that nothing we do makes any difference anyway?

The Stoics came up with a pretty good response.[48] They claimed that, although everything has antecedent causes, things are not always necessitated by their antecedent causes. A cylindrical roller has the capacity to roll downhill. Someone can push it to start it rolling, but that person has not given it the capacity to roll, which is simply an attribute of what it is to be a cylinder. So, when an impression of some kind impinges on us (either a sense impression or an internally generated thought), it is bound to make a mark, but we do not have to give the impression the kind of assent that leads to action. The sight of a beautiful woman provokes lust in a man who lacks self-control; her beauty is the antecedent cause, but his reaction is still up to him, because it is part of his makeup, not part of the antecedent cause.

In effect, then, there are two kinds of causes, external and internal. The external cause is the person pushing the roller; the internal cause is the nature of the roller.[49] The external cause is the impression that impinges on me; the internal cause is my individual nature or character and the use to which I put my

---

48. In technical terms, it is called "compatibilism." Two book-length studies are: S. Bobzien, *Determinism and Freedom in Stoic Philosophy* (Oxford University Press, 1998); R. Salles, *The Stoics on Determinism and Compatibilism* (Ashgate, 2005).

49. Marcus alludes to this point at 10.33.

faculty of assent. So, although the things that happen to us are entirely predetermined, our responses to these things are not. They are "up to us" (5.5, 5.33, 6.32, 6.41, 7.2, 7.54, 8.17, 8.34, 9.40, 10.32, 11.37, 12.22), and therefore things that are up to us, or within our power, or subject to our will, make up the domain of morality and culpability. And an important implication of the roller analogy is that if you change your disposition, you will react differently: the source of virtue is internal.

I have used the word "assent" a couple of times. This was a key term in Stoicism, and Marcus is comfortable using it (3.9, 5.10, 7.55, 8.7, 11.37).[50] When a mature, rational human being receives an impression, it is assessed by the "command center," a Stoic term for the rational faculty, seen as the faculty that processes impressions and initiates action.[51] The incoming impression presents itself as providing information about the world; it comes in the form of a proposition such as "There's a cat on the kitchen counter." The command center has a choice between assenting to or withholding assent from the proposition; it might withhold assent, for instance, if it realized that what seemed in the dim light to be a cat was actually a bundled towel. And assent gives

---

50. On assent—"the linchpin of the Stoic system"—see especially Brennan, *Stoic Life*, 51–61.

51. See especially 5.27. Marcus uses the term often and talks also of the "command center" of the universe (6.36, 7.75, 9.22). On about a dozen occasions, he also calls the command center a person's inner "guardian spirit," and once "the ruler within us."

rise to an impulse that leads to action;[52] you might shoo the cat out of the kitchen. It is immediately clear how assent is critical for morality: rational, virtuous behavior results from assenting to impressions that correctly judge the value of the source of the impression. Each of the virtues is a state of the soul, which, being material (even if made of refined matter), has the ability to move the body to action. So virtuous behavior takes place when the soul assents to correct propositions, leading to impulses that initiate action in the real world.

The Stoics were as notorious in their own time as they still are for holding out as an ideal the state of *apatheia*, complete freedom from passion (1.9, 6.16, 11.18);[53] we still use the word "stoical" for rational calmness in the face of situations that would normally

---

52. "Impulse" is the standard translation of *hormē*, and it is acceptable as long as the reader appreciates that it does not necessarily imply impulsiveness, and whereas in common English we do not have to act on our impulses, in the Stoic use of the term an impulse necessarily leads to action. Marcus uses the term in *Meditations* a great many times. We can now see that when he says that he wishes in some way to correct his impulses (as at 2.2, 2.16, 3.6, 3.16, etc.), this is shorthand for wishing to correct the beliefs that lead to impulses, and so coincides with his repeated insistence that nothing is bad unless he thinks it so.

53. I have translated *pathos* as "passion" rather than "emotion" because it is more literal (passion is something that happens to one as a passive, reactive subject, and so is *pathos*) and, as the more forceful term, helps to explain why the Stoics saw many *pathē* as forms of psychic sickness.

generate an emotional reaction.[54] As a form of impulse, passions should be under our control; we should not get carried away by them. In the Stoic view, the problem with the passions, the most prevalent kind of impulse, is not just that they are likely to disturb the cool processes of rationality,[55] and therefore dislodge one from the path of virtue (as at 2.5, 2.13, 3.4, 8.48, 12.19), but also that they are, or come with, mistaken beliefs about the value of whatever it is to which the passion attaches. They are a form of overhasty assent to a mistaken proposition.[56] In short, the passions are in fact value judgments, and they assign importance to things that are indifferent (11.37). Hence, Marcus rejects passion in general (e.g., 12.19), as well as specific passions such as fear, anger, and sexual desire.

If you are afraid of something, for instance, you think that it is going to be bad for you, when in fact, since it is neither virtue

---

54. Mr. Spock from *Star Trek* springs to mind. Apart from works listed in the Recommended Reading, an interesting study dedicated to Marcus is T. Engberg-Pedersen, "Marcus Aurelius on Emotions," in *The Emotions in Hellenistic Philosophy*, ed. J. Sihvola and T. Engberg-Pedersen (Springer, 1998), 305–337.

55. The Stoics saw the human soul as unified, and so did not separate passion and reason in a Platonic fashion as two distinct parts of it. It is the same soul that reasons, desires, wills, remembers, perceives, and feels. So, strictly speaking, passions are not the enemies of reason, but are forms of perverted reason, or misjudgments.

56. This is one reason why Marcus sets himself various exercises designed to slow down assent until he has a clear view about the source of the impression. For these exercises, see pp. lvi–lvii.

nor vice, it is neither good nor bad.[57] Even your child's death is actually a matter of indifference and should be treated as such (9.40). Your child is a gift to you from the universe (12.26), and so never really belonged to you; its death was chosen by the universe, and the universe is good. Substituting these propositions helps counteract the tendency to passion. So a Stoic, unless he or she is a perfected sage, is aware of the passion and its propositional content ("My child's death is going to upset me"), but withholds assent from it and substitutes a more rational proposition.[58] This

---

57. The Stoics recognized four categories of passion: fear (with reference to an apparent bad in the future), desire (with reference to an apparent good in the future), pleasure (with reference to what we believe to be good and believe we now have), and distress (with reference to what we believe to be bad and believe we now have). The other passions were regarded as subspecies of these four. It is less clear how they accommodated passions that are focused on the past, such as guilt and shame, but see Graver, *Stoicism and Emotion*, 191–211. Whether we feel pleasure or distress, fear or desire, depends on whether we accept or do not accept the way things present themselves to us, our impressions. Hence, in one and the same situation, one person will feel pleasure while another will not. But what makes reason weaker in one person than another? Largely upbringing, and so the Stoics stressed the importance of a good education. This helps to explain why Marcus thanks his teachers in Notebook 1. But upbringing was not the only factor: innate biases, inherited from parents and turned habitual by repetition, also played a part. See Graver, *Stoicism and Emotion*, 149–171.

58. As Marcus often says, nothing is good or bad unless you think it so. Entry 9.13 is a particularly clear statement, but the notion is deployed many times throughout *Meditations*.

seems to be how Marcus understands the teaching, because at 1.9 he praises one of his teachers, not for never feeling passion, but for never *presenting* in a passionate way.

However, some feelings were acceptable. Thinking that an indifferent is good or bad is false; so a sage, who has no false beliefs but only knowledge, experiences no passion. He does, however, experience three "good feelings" (*eupatheiai*): volition (the rational pursuit of something), caution (the rational avoidance of something), and joy (rational elation).[59] Each of the three has subspecies that were therefore considered acceptable passions: kindness/benevolence, which Marcus constantly stresses, was considered a form of volition, as was friendliness; modesty and reverence were forms of caution; a sense of humor and cheerfulness were forms of joy. A dispassionate or impassive person, in the Stoic sense, is not an unfeeling zombie, but an individual who is guided by detached reason and experiences only sane passions.

A PERSONAL STOICISM

What did Marcus make of all this? As I have said, he was not writing a handbook of Stoicism. None of the ideas sketched in the previous section is discussed or developed in *Meditations*, but on every page they color the entries. Let's consider four prominent themes of the book. Marcus touches on many issues, but each of these four topics has dozens of entries devoted to it.

---

59. See Graver, *Stoicism and Emotion*, 51–59, 81–83.

They are anger management, death, the paltriness of fame and the world in general, and his treatment of others. Anger and fear of death had garnered a great deal of attention from professional philosophers, who were concerned with the impediments to happiness, and the innate sociability of human beings lagged not far behind, but the point is that, for Marcus, all four are deeply personal concerns. But he always puts a Stoic spin on them, and he always finds that Stoicism either affords him consolation or spurs him to try to do better.

Marcus was frequently annoyed by the people with whom he was required to associate. He even sets himself the exercise of "seeing into their souls" to recognize their baseness (e.g., 4.38, 6.53, 7.62, 9.18, 9.27, 9.34). In over fifty entries of *Meditations*, he confesses to finding it difficult to control his temper and chides himself for it. He finds Stoic principles helpful in a number of respects:[60] bad people cannot help themselves because, given their mistaken views about what is and is not important, they have no choice but to behave badly (6.27, 6.57, 7.26, 10.30); they cannot harm him, since all harm is self-inflicted and due to one's own false beliefs—in other words, it is his own anger that harms him (2.1, 2.11, 4.7, 7.22, 8.29, 8.55, 10.25, 11.20); even bad men must have a place in the universe, since the universe is subject to rational providence (6.1, 6.42); they are kin, rational creatures just like himself, and so deserve to be treated with kindness and justice (2.1); and in any case he should accept whatever the gods put

---

60. Most of these are summarized in 11.18, which is a devoted to anger management.

in his path (5.8, 11.13). In more commonsensical, less Stoicized moments, he also reminds himself that he is no better than them (7.26, 10.30), that given the shortness of human life their flaws are trivial and his anger meaningless (5.23, 11.18), that he may have misunderstood the situation or not have the whole picture (9.38, 11.18), and that he should show them where they are going wrong rather than lose his temper (5.22, 5.28, 6.27).

More than sixty entries touch on death and the transience of all things. This was a particularly acute issue for Marcus, who was consumptive and aware that he might die young. It is this that gives *Meditations* its frequent sense of urgency: there is no time to lose (2.4–2.6, 3.1, 3.14, 4.17, 4.37, 10.15). He draws on Stoicism often to console himself that death is a natural process, no more than the disintegration of the elements of which he is made (especially 2.11, 2.12, 9.3); in fact, he claims, the death and disintegration of any creature is actually good for the universe, because it allows it to create something new out of its elements and so perpetuate the divine plan (2.12, 7.25), and because what is good for the whole cannot be bad for a part (2.3, 6.54, 10.6). He reminds himself that everything that is born must die (4.48, 6.47, 9.31), even the universe itself, so death can be no bad thing (2.11, 6.28, 9.1, 10.7, 12.23, 12.34). He consoles himself with the thoughts that death is either oblivion or transference to an afterlife, neither of which is bad (3.3, 8.58), and invents arguments for the conclusion that death cannot be truly bad (2.11). In short, Stoicism taught him that death was an indifferent, nothing to fear.[61]

Upper-class Romans were obsessed with the perpetuation of their family names, and Marcus wanted to be remembered as a good emperor.[62] So he has to remind himself that fame is an indifferent (9.1, 9.30, 10.30). Memories fade, and no one is remembered for long (2.17, 4.3, 4.19, 7.34). Fame is assigned by other people, who may be rotten (2.12, 3.10, 4.3, 6.16, 7.34, 8.44), so that to seek fame is to make oneself dependent on others, which is the opposite of the Stoic ideal of being an independent moral agent, focused only on matters that are "up to him." Fame is at best an epiphenomenon, no more than icing on the cake, but what is important is the cake, making sure that your actions are virtuous, whether or not you are remembered for them. And as a remedy against thoughts of fame or any concern with what the future might hold, he reminds himself that all we have is the present moment (2.14, 3.10, 12.26).

Finally, as emperor, one of Marcus's chief concerns was, naturally, his dealings with others. Very often, as I have said, he

---

61. Stoic discussions of death and suicide are analyzed by A. G. Long, *Death and Immortality in Ancient Philosophy* (Cambridge University Press, 2019).

62. "He was very concerned to ensure that he had a good reputation" (*Historia Augusta: Marcus* 20.5).

finds people contemptible (e.g., 5.10, 5.28, 9.3, 9.42), but he draws on Stoic theory to remind himself that it is natural to care for others (5.31) or at least tolerate them (5.20). As a consequence, he urges himself to love them and treat them well (6.39, 7.13, 9.27, 10.36), to focus on their good features (6.48), and in general to be more objective (7.26, 9.42) and to avoid high-handedness (6.30) and suspicion (6.20). Earlier Stoics had recognized the social virtues of benevolence and so on, but Marcus naturally puts more emphasis on them.[63] Human beings are meant to serve one another (5.16, 5.30, 7.55, 8.59, 9.1, 9.9, 11.18); kindness, love, and affection for others are, as we have seen, passions that he finds acceptable. He tells himself: "Find joy and rest in one thing alone: in moving from one socially useful act to another, while remaining mindful of God" (6.7). And he urges himself to be an egoless emperor (7.73, 7.74, 9.42, 11.4).

Marcus clearly found Stoic theory helpful in a number of respects. He reinforced these theoretical frames of reference with a series of practical exercises, which helped to make the theories real. Probing questions allow him to delve under the surface and gain objectivity (3.11, 8.11, 10.9). Reducing things to their bare essentials helps him see them for what they are (3.11, 4.21, 6.13, 7.29, 9.25, 9.37, 12.2, 12.8, 12.10, 12.18, 12.29). A cosmic, long-term perspective—the view from above, as it were (7.48,

---

63. See G. Reydam-Schils, "Marcus Aurelius' Social Ethics," in *Meditations and Representations: The Philosopher and Emperor Marcus Aurelius in an Interdisciplinary Light*, ed. M. van Ackeren and J. Opsomer (Reichert, 2012), 111–132.

9.30, 12.24)—shows him the impermanence of things and their repetitive sameness, the immensity of time, the paltriness of the world and its inhabitants, the absurdity of seeking fame, and the meaninglessness of death, which is no more than a rearrangement of eternally existing elements (3.10, 5.24, 6.36, 7.48, 9.30, 9.32, 11.1, 12.24).[64] An alternative perspective—the view from inside, as it were—shows him how all things are interconnected (4.40, 6.38, 7.9).

Marcus was trying to encapsulate the magnificent vision of human life and its cosmic setting that Stoicism afforded and to see how it applied to his personal quest for happiness and his desire to be a good emperor. Of course there would be setbacks, but there is no point in making things worse for yourself by worrying about things that are not within your control. You have to make the best of the lot the gods have assigned you. You must depend on yourself as much as you can and avoid treating indifferents as important or being ruled by your feelings. Your rational faculty can help you select a path through life that will lead you to happiness. *Meditations* shows us a man who was engaged against the odds in an ongoing quest for self-perfection, and although it was written entirely for himself, it encourages others to do the same, shows them a path, and casts a little light on the way ahead.

---

64. On this cosmic perspective, see T. Bénatouïl, "*Theōria* and *Scholē* in Epictetus and Marcus Aurelius: Platonic, Stoic or Socratic?" in *Plato and the Stoics*, ed. A. G. Long (Cambridge University Press, 2013), 147–173.

MEDITATIONS

NOTEBOOK 1[1]

---

1. This first notebook is very different from the reflections and precepts that make up the rest of the book, though there is a common core in Marcus's concern with his own self-improvement. Marcus uses this notebook to give a selective account of his education, to acknowledge the people who, in retrospect, seemed to have had the most influence on his early life, and to inspire himself to emulate them. Moreover, this notebook is structured and planned, whereas the rest of the book usually consists of unordered jottings. The structure of this first notebook is not so much chronological as thematic: entries 1–4: family members; 5–11: educators; 12–15: friends; 16: Antoninus as preparing Marcus for emperorship; 17: the gods. The idea of such a survey might have been triggered by his writing of 6.30 and 6.48, so that it is a kind of offshoot of the rest of the book, despite being placed first. Stoics believed that one's character was greatly conditioned by the people one met early in life (the soul being a tabula rasa at birth, with only dispositions for future knowledge and behavior), so Marcus is thanking these people for having put him on the path of philosophy and making it possible, or at least easier, for him to become a man of virtue and a good emperor.

[1] From my grandfather Verus:[2] nobility of character and evenness of temper.

[2] From what I've been told and remember of my natural father:[3] modesty and manliness.

[3] From my mother:[4] reverence for the gods, generosity, and the ability to abstain not only from wrongdoing but even from contemplating it; also, a frugal lifestyle, far removed from the habits of the rich.[5]

[4] From my great-grandfather:[6] not studying at places where teaching was publicly available; being taught by good teachers at

---

2. For sketches of the people Marcus names, see "The People and Gods of *Meditations*," 293–310. The lists that follow in this first notebook are not entirely consistent in syntactical terms. Usually, one can understand "I learned the value of" as the missing clause, but Marcus gradually introduces more and more character sketches of the people he is writing about, and for these "I benefited from" often works as the filler. But it is best to read each entry of this first notebook just as a list, a series of bullet points, without worrying too much about the precise syntax. See also the first note to 1.17.

3. Also called Marcus Annius Verus; he died when Marcus was quite young. Marcus was then brought up by his grandfather, yet another Marcus Annius Verus.

4. Domitia Lucilla.

5. Despite the fact that Lucilla herself was one of the wealthiest women in Rome.

6. Lucius Catilius Severus, his mother's step-grandfather, a two-time consul, the governor of Syria, and proconsul of Asia. He clearly played a part in Marcus's upbringing, and for a while in his early years Marcus added "Catilius Severus" to his name in homage.

home; and the recognition that education is something on which one should spend freely.[7]

[5] From my tutor:[8] supporting neither the Greens nor the Blues,[9] and neither the Lights nor the Heavies;[10] endurance of hardship, reduction of one's needs, working with one's own hands; minding one's own business and turning a deaf ear to malicious gossip.

[6] From Diognetus: not getting carried away by empty enthusiasms; skepticism about the claims made by wonder-workers and sorcerers for things like spells and the exorcism

---

7. There was quite a vigorous debate among the upper classes of Rome about the relative value of being taught at home or in school.

8. Probably a slave (and hence unnamed?), responsible for steering Marcus's earliest years.

9. The Greens and the Blues were the two dominant teams of chariot racers; there were also Reds and Whites. The sport aroused great passion in imperial Rome, and furious, and sometimes violent, rivalry among opposing fans. Many emperors were known partisans of the Greens or the Blues, failing to recognize the importance of impartiality for an emperor..

10. Some gladiatorial contests pitted lightly armed against heavily armed fighters. At 6.46, Marcus reveals that gladiatorial fighting disgusted him (see also Cassius Dio, *Roman History* 72.29.3), and as emperor he restricted the number of shows per year. Several previous emperors had actually taken part in gladiatorial combat (as Marcus's son Commodus would as well), though of course their opponents always submitted so that the emperor would win.

of spirits;[11] not keeping quails for fighting or being excited by such pursuits; tolerating plain speaking; being oriented toward philosophy and attending the lectures of, above all, Baccheius, but also Tandasis and Marcianus;[12] writing essays from an early age; being drawn to the pallet, the skin coverlet, and everything else that goes with a Greek-style upbringing.[13]

[7] From Rusticus: understanding the importance of correction and treatment of one's character;[14] not being diverted

---

11. Despite this, an Egyptian magician called Arnuphis was a prominent member of Marcus's court.

12. These lecturers are otherwise unknown. Some editors replace the name "Tandasis" with a known teacher of Marcus, Basileides of Scythopolis.

13. The word Marcus uses was commonly used for the notoriously tough training regime Spartan boys and men underwent. Asceticism was encouraged by both the Stoics and the Cynics. Marcus was about twelve years old when he began to be attracted to Greek ways and Greek philosophy, though it was probably another ten years or so before he became an actual practitioner.

14. For philosophy as therapy, see the Introduction, xxxvii–xxxviii.

by an interest in sophistry;[15] not writing about philosophical theories, or delivering homilies designed to get someone to change his life, or ostentatiously playing the ascetic or the philanthropist to impress people; avoiding rhetoric, the composition of poetry, and highfalutin language; not walking around at home in fancy clothes or doing anything of that kind; adopting an unaffected style in one's letters (as in the letter written by him from Sinuessa to my mother);[16] being forgiving and ready to get back on good terms with angry and offensive people as soon as they're prepared to simmer down; reading attentively, not being satisfied with skimming a book at a general level, and not readily assenting

---

15. By "sophistry" here, Marcus chiefly means rhetoric, which was taught and practiced in his day by a class of intellectuals called "sophists." Although Marcus turned from rhetoric to philosophy, as emperor he often needed to rely on rhetoric (see 8.30), and since many of the sophists were eminent people in the empire and in their home towns, Marcus often had official business with them. So "sophist" was an honorific title, though the label had been tainted by Plato's and Aristotle's criticisms of earlier "sophists." In Marcus's day, they were in demand as keynote speakers for all kinds of public occasions, they traveled all over the world giving display speeches, and the sons of the best families might be apprenticed to them.

16. Sinuessa was a seaside town north of Naples. The bracketed aside is one of many features of the book which show that it was written for Marcus alone, not for publication, since the public would not have access to Rusticus's letter to Marcus's mother. Writers contemporary with Marcus had developed letter writing into an elaborate art form.

to superficial interpretations; and reading Epictetus's *Discourses* (he shared his personal copy with me).[17]

[8] From Apollonius: self-reliance and indisputable immunity to the dice-rolls of fortune;[18] focusing exclusively and ceaselessly on reason; remaining always the same person whether one is in acute pain, or losing a child, or chronically ill; seeing clearly, in a living example, that it's possible for one and the same person to be both highly energetic and able to relax; not resenting having to explain something; observing a man who plainly regarded his expertise and skill at the exposition of philosophical theories as the least of his gifts; and learning how to accept apparent favors[19]

---

17. It is not clear that these are Epictetus's *Discourses* as we have them. The word translated as "discourses" means literally "written versions of lectures." This is what our *Discourses* are—they were put into book form by a disciple of Epictetus called Arrian (Lucius Flavius Arrianus)—but there were other such notes in circulation, including another four books' worth from Arrian, supplementing the four books of *Discourses* that we have. Hence the existence of fragments of Epictetus from books that we no longer have. Rusticus may have attended Epictetus's lectures and taken notes. But most of Marcus's references to Epictetus in *Meditations* do seem to come from Arrian's version.

18. Apollonius is being described almost as a "sage," the Stoic term for an enlightened person. Only a sage is beyond the reach of fortune or any kind of accident. The idea originated with Socrates, at Plato's *Euthydemus* 279c–280b.

19. The favors are called "apparent" presumably because, for a Stoic, they belonged to the populous class of things that were "indifferent" or morally neutral; see the Introduction, xl–xli.

from friends without thereby becoming their inferior or hurting their feelings by rejecting them.

[9] From Sextus: kindness; the example of a household governed by paternal authority; the true meaning of living in accord with nature;[20] an unfeigned grace; paying solicitous attention to friends; tolerance of ordinary people and those whose opinions are not guided by philosophical theories; accommodating oneself to everyone (this was a feature which made his conversation more soothing than any flattery and yet at the same time made his companions treat him with the greatest respect); the convincing and methodical explication and systematization of the essential principles of life; never presenting as angry or in the grip of any other passion, but being simultaneously completely impassive and yet highly affectionate;[21] praising without making a song and dance about it; and wearing one's learning lightly.[22]

---

20. The usual Stoic way of describing the ideal philosophical life, commonly recurring in *Meditations* (see, e.g., 1.17, 7.56, 10.15, 12.1 and the Introduction, xlv).

21. Although the Stoics regarded passions as forms of mental sickness, certain emotions or emotion-based practices were acceptable. See the Introduction, xlix–lii. Otherwise, passions were "irrational movements of the soul" or "impulses that have got out of hand."

22. The foundation of interpersonal relationships for Marcus is the fact that all men are equally rational creatures and therefore should be treated with kindness, even if they go wrong. But Marcus found such kindness difficult, and often chastises himself for failing (e.g., 4.37, 5.5, 6.30, 6.39, 7.13, 7.63, 8.8, 9.27, 11.13).

[10] From Alexander the language teacher: refraining from criticism; not jumping down a person's throat and lambasting him when he makes a mistake in his vocabulary, syntax, or pronunciation, but adeptly introducing the correct form, the one he should have used, when responding to or confirming what he said, or when discussing the matter further with him—the matter itself, not his expression—or by finding some other tactful way to remind him.

[11] From Fronto:[23] understanding the nature of despotic malice, deviousness, and hypocrisy, and the realization that,

---

23. Despite the warm relationship between Marcus and Fronto, as revealed by the surviving letters between them, it is noticeable how few of life's important lessons Marcus felt he had learned from Fronto compared to, say, Rusticus (1.7). This reflects Marcus's turn away from rhetoric (as taught by Fronto) and toward philosophy (under the influence of Rusticus, in the first instance), and it is perhaps significant that, of Marcus's four rhetoric teachers, Fronto is the only one he mentions, whereas he mentions all six of his philosophy teachers. In their letters, Fronto tried to persuade him that the two disciplines were compatible, but Marcus did not agree, on the grounds that a rhetorician has to be self-satisfied, whereas for a philosopher there is always farther to go. On Marcus's attitude toward rhetoric and sophists, see E. Bowie, "Marcus Aurelius, Greek Poets, and Greek Sophists: Friends or Foes?" in *Intellectual and Empire in Greco-Roman Antiquity*, ed. P. Bosman (Routledge, 2019), 142–159.

on the whole, our so-called Patricians are rather lacking in affection.[24]

[12] From Alexander the Platonist: the general avoidance, except when absolutely necessary, of telling anyone, to his face or in a letter, "I'm too busy"; and not making this kind of excuse for constantly evading the obligations that arise out of one's relationships with one's fellows, by using "the pressure of circumstances" as a pretext.

[13] From Catulus: not ignoring a friend's criticism, even if it happens to be unreasonable, but actually trying to restore normal relations with him; wholehearted praise for one's teachers, of the kind that is recorded for Domitius and Athenodotus; and genuine love for one's children.

---

24. The Patricians of Rome were the ruling class; they either belonged to old noble families or had been recently elevated by an emperor. In one of his extant letters (Haines II.156), Fronto went further, denying that affection was a Roman attribute at all, or even that there was a Latin equivalent for the Greek word. Marcus tried to look for nobility of soul in the Roman aristocracy, not just nobility of wealth and birth, and even married his daughter Lucilla (after her first husband, Lucius Verus, had died) to a Knight, a member of the next order down from the Patricians.

[14] From Severus: love of family, love of truth, and love of justice; that, thanks to him, I came to know about Thrasea, Helvidius, Cato, Dion, and Brutus,[25] and conceived the notion of a political system with the same laws for all, governed on the principles of personal and political equality, and of a monarchy

---

25. Most of these men were famous, philosophically inspired martyrs to the cause of preserving or restoring the Roman Republic in the face of sole rule or the threat of it; see "The People and Gods of *Meditations*," 293–310. Marcus fails to mention here that his friend Rusticus's grandfather, Junius Arulenus Rusticus, was another martyr, executed under Domitian. It says a lot about the changed face of the imperial throne under the "good emperors" (see the Introduction, note 16) that the philosophy of the opposition to imperial rule in the first century had become the personal philosophy of an emperor. What was Marcus's interest in these men? Perhaps they were reminders of the opposition he would arouse if, as emperor, he turned autocratic. Perhaps, also, they were reminders that it is possible for politics to be a field where idealism is not misplaced. In his biographies of Dion, Cato, and Brutus, Plutarch of Chaeronea had presented them as potential philosopher-kings, and though the ideal would prove impossible to put into practice, it was said that Marcus was attracted to the possibility that he might become one (*Historia Augusta: Marcus* 27.7). On the relation between philosophy and practical politics at Rome, see M. Griffin, "Philosophy, Politics, and Politicians at Rome," in *Philosophia Togata*, Vol. 1, ed. M. Griffin and J. Barnes (Oxford University Press, 1989), 1–37.

that chiefly prizes the freedom of its subjects.[26] Also from him: a constant and consistent prizing of philosophy; a readiness to do good to others and a liberal generosity; optimism, and confidence that one is loved by one's friends; his candor with those who got a dressing-down from him; and the way in which his friends never had to guess his likes or dislikes, since he didn't disguise them.

[**15**] From Maximus: self-mastery and total immunity to passing whims; cheerfulness in all circumstances, even when ill; an integrated character, both gentle and dignified; doing what one has to do without complaining; how everyone trusted him to mean what he said, and to do what he did with the best of intentions; never being astonished or alarmed,[27] never hurrying

---

26. Marcus always took care not to turn his monarchy into a tyranny, modeling himself on Antoninus Pius; see 6.30. The terms Marcus uses here are all taken from Greek democratic discourse, but, as emperor, Marcus was not of course advocating pure democracy but what Plato called "geometric" equality (*Laws* 757b–c), where all citizens— emperor, senators, ordinary people—get their due (see also 1.16). And, according to the political theorizing of the time, ordinary people could be largely discounted, so that it is quite likely that, when Marcus talks of "political equality," he means no more than the regular rotation of high office among members of the ruling elite. Wise, law-abiding monarchy was held by a number of thinkers of the imperial period, from various schools, to be the best constitution; see, for example, Dio Chrysostom, *Orations* 1–4.

27. Calm acceptance was, in Marcus's view, better than being taken aback or surprised by events; see, for example, 7.26, 12.13. Surprise is a sign of not serenely accepting every experience in your life as assigned to you by the gods and of ignorance about the way things are.

or hesitant or helpless, never showing a downturned mouth or a fawning grin—or, to put it another way, never grumpy or mistrustful; being benevolent, forgiving, and honest; making it clear that he was inflexibly upright rather than in need of straightening by others;[28] how people could never take him to be looking down on them, but at the same time could never have consented to thinking of themselves as his superiors; a good sense of humor.

[16] From my father:[29] calmness and an unshakable adherence to deliberately made decisions; indifference to the empty glory of so-called honors; industriousness and perseverance; a willingness to listen to any proposal that is in the interest of the state; impartiality in giving everyone his due;[30] knowing by experience when to tighten the reins and when to slacken them;

---

28. Such uprightness is also held out as an ideal at 3.5 (end) and 7.12.

29. The emperor Antoninus Pius, who adopted Marcus. See also 6.30 for another similar tribute to him. There is an overall movement in this long entry from Antoninus's public life as emperor to his private life. It constitutes "one of the noblest tributes that a great man has paid to another" (Farquharson, *Meditations of Marcus Aurelius Antoninus*). It is also a unique document, an assessment of a Roman emperor not by a biased historian but by one who knew him intimately. Notice that Marcus's ideal ruler is not a philosopher-king but more of a well-bred Roman gentleman who applies common sense to his rulership.

30. A common philosophical definition of justice, adopted by the Stoics, was "giving everyone their due."

that he put a stop to homosexual affairs with teenagers;[31] how he used considerately to excuse his friends from always having to dine with him and from the obligation of accompanying him on journeys out of town, and how he behaved no differently toward them after they had been unavoidably absent for some reason or other; diligence and patience in looking into matters arising from council sessions,[32] so that one could never accuse him of giving up the investigation and being satisfied with first impressions; the ability to retain friends, and never being fickle or playing favorites; self-sufficiency in all situations, and joyfulness; the ability to provide for events well in advance and to arrange everything in advance, down to the smallest details, without making a big production out of it.

How he reduced public acclamations and all forms of flattery during his reign;[33] his unceasing watch on the needs of the empire, his stewardship of its resources, and his tolerance

---

31. Pederasty was justified by reference to longstanding Greek practices, but it was anathema to many Romans. The two emperors before Antoninus, Trajan and Hadrian, had both been fond of boys; Hadrian's love for Antinous is particularly well known. There are a number of other implicit contrasts with Hadrian in this entry, and with other emperors: see Rutherford, *Meditations*, 107–110.

32. An emperor was supported and advised by a Privy Council.

33. Acclamations of the emperor came in two forms. The Senate (up to six hundred members) might chant ritual phrases of thanks and flattery; and ordinary people might cry out, "May the gods preserve you!" or some such prayer as the emperor passed.

of the criticism he received for these and similar measures;[34] his freedom from superstition in approaching the gods, and his refusal, when dealing with men, to pander to the masses with demagoguery and obsequiousness; his sober reliability in all things, lack of vulgarity, and ability to resist new fads; his ability to enjoy the material comforts of life, which fortune gave him in abundance, in an unpretentious way, but also without apology, so that he simply accepted them as matters of fact when he had them and felt no lack when they were gone;[35] the fact that no one could call him a sophist, a canter, or a pedant, but only a mature and peerless man, beyond the reach of flattery, and competent to manage others' business as well as his own.

Then there was the way he honored genuine philosophers, and avoided either condemning the charlatans or being taken in

---

34. He was accused above all of being stingy (Cassius Dio, *Roman History* 70.3.3).

35. Strictly, the "material comforts of life" were "indifferents" (see the Introduction, xl–xli). Marcus would not have counted it to Antoninus's credit if he had desired and sought these things, but few Stoics were so strict (or were such Cynics) that they did not enjoy them if they came their way.

by them;[36] also, the fact that he was good and witty company, without taking it too far; the moderate degree of attention he paid to his bodily needs, stemming not from a strong attachment to life or from vanity, but from a true estimation of their importance, the upshot being that, thanks to his own ministrations, he reduced to a minimum any need of doctoring or medicines and treatments; above all, the way he deferred without a trace of resentment to those with some special ability, such as eloquence, or expertise gained from the study of law or human behavior or some other subject, and being supportive of their pursuits,[37] so that each of them could achieve distinction for his accomplishments in his field; doing everything in compliance with tradition, without deliberately making it obvious; also, not chopping and changing, but remaining true to the same places and practices; his ability immediately to recover his vim and vigor and return to his usual routine after attacks of migraine; the

---

36. Philosophers commonly approached emperors in the hope of patronage. Philosophy in Marcus's day was a way of saving your soul, so when Marcus talks of fake philosophers, we can get a sense of what he means by thinking of the fake gurus of the 1970s and onward. The stakes were the same in both cases: a wrong choice could blight your life. There are traces of such pseudo-philosophers in 5.18 and 9.29. Antoninus was no philosopher himself, so he presumably distinguished between true and false philosophers by their moral character or lack of it. Marcus too was said to be good at spotting charlatans (Cassius Dio, *Roman History* 71.32.5).

37. Financial support was always an emperor's chief way of expressing approbation or admiration.

fact that there was little he couldn't talk about, because it was the exception rather than the rule for him to have secrets, and then the only ones he had were state secrets; being conscientious and professional when it comes to matters such as the provision of entertainments, the contracting of public building projects, and the distribution of largesse, as a man whose focus is on only what needs to be done, not on the glory to be gained by doing it.

He was regular in his bathing habits,[38] not given to adding to his residences, careless about what he ate, unconcerned about the cut and color of his clothes, and indifferent to the physical attractions of his slaves. The fact that his clothes were brought up to him from his country estate at Lorium,[39] and a great many

---

38. This seems an odd thing to praise him for, but two previous emperors, Caligula and Nero, were notoriously erratic in this respect. Besides, in the biographical tradition, apparent trivia were rightly taken to be at least as revealing of a person's character as his major public deeds. At 6.30, Marcus commends Antoninus even for his regular bowel movements.

39. In Etruria, about twelve miles west of Rome. His clothes, then, were made by slaves on this family estate rather than being expensively bought.

details of his life in Lanuvium;[40] the way he treated the apologetic customs officer in Tusculum,[41] and his social graces in general.

There was no trace of stridency, obduracy, or impetuousness in him, nor was he the kind of man who, as they say, "gets in a sweat." All his tasks were divided up and carefully thought through, as though he had all the time in the world, and carried out in an unperturbed, orderly, and resolute manner, in ways that suited whatever needed doing. The tale told about Socrates might be applied to him—that he had the ability both to refrain from and to enjoy the things that most people are too weak to refrain from and too inclined to enjoy.[42] Strength of will—the ability to persevere in the one situation and remain sober in the other—of the kind that was displayed by Maximus in his illness.[43]

---

40. Antoninus was born in Lanuvium, southeast of Rome, but was brought up on the estate at Lorium. Before becoming emperor, Marcus too divided his time between the two estates.

41. A Latin town about ten miles southeast of Rome and, as a hill town, a favorite haunt of Romans in the heat of the summer. We have no further knowledge of this incident with the customs officer; again, Marcus is writing for himself. The story is presumably meant to illustrate Antoninus's kindliness; perhaps the customs officer apologized for not being suitably dressed.

42. If this is not an apocryphal story about Socrates (of which there are many), it may be an echo of Xenophon, *Memorabilia* 1.3.15.

43. This is the Maximus of 1.15, and his illness was mentioned there as well, but we do not know the details.

[17] From the gods:[44] the goodness of almost all the people in my life: grandparents, parents, sister,[45] teachers, members of my household, relatives, and friends, and that I never stumbled into offending them, despite having the kind of nature that might well have led me to do so, but, by the grace of the gods, the conditions never occurred that would have put me to the test; that I spent no longer than I did being brought up with my grandfather's mistress;[46] that I preserved my youthful innocence and didn't become a man ahead of time, but was even rather late in doing

---

44. Now the missing phrase appears to be "I am grateful for," but it is important to see that this is not the filler for the earlier entries, because Marcus would never have claimed to possess all the attributes that he admired in others. It is quite wrong to translate, as some do, "From him [Apollonius, in 1.8] I acquired the habit of unshakable composure," because the rest of the notebooks plainly show that Marcus did not have the habit of unshakable composure. In the rest of the book he is usually concerned with self-correction, but he was also open to correction by others (e.g., 4.12, 6.21; justified in Stoic terms at 8.16). It is only now that, for the first time, he is talking directly about himself, in this culminating entry, which is almost a prayer of thanksgiving.

45. Annia Cornificia Faustina, Marcus's only sibling, was a couple of years younger than him. She died young, in 152, leaving two children.

46. Name unknown. She was not brought into the household until Verus's first wife had died, as a kind of common-law wife. She might have been a lot younger than Verus, and, in context, Marcus seems to be implying that there was a sexual current between them. Marcus left Verus's household when he was adopted, shortly before his seventeenth birthday, by the emperor Hadrian.

so;[47] that I was subject to a ruler and a father[48] who was to strip me of all vanity and make me realize that one may live in a palace without requiring bodyguards,[49] flashy clothing, torchlight, statues, and similar trumpery, and that an emperor can make his life almost as circumscribed as that of a private citizen without thereby debasing himself or being less active in carrying out the duties that are required of him on behalf of the state.

That I had a brother[50] who was the kind of man who could rouse me to take care of myself, and who also delighted me with his respect and affection; that my children weren't born mentally defective or physically deformed; that I went no further than I did with rhetoric, poetry writing, and the other pursuits that might well have absorbed me if I'd found myself making progress on that path; that I lost no time in establishing my tutors in the social rank to which I thought they aspired and didn't fob them off with the hope that, since they were still young, I would see to it later;[51] that I got to know Apollonius, Rusticus, and Maximus.

---

47. As several of the entries in the book show, Marcus was rather a prude about sexual matters. A little later in this entry, for instance, he thanks the gods that he was "cured" whenever he felt erotic passion.

48. Antoninus.

49. The famous Praetorian Guard.

50. His brother by adoption, and co-emperor, Lucius Verus.

51. He raised them to senatorial rank, especially by making them aediles or praetors.

That I had a vivid and often-repeated sense of what it is to live life in accord with nature,[52] such that, so far as concerns the gods (that is, the gifts I received from them, the ways in which they helped me, and the thoughts I had about them), nothing is stopping me from living in accord with nature right now, and, if I fall short of this ideal, that is my own fault and due to my failure to observe the reminders—one might almost say the instructions—that I've been given by the gods.[53]

---

52. On living in accord with nature, see the Introduction, xlv. In 1.9, he attributes his understanding of living in accord with nature to Sextus, not to the gods; presumably the two worked on him in parallel.

53. This is Marcus's way of expressing what might otherwise be expressed as a kind of innate knowledge: "We come into the world with no innate conception of a right-angled triangle or of a quarter-tone or half-tone.... But everyone who comes into the world has an innate conception of good and bad, right and wrong, proper and improper, and of happiness, of rightness and appropriateness, and of what he ought to do and avoid doing" (Epictetus, *Discourses* 2.11.2–4).

That my body has lasted so long, given the kind of life I've lived;[54] that I didn't touch Benedicta or Theodotus,[55] and that later in life as well, whenever I felt erotic passion, I was cured;[56] that, although I was often angry with Rusticus, I didn't take it further and do anything I might have regretted; that my mother, who was to die young, at least spent her final years living with me; that whenever I wanted to help someone who was in need of money or something, I was never told that I didn't have the resources to make it happen; that I myself never fell into similar

---

54. On Marcus's life, see the Introduction, xiv–xxiii.

55. Probably slaves of the imperial household. It was understood that masters could have sex with their slaves: see, for example, 3.2. Marcus assumes the possibility of sex with both men and women, but this does not make him "bisexual," in our terms. In ancient times, sex was classified less by gender and more by who did the penetrating and who was penetrated. Despite his apparent attraction toward Theodotus, Marcus was basically homophobic: 3.16, 5.10, 6.34. Homosexual practices were widely tolerated in imperial Rome, but many, like Marcus, found them distasteful. In Marcus's case, this dovetailed with his desire, as a Stoic, to see himself and others restrain themselves and not give in to bodily urges.

56. Notice the implication that Marcus was not in love with his wife. This was normal, especially for arranged marriages at the highest levels of society. One married for reasons of political alliance and to perpetuate the family with noble stock; one fell in love, or lust, with others.

need and had to be helped by someone else; that my wife[57] was the kind of woman she was, so biddable, affectionate, and unaffected; that I had no lack of suitable tutors for my children.[58]

That I was given help in my dreams, especially how to avoid spitting blood and getting dizzy;[59] the response of the oracle in Caieta, "Just as you use yourself";[60] that when I was first attracted to philosophy, I didn't fall into the hands of a sophist, nor did

---

57. Annia Galeria Faustina, the daughter of Antoninus Pius. They married in 145, and she died in 175 in Asia Minor, as she and Marcus were returning to Rome from a tour of the eastern provinces of the empire.

58. Some of what Marcus thanks the gods for seems relatively trivial, but Marcus is reminding himself to be grateful for everything the gods have ever given him. In Notebooks 2–12, this is expressed as welcoming or accepting every experience that has been allotted to one by the gods.

59. Dreams that expressed or hinted at cures for illnesses were such a recognized aspect of the ancient Mediterranean world that, apart from private visions of the kind Marcus experienced, there were many healing temples where one could go and spend some nights until one was vouchsafed such a dream. It sounds as though Marcus was consumptive, and he died relatively young.

60. The text here is very uncertain. There was an oracle of Apollo at Caieta (modern Gaeta, north of Naples). Quite what Marcus's question to the oracle was is anyone's guess: "How should I use others?" perhaps.

I shut myself away and study history, or analyze arguments, or occupy my time with the study of celestial phenomena.[61]

For none of the blessings I've listed are possible without the help of the gods and of fortune.[62]

———

61. See also Xenophon, *Memorabilia* 1.1.11–16 and 4.7.5–6 on Socrates, and Epictetus, fragment 1 Schenkl ("Matters beyond our ken we should ignore"). Logic and physics (the nature of the universe) were, however, core disciplines for many Stoics. At 7.67, Marcus again confesses his lack of interest in these fields; see also 8.1. He may have felt himself not clever enough to understand it all: see 5.5.

62. Although the Stoics believed in a single God, the Rational Mind that providentially guides the entire universe and all that it contains, they accepted the existence also of the plural gods of the Greek and Roman pantheons as fragments of this Reason, each responsible for a different province of the universe.

NOTEBOOK 2

Written Among the Quadi on the River Granua. 1.[1]

---

1. The Marcomannic Wars (see the Introduction, xxi–xxii) occupied much of Marcus's reign. The Quadi, from modern Moravia, had been defeated by 174, but they rebelled again in 177, and Marcus had just successfully defeated them when he died in 180. The Granua is the modern river Hron in Slovakia. Only this notebook and the next have such headings; if Marcus wrote more, they are lost. The "1" at the end of the inscription probably means "Notebook 1," the first notebook to be written; but the later addition of what is now Notebook 1 made this former first notebook Notebook 2. If there are primary themes to this notebook, they are Marcus's relations with the divine and his neighbors, and his urgent need to reform himself. In other words, it is to a certain extent a book of fundamental principles. The first four entries of this notebook have been turned into an excellent rap song (not in my translation) by Akira the Don.

[1] At the start of the day[2] tell yourself: I shall meet people who are officious, ungrateful, abusive, treacherous, malicious, and selfish. In every case, they've got like this because of their ignorance of good and bad.[3] But I have seen goodness and badness for what they are, and I know that what is good is what

---

2. There are more thoughts about how to start the day at 5.1 and 10.13; the anticipation of future ills was an acknowledged practice within Stoicism, a way of lessening their impact when or if they occurred. This entry follows a pattern typical of *Meditations*: Marcus confronts a problem (the unpleasantness of the people he has to deal with as emperor) and comes up with a solution. Here the solution is to be a better person than them. How to cope with offensive people is a recurrent theme of the notebooks (e.g., 5.28, 9.42, 10.30, 11.9, 11.13, 11.18), as is anger management in general. In fact, the curbing of anger is such a strong theme in the book that we can safely conclude that Marcus had a short temper.

3. The Stoics followed Socrates in holding that virtue was knowledge and vice, ignorance. If one truly knows what is right and what is wrong, one will not be swayed by other factors to do wrong. People do wrong and go wrong out of ignorance and false beliefs. If I choose to smoke cigarettes, I do not do so because I believe them to be bad for me, but because of the belief that the pleasure of smoking outweighs any pain, current or future. Ultimately, what I want is not the cigarette but the good, and so, if I choose something that is in fact bad, it is not because I want something bad, but because I have a false belief about what is good for me (in this case, pleasure). This nest of ideas recurs frequently in various forms throughout the book.

is morally right, and what is bad is what is morally wrong;[4] and I've seen the true nature of the wrongdoer himself and know that he's related to me—not in the sense that we share blood and seed, but by virtue of the fact that we both partake of the same intelligence, and so of a portion of the divine.[5] None of them can harm me, anyway, because none of them can infect me with immorality,[6] nor can I become angry with someone who's related

---

4. This is the fundamental tenet of Stoicism: the only thing that is truly good is virtue, and the only thing that is truly bad is vice. Everything else that we might think "good" or "bad" is in fact an "indifferent," morally neutral, though indifferents occupy a scale of value and are to be preferred or rejected according to whether they support or hinder an aspirant to virtue.

5. For Stoics, as Marcus makes clear, a person's true self is the rational mind, which is a splinter of the Rational Mind that is God or Zeus and that steers the whole universe for the best. All humans are therefore kin because they all partake of the same divinity. The idea recurs frequently in the book, along with some of its consequences in terms of what it implies for one's relations with other people. This true self, as the god within, is prominent in Notebooks 2 and 3, and then appears little until Notebook 12.

6. Marcus is alluding to a famous saying of Socrates, from Plato's *Apology of Socrates* 30c–d: "My accusers cannot harm me, because in my opinion it is contrary to divine law for a better man to be harmed by a worse one." In a different paraphrase, the saying forms the final words of Epictetus's *Handbook*. The inability of anyone or anything external to do one harm is a recurrent theme of the *Meditations*. It also follows that the only harm we suffer is the harm we do to ourselves by doing wrong, which is to say by assenting to false and injurious beliefs. See, for example, 2.16, 4.26, 6.21, 8.55, 9.4, 9.38.

to me, or hate him, because we were born to work together, like feet or hands or eyelids, like the rows of upper and lower teeth.[7] To work against each other is therefore unnatural—and anger and rejection count as "working against."[8]

[2] This thing that I am, whatever we are to call it, is flesh, spirit, and the command center.[9] Forget your books—and don't

---

7. The analogy between parts of the body and human beings as parts of a greater organic whole is common in the book.

8. For Marcus, a person's spiritual development is revealed not just by her increasingly rational selection among the choices with which she is faced, but also by her increasing avoidance of negative passions in favor of those that allow her to cooperate with fellow human beings. It is an essential aspect of Stoicism that every individual always has choice—hence the tone of the entire *Meditations*, in which Marcus urges himself to make the right choices. We choose at every moment to be puppets or our own puppet masters (to borrow a recurrent image deployed by Marcus).

9. The same tripartite distinction at 3.16, 12.3, and 12.14. The Stoics were thorough materialists: even our souls are made of air, a physical substance, as is the "command center," because it is a part of our soul. Otherwise, they reasoned, how could a thought, generated in the soul, cause our bodies to move? The command center is the highest, divine, rational part of the soul, the same as the god within of the previous entry. The command center is one's mind, or self, or center of consciousness, responsible for all mental processes, but not for automatic bodily processes. It was usually thought to be located in the heart.

let it upset you—that's not allowed.[10] Instead, as one on the point of death, despise the flesh: it's just blood, bones, and a network of nerves, veins, and arteries.[11] Then consider what spirit is: no more than air, and never constant, continually belched out and gulped back in again. So that leaves the third ingredient, the command center. Look at it this way: you're elderly; put an end to allowing its enslavement; put an end to being tugged here and there like a puppet at the prompting of selfish impulses;[12] put an end to

---

10. This notebook was very likely written out on campaign. Marcus did not have his complete library to hand, and he was obviously missing it. But its lack enabled him to focus, in true Stoic fashion, on being virtuous, rather than on being learned. Disparagement of book learning is an especially prominent theme in Epictetus's *Discourses*.

11. By Marcus's time, these aspects of human anatomy were known, but their true functions were not perfectly understood. Note the asceticism implicit in "despise the flesh." Marcus had little but disdain for his body (see also 3.3, 7.68); it seemed to him little more than a source of pain and discomfort (e.g., 5.26, 7.14, 7.66, 9.41, 12.1), and filth (8.24) or, on the contrary, of tempting pleasures (e.g., 5.26, 11.19).

12. Marcus liked the puppet analogy and used it in several other places: 3.16, 6.16, 6.28, 7.3, 7.29, 10.38, 12.19. He was probably thinking not so much of the kind of puppet that dangles from strings and is manipulated by a human agent as of the kind, popular in his day, that goes through its motions after being wound up, with its strings pulled by, for example, falling weights. In other words, his point is that it is a thoughtless, mechanical kind of action. See S. Berryman, "The Puppet and the Sage: Images of the Self in Marcus Aurelius," *Oxford Studies in Ancient Philosophy* 38 (2010): 187–209.

both complaining about your present fate and shrinking from the future.[13]

[3] The gods' works are filled with providence; the works of fortune aren't independent of nature or of the interlacing and intertwining of things under the direction of providence.[14] It is the source of everything, including necessity and the well-being of the universe, the whole of which you are a part. What is good for every part of nature is what is supplied by the nature of the whole and what preserves the whole; and what preserves the whole is the changing of the compounds no less than the changing of the

---

13. As later entries make clear, this is a form of impiety, because it is in effect not accepting the lot the gods have assigned you: see, for example, 5.8, 9.1 (especially), and 11.20. This, though unstated, is the link between this entry and the next.

14. In a world governed by the rational providence of God, what place is there for fortune? For Marcus (see especially 3.2), fortune manifests in the apparently random effects of natural processes. But since they are natural processes, if we had full understanding, we would see God's hand at work there too, and not ascribe them to chance. The Stoics were determinists: every event is part of an unbroken chain of causation, extending back and forward forever. "Providence is God's will, and furthermore God's will is the sequence of causes" (Calcidius, *On Plato's Timaeus* 144). On Stoic determinism, see the Introduction, xlvi–xlviii.

physical elements.[15] Be content with these doctrines; make them your constant guiding principles. Get over your thirst for books, so that you don't die grumbling, but with true serenity and with heartfelt gratitude to the gods.

[4] Remember how long you've been putting this off and how often the gods have given you due dates of which you've not taken advantage. It's high time now for you to recognize what kind of universe you're a part of, and what kind of universal directing power you're an emanation of, and that a limit has been set on your time, and if you don't use it to dispel the mists it will pass, and you will pass, and the opportunity won't come again.

[5] You must always consider, with Roman and masculine doggedness, how to tackle any matter that arises with scrupulous and unfeigned grace, affection for others, generosity, and justice,

---

15. The elements (earth, water, air, fire) that, in infinite combinations, make up every item in the universe are constantly breaking apart (which is death) and recombining. The main lessons Marcus wants to learn from this—often repeated in the book—are that everything is transient and that death is not to be feared. Death—the dissolution of the compounds that we are—is just as much a natural and therefore beneficial process as the combining and recombining of the four elements.

and how to spend no time over all other incoming impressions.[16] That will happen if you treat every act as though it were the last of your life[17]—which is to say, if you're free from all stray thoughts[18] and from any deviation, under the influence of passion, from the principles established by reason, and if you're free from hypocrisy, self-love, and dissatisfaction with your lot. And look! There are only a few things that a person has to master in order to gain the ability to live a contented and god-fearing life.[19] Even the gods will require nothing more from someone who adheres to these few principles.

[6] Treat yourself with contempt, soul of mine—yes, contempt! The time has passed for you to respect yourself. For

---

16. "Impressions" translates *phantasia*, a technical term within Stoicism. The word covers all objects of awareness, anything that impresses itself on our minds or appears to us: sense perception (seen as a sensory mode whereby the mind receives impressions) and all forms of thinking, memory, and imagination. In each case, what is impressed on or presented to the mind effectively comes, according to the Stoics, in a propositional form: "There's a bull in the field." We then mentally accept or reject that proposition, leading to an "impulse" to take appropriate action. An action is the consequence of assenting to the impulse that it is the appropriate thing to do.

17. Marcus found this exercise useful and repeats it at 2.11 and 7.69.

18. The value of mental focus and always acting purposefully is a recurrent theme of the book. It is a matter, as Marcus puts it in 11.21, of "always being the same man."

19. At 4.3, Marcus again consoles himself with the thought that the stages on the road to enlightened sagehood are few, even if difficult. See also 3.10 and 7.67.

no one lives long, and this life of yours is all but spent while you dishonor yourself and make your happiness depend on the souls of others.[20]

[7] Do you get sidetracked when external things intrude? Free yourself from them, in favor of learning something new and worthwhile, and stop your purposeless wandering. But now there's another kind of meandering that you need to guard against: people who've become world-weary, and lack a goal to which they can direct every impulse and, in general, every impression, act in ways that are as meaningless as their words.

[8] One doesn't commonly see people becoming miserable as a result of not taking note of what's going on in someone else's

---

20. He is urging himself to be a self-reliant moral agent. The Greek word *psykhē* is notoriously impossible to translate, because it corresponds with no single thing in English. It is the "soul," the animating part of a person and the true self; it is the conscious self or "mind," which thinks, remembers, feels, imagines, and so forth; sometimes it is "temperament" or "character." It is a blanket term for the inner conscious and unconscious parts of a person, and hence is frequently distinguished from and coupled with the body. It is important to try to capture the capaciousness of the Greek term, and so I have mostly used "soul," but sometimes "mind" (and occasionally "heart," as in "wholehearted"). Marcus too uses "soul" and "mind" (*dianoia, nous*) interchangeably when he is talking about the rational faculty of the soul. He also occasionally substitutes "spirit" for "soul," especially when he says that we are made of "body, spirit, and mind." The human soul is made of pure *pneuma*, spirit, which is at the same time the stuff that permeates all creation and maintains it.

soul, but anyone who's unaware of the activity of his own soul can't help but be miserable.[21]

[9] Here are things you should always bear in mind: what the nature of the whole is; what my nature is; how my nature is related to the nature of the whole; what kind of part it is of what kind of whole; and that no one is stopping you from being in accord with the nature of which you are a part, in all you ever say or do.[22]

[10] Theophrastus spoke as a true philosopher when, in the course of his comparison of offenses (a comparative exercise that is quite commonly undertaken),[23] he said that the sins of desire

---

21. As in the previous entry, Marcus is talking about the importance of having an aim in life, and one that corresponds to the reality of things; otherwise, one's soul moves aimlessly in various useless directions. Happiness, the avoidance of misery, depends on aligning oneself with the rational ordering of the universe. Everything else is "flowers by the wayside." Almost all ancient Greek philosophers agreed that happiness was the goal and that it depended on the secure possession of goods; the Stoics differed in claiming (following Socrates) that the only thing that is good is virtue. This constitutes or is sufficient for happiness because it puts us in a harmonious and joyful relationship with the powers that govern and guide the universe.

22. Marcus often reminds himself that he is or should be an independent moral agent: for example, 3.12, 4.49, 5.29, 6.58, 8.32, 9.11, 10.32, 12.25. In a rush to jot down his ideas, Marcus used both the first and the second persons for himself, both "I" and "you"; we will find him doing so quite often in the book, but the "you" predominates.

23. Marcus's tone is wry: for a Stoic, all sins are equally bad, just because they are not virtue.

were more serious than the sins of anger. He argued that an angry man abandons reason because he's distressed, experiencing some internal psychic contraction,[24] while a man whose wrongdoing is caused by desire is more self-indulgent, because he's been defeated by pleasure,[25] and is less manly in his wrongdoing. He was right, then, and thinking like a philosopher, to say that wrongdoing that's accompanied by pleasure is more deserving of blame than wrongdoing that's accompanied by distress. To put it generally, the latter case seems to be one where someone has had wrong done to him first, and his pain compelled him to get angry, whereas in the former case he felt impelled of his own accord to do wrong and acted as he did because he was carried along by desire.[26]

––––––––––

24. "Distress is an irrational contraction" (Andronicus, *On Passions* 1).

25. "Being defeated by pleasure" was the standard Greek way of expressing weakness of will, from the time when Plato first introduced the topic as a matter for philosophical speculation. See also, for example, 2.16, 2.17.

26. Theophrastus was in fact following his teacher, Aristotle. At *Nicomachean Ethics* 1149a, Aristotle said: "Lack of self-control with regard to anger is less shameful than the kind that relates to desire." It seems odd for Marcus apparently to be agreeing with Theophrastus's ranking, when for a Stoic both desire and anger are to be avoided. It is possible that he was bearing in mind the Stoic doctrine (Stobaeus, *Anthology* 2.90–91) that anger is in fact an offshoot of desire, and was therefore ranking anger as less of a problem than desire. This entry forms an important plank in the argument some scholars develop that Marcus was not a pure Stoic.

[11] Everything you do and say and think should be predicated on the possibility of your imminent departure from life.[27] But, if the gods exist,[28] leaving this world can't be something to fear, because they wouldn't let anything bad happen to you. On the other hand, if they don't exist or have no care for the human race, why live in such a world, devoid of gods and divine providence?[29] But in fact they do exist and they do care for the human race, and they've made it entirely up to each of us to avoid experiencing anything truly bad.[30] And if anything else were bad, they would also have made sure that it was our choice whether or not to experience that too. (But how could a man's life be made worse by anything that doesn't make him a worse

---

27. The first of very many entries in the book offering Marcus, who was often ill, consolation in the face of death. Over 10 percent of the entire book is given over to the subject of death.

28. Marcus is not here doubting the existence of the gods, but supplying a premise for his argument. For more on the gods, see especially 1.17, 6.44, 9.27, 9.40, 12.5, 12.28. The Stoics saw little theoretical incompatibility between their doctrines and normal Roman religious beliefs, but their theology, with its identification of the gods with providence and fate, undermined the functions of petitionary and propitiatory prayer and sacrifice. Notice, in this entry, the equivalence between the gods and what Marcus here calls "the universe."

29. Marcus also doubts the value of remaining alive in a godless universe at 6.10.

30. For Stoics, the only truly bad thing is moral vice, and the ability to avoid that and seek virtue is entirely up to us. We choose at every moment what to do and what to regard as bad. All harm is therefore self-inflicted. See also 6.1, 9.42, and 11.8.

person?)[31] The universe would have neglected this only if it were ignorant, or if it had knowledge but lacked the ability to guard against it or correct it; but neither of these is the case. Nor could it have committed such a great wrong, out of either impotence or incompetence, as to let good and bad things be the lot equally of good and bad people without distinction. But death and life, glory and obscurity, pain and pleasure, wealth and poverty— all these things come to good and bad people alike, since they are morally neutral in themselves, and this proves that they're neither good nor bad.[32]

[**12**] How rapidly everything vanishes, physical bodies lost in the universe and the memory of them lost in eternity! Look at the nature of every object we perceive, especially those that entice us with the prospect of pleasure, frighten us with the prospect of pain, or are celebrated by humans in their vanity! How worthless, vile, sordid, and short-lived things are, just corpses![33] It is for the intellectual faculty to consider what kind of people they are, those whose views and voices confer fame or obscurity;

---

31. There is a similarly moral interpretation of being harmed at 4.8.

32. They are "indifferents," morally neutral: Introduction, xl–xli. There seem to be three consolatory thoughts about death in this entry, related but not always fully formed: the gods are good and therefore govern a good universe, so death cannot be bad; an aspect of their goodness is our ability to avoid anything truly bad, but we cannot avoid death, so it cannot be truly bad; death is one of a host of indifferents, neither good nor bad.

33. The shoddiness, paltriness, and vulgarity of the world is a recurrent theme.

what death is, and the fact that, if one sees it for what it is and, by analyzing the concept, dissolves the impressions that adhere to it, one will stop believing it to be anything other than a natural process[34]—and there's nothing to fear about natural processes unless you're a child[35]—though in fact not only is it a product of nature, but it also does nature good;[36] and how a human being makes contact with God, with what part of himself, and in what condition this part of him must be to do so.

[13] There's nothing more pathetic than a man who's always running around and poking his nose in everywhere—investigating "the nether regions of the earth," in the poet's words[37]—and using outside signs to infer what's going on in his neighbors' souls, without realizing that all he needs to do is focus on his own inner

---

34. Death is a natural process simply because of the natural law that everything that is born will die. See the Introduction, liv–lv, for other ways in which Marcus consoled himself in the face of impending death. "Death is not frightening; what is frightening is the idea that death is frightening" (Epictetus, *Handbook* 5).

35. He is thinking of things like thunder and lightning.

36. How does my death benefit nature? Chiefly (and frequently repeated in the notebooks) by replenishing the stock of physical elements so that more creatures can be made; at 6.15 and 7.25, Marcus speaks in this context of the renewal of the world. As often elsewhere, Marcus is inviting himself to reconsider death in a new, positive light.

37. Pindar of Boeotia (518–c. 440 BCE) was the most famous lyric poet of the Greek world. This snatch of a poem is fragment 292 Snell. Marcus uses it merely as a vivid metaphor for poking one's nose in where it has no business.

guardian spirit[38] and take proper care of it. Caring for it is keeping it unsullied by passion, purposelessness, and dissatisfaction with the activities of gods and men; for the goodness of the gods is such that their acts are to be respected, and human kinship means that men's acts are to be welcomed. There are times, however, when human acts are also rather pitiful because of their ignorance of good and bad, which is as much of a disability as being blind to the difference between white and black.[39]

[14] Even if you were to live for three thousand years or ten times as long, remember that the only life anyone loses is this one, the one he's living, and the only life anyone lives is the one he loses. It follows that the longest life and the shortest life come to the same thing.[40] The present moment is equal for all, and therefore its passing is equal for all, and therefore what is lost

---

38. Another term for what elsewhere is called the "command center" within oneself. The idea that each of us has our own guardian spirit may be Pythagorean in origin, but it was promoted especially by Plato; see, above all, the great myth that concludes his *Republic*, and *Timaeus* 90a.

39. Marcus does not mean that moral ignorance is as involuntary as color blindness—though it may be pitied (as also in 2.1). In moral matters, there is always choice.

40. The life of a mayfly and the life of an elephant are exactly equal—both one life long; see also 4.50 and 9.33. The American novelist Kurt Vonnegut puts this insight to use in several of his books.

turns out to be a mere instant.[41] After all, no one can lose either the past or the future, because no one can lose what he doesn't have. So there are two points for you always to bear in mind: first, that everything is the same in kind throughout all eternity, and recurs cyclically,[42] and that it makes no difference how long you see these same things, whether it's a hundred years or two hundred years or infinite time; second, that both the longest-lived and the shortest-lived lose an equal amount of time, because the present is the only thing one can lose, since that is all one has, and no one can lose what he does not have.

---

41. We have seen Marcus consoling himself in 2.12 with the thought that death cannot be a bad thing because it is a "work of nature." Now he consoles himself with the thought that death is no more than the loss of a single moment; see also 3.10 and 12.26 (end).

42. Stoics believed in eternal recurrence—that the physical universe goes through an endless sequence of cycles, each ending after an immensity of time in total conflagration, with exactly the same events happening in each cycle. Their thinking was perhaps that, since *ex hypothesi* the world is, thanks to God's providential goodness, as good as it can be, any variation in its next iteration would be less than good. Marcus alludes to the theory quite often in the book. In modern times, the theory features in the work, among others, of Friedrich Nietzsche and P. D. Ouspensky (and even crops up in the 1993 film *Groundhog Day*). For more on eternal recurrence, see A. A. Long, "The Stoics on World-Conflagration and Everlasting Recurrence," in his *From Epicurus to Epictetus: Studies in Hellenistic and Roman Philosophy* (Oxford University Press, 2006), 256–282.

[15] "Everything is as you take it to be."[43] As a response to Monimus the Cynic, this is self-evident, but the value of the saying is also obvious, if one accepts what is wholesome about it, its truth and no more.

[16] The human soul dishonors itself, first and foremost, when it becomes, to the extent that it can, a growth and a tumor, as it were, on the universe. To resent anything that happens is to set oneself apart from nature, of which the various individual natures of everything else are parts.[44] A second case is when it rejects another human being or even opposes him with malicious intent; this is what the souls of angry people are like.[45] Third, it

---

43. This famous saying is repeated or alluded to at 12.8, 12.22, and 12.26. Monimus adopted the skeptical view that there is no objective way to tell true from false, good from bad, and so on, on the ground that everything is as you take it to be. The Stoics turned his words back on themselves: if everything is only as any individual takes it to be, then his assertion applies only to himself, not to others. At the same time, as Marcus goes on to acknowledge, there is some "wholesomeness" to Monimus's assertion insofar as it coincides with the Stoic view, frequently alluded to in the notebooks, that judgments about the world are entirely up to us.

44. Since for a Stoic the universe is a single, ordered whole, interrelated in all its parts (e.g., 4.45, 12.30) and governed by divine Reason, then to resent anything that happens is to set oneself apart from the universe. See also 4.29 and 11.8.

45. So, to be alienated from just one person cuts one off from the community of rational beings as a whole because it is not living in accord with nature.

dishonors itself when it's defeated by pleasure or pain.[46] Fourth, when it dissembles and does or says anything in an affected or dishonest manner. Fifth, when it fails to direct any of its actions or impulses toward a goal, but instead acts without purpose and without attention, when even the slightest actions should be carried out with reference to the end.[47] And the end for rational beings is to follow the reason and rule of the most venerable of all cities and communities.[48]

---

46. Notice how Marcus in this entry combines behaviors that affect other people and those that affect only ourselves: we need to behave virtuously in both respects. Our personal inward growth has to be paralleled by increasingly correct behavior toward others. Here, with the mention of pleasure and pain, we again meet the idea that the passions, or almost all of them, are forms of psychic sickness that warp our true nature and prevent us from "living in accord with nature."

47. There is a similar list of offenses against oneself at 9.1.

48. Marcus means the world itself, which the Stoics thought of as a great city or state, a *cosmopolis*, of which all people are citizens; see also 3.11, 4.3, 4.23, 4.29 (very similar thoughts to those of this entry), 10.15, 12.36. The city is ruled by reason, embodied as law (4.4, 8.2, 10.25, 12.36).

[**17**] A person's lifetime is a moment, his existence a flowing stream,[49] his perception dull, the entire fabric of his body readily subject to decay, his soul an aimless wanderer, his fortune erratic, his fame uncertain. In short: the body is nothing but a river; the soul is dream and delusion; life is war and a sojourn in a strange land; and oblivion is all there is to posthumous fame.[50]

---

49. Marcus is referring to the famous saying of Heraclitus of Ephesus (c. 500 BCE) that "Everything is flowing." The Stoics (especially Cleanthes) looked back to Heraclitus as one of their forebears. Either directly or by interpreting his work, they found themselves supported by him in thinking of fire as an active principle, which starts the cosmogonic process, organizes the universe, and brings the universe to an end by means of periodic conflagrations. They agreed that everything was in flux, both locally and overall—just permutations of fire—so that there was unity underlying the unstable plurality of the world. They agreed that the universe was governed by *logos*, Reason, and that human *logos* was a fragment of *logos*-at-large. They even tried to claim that Heraclitus was a determinist. Marcus in particular felt himself indebted to Heraclitus, whom he considered a great sage (3.3, 4.46, 6.42, 8.3). He employs Heraclitus's image of a river to represent universal flux (2.17, 4.43, 5.23, 6.15, 7.19) and alludes to other famous Heraclitean dicta at 6.17, 6.57, and 9.28. He agrees with Heraclitus that the senses are unreliable (2.17) and that the true nature of things is hidden (5.10).

50. Marcus frequently recurs to the topic of fame and its evanescence—so frequently that it seems fame was something he was tempted by. As here, he generally dismisses fame as worthless, but there was some debate on the matter. Could one, perhaps, not become famous for being virtuous, as Socrates was for the Stoics? Was even a moderate degree of public recognition forbidden?

What, then, can escort us safely on our way? Only one thing: philosophy.[51] This consists in keeping the guardian spirit within us safe from assault and harm, never swayed by pleasure or pain, purposeful when it acts, free from dishonesty or dissemblance, and never dependent on action or inaction from anyone else. It also consists in accepting what happens, the lot one has been assigned, as coming from the same source as oneself, and in always awaiting death with a serene mind, understanding that it's no more than the disintegration of the elements of which every living creature is a compound. If there's nothing unusual in the elements themselves changing moment by moment one into another, why should the alteration and disintegration of them all be a cause for anxiety? It's in accord with nature, and nothing that's in accord with nature is bad.

---

51. This is an important passage for understanding how Marcus thought of philosophy. It had been established for hundreds of years, since the fourth century BCE, that for anyone who wanted to be happy and fulfilled as a human being (as all do) and was prepared to work at it (as few do), philosophy was the essential tool. "Who can doubt that, although life is given to us by the immortal gods, the gift of living well is given by philosophy?" (Seneca, *Letter* 90.1).

NOTEBOOK 3

Written in Carnuntum[1]

[1] One must take into consideration not only the fact that life is being used up day by day and there's less of it left, but also that, if one were to live longer, there's no guarantee that one's mind will remain unaffected and capable of understanding the way things are in themselves, or the concepts that guide one's experience of matters both divine and human. The early

---

1. Carnuntum (near modern Hainburg in Austria) was the capital of the Roman province of Pannonia Superior. Marcus made it his headquarters in the early 170s for the Marcomannic Wars, and the site is now an excellent archaeological park. Carnuntum lay on the Danube, which was the boundary of this part of the Roman Empire, with hostile Germanic tribes such as the Quadi on the northern side. Life in the headquarters was more peaceful than life on the front line, and this perhaps explains the relatively light and constructive tone of this notebook, which focuses above all on what it is to be a good man.

symptoms of senility don't involve the failure of things like transpiration, digestion, sense perception, or impulse;[2] the first to go are abilities that require a well-trained mental faculty, such as making proper use of oneself, accurately estimating the limits of appropriate behavior, analyzing one's impressions, and understanding whether the time has come to take your leave of this life.[3] You must have a sense of urgency, then, not only because at each moment you're drawing closer to death, but also because your understanding of the world around you and your ability to pay attention to it will come to an end before you do.

[2] One should also take careful note of things such as the fact that even the by-products of natural phenomena have a certain charm and attractiveness. For example, in the process of baking bread, the loaf breaks open in some places, and although these cracks in a sense represent a failure of the baker's art, they

---

2. That is, the faculties that, according to Stoicism, we share with plants (transpiration is breathing through pores; see 6.16) and animals.

3. Suicide was considered by Stoics the rational and right thing to do if the gods willed it—that is, if it became impossible for a man to live in accord with nature and be virtuous (for instance, if he was insane, badly maimed, or utterly destitute) or to continue to serve friends or country. Both the founders of Stoicism, Zeno of Citium and Cleanthes of Assos, were said to have killed themselves, and Cato and Brutus (see 1.14) were also famous Stoic suicides. On Xenophon's (but not Plato's) account of Socrates's trial and death, Socrates in effect killed himself. The Stoic writer Seneca regarded suicide as the ultimate justification of a person's freedom and eventually put this theory into practice. Marcus contemplates the possibility again at 5.29, 8.47, 9.2, 10.8, 10.22, 10.32, and 11.3.

do somehow catch the eye and, in their own way, stimulate the desire to eat the bread. Or again: when figs are fully ripe they split open, and in the case of ripe olives the very fact that they are on the verge of rotting gives the fruit a specific kind of beauty. The same goes for ears of wheat bowing down to the ground, a lion's wrinkled brow, a boar foaming at the mouth, and many other things. They are hardly lovely if viewed in isolation, but they enhance the appeal of the natural phenomena of which they are concomitants, and so we find them attractive.

So there's almost nothing that a sensitive person, with a deep enough understanding of the workings of the universe, will fail to find pleasing in its manifestations, including these incidental concomitants. He gets as much pleasure from seeing the gaping jaws of actual wild beasts as he does from the secondhand representations of them by painters and sculptors.[4] He's able to see a kind of perfection and beauty in the elderly of both sexes, and to view the sexual attractiveness of his slaves with chaste eyes.[5] And although most people will find few such cases plausible, that's because they are not genuinely familiar with nature and its works.

---

4. The lion's jaw recurs in 6.36, again as something usually found terrifying. In his *On the Parts of Animals*, Aristotle says: "It would be illogical and absurd to take pleasure in contemplating reproductions of creatures . . . and not to find it more enjoyable to contemplate the creatures themselves, which nature has made" (645a).

5. Because he will see their allure simply as a by-product of natural processes. Compare 1.16 on Benedicta and Theodotus.

[3] Hippocrates cured many an illness, before dying of an illness himself. The Chaldaeans[6] foretold the deaths of many people, but were then overtaken themselves by their death days. Alexander, Pompey, and Julius Caesar wiped out entire cities by the dozen, and slaughtered hundreds of thousands of horsemen and foot soldiers in battle, and one day they too passed away. Heraclitus, as a natural scientist, wrote a great deal about the destruction of the world by fire, and died with his insides filled with water, wrapped in a poultice of cow dung.[7] Democritus was killed by lice, and lice of another kind killed Socrates.[8] What to make of this? You embarked, set sail, and reached land. Step ashore. If it takes you to another life—well, nothing is devoid of

---

6. A priestly caste of astrologers from Babylon. Doctors and astrologers head the list at 4.48 as well.

7. This was a famous tale about Heraclitus's death, popular because of the ironic contrast between his emphasis on fire and the fact that he died of dropsy. By the same token, the cow-dung poultice contrasts with the loftiness of his theories. Cow-dung poultices are still in use in various parts of the world.

8. Democritus was not the only person from ancient times who was said to have died from an infestation of lice (phthiriasis), but it is not clear what sickness is being referred to, unless it is simply that he contracted typhus or something from the louse bites. In Democritus's case, his death is presumably, like Heraclitus's, supposed to be ironic: the inventor of atomic theory was killed by tiny little things. The "lice" that killed Socrates were the Athenian people, who condemned him to death in 399 BCE.

gods, even there. If it takes you to a state of insensibility,[9] you'll no longer have to endure pain and pleasure, and you'll no longer be in thrall to a bodily vessel that is as far inferior as that which is serving it is superior. For the latter is mind and guardian spirit, while the former is earth and blood.

[4] Don't waste what remains of your life thinking about other people, unless you do so with reference to the welfare of the state—I mean wondering what so-and-so is doing and why, or what he's saying, what he's thinking, what his designs are, and so on, which distracts you from paying attention to your own command center.[10] You have to exclude everything purposeless and random from the sequence of your thoughts, but especially and above all anything prompted by idle curiosity or ill will. You must get into the habit of restricting your thoughts to those that are such that if you were suddenly asked, "What are you thinking?" you could answer, frankly and without hesitation, "X" or "Y," and it would immediately be clear from your reply that all your thoughts are guileless and kindly, the thoughts of a

---

9. The full range of postmortem possibilities are "dispersal, extinction, or survival/change of place" (8.25, 11.3). But dispersal is the possibility that Marcus attributes to an Epicurean worldview, and so here (and at 5.33) he offers himself only the two Stoic possibilities. The choice of "extinction or survival" was famously postulated by Socrates in Plato's *Apology of Socrates*, at 40c–41c.

10. See 2.13 on caring for one's own command center. This entry and those that follow (up to 3.14) outline the kind of behavior Marcus expects of himself as a good man and a good ruler. Self-sufficiency is particularly emphasized here and in the next few entries.

sociable[11] creature who disdains pleasurable or any kind of self-indulgent fantasies and is untouched by rivalry, malice, suspicion, or anything else that one would blush to admit one had in mind.

Such a man—that is, one who has stopped postponing the time to focus on what is best in the universe—is indeed a kind of priest and minister to the gods.[12] He draws on that part of himself, lodged within him, that makes it possible for him to be uncorrupted by pleasures, unscathed by any pain, untouched by disrespect in all its forms, unaffected by immorality in all its forms, an athlete contending for the greatest of all prizes (that of never being thrown[13] by passion), deep-dyed in justice, able to welcome with all his heart every experience that comes his way and is allotted to him, and able to confine wondering what someone else is saying or doing or thinking to very rare occasions, only when the welfare of the state makes it absolutely imperative.[14]

---

11. Sociability was a Stoic virtue because it stemmed from recognition that we are all kin and members of the same community. It was particularly the Roman Stoics who emphasized it (and kindness, for instance) as a way to offset the austere aloofness of traditional Greek Stoicism and to reconcile Stoicism with the traditional Roman virtues of service to the state and care for friends and family. They tried to combine spiritual detachment with engagement with daily life.

12. Because the gods, being good, are responsible for "what is best in the universe."

13. Wrestling was so popular in the ancient Greek and Roman worlds that metaphors from the sport are common.

14. Marcus is effectively describing a Stoic sage, such as he aspired to be.

He does no one's work but his own, and thinks continually about the lot that has been woven for him by the universe,[15] making sure that the former is done well and convinced that the latter is good, because the fate that has been assigned a man is not only carried with him, but carries him with it.[16] He bears in mind also the kinship of all rational beings, and that even though it's natural for a man to care for all his fellow men, yet he must not welcome everyone's opinions, but only the views of those who live in agreement with nature.[17] As for those who live otherwise, he constantly reminds himself what they're like at home and in

---

15. The metaphor of weaving (see also 2.3) is prompted by the fact that one of the three Fates in traditional Greek religion was Clotho, the weaver. The other two were Atropos (the implacable) and Lachesis (she who allots).

16. The guardian spirit, or command center, is an internal part of a person, and in this sense is carried along with her, but it is also that which steers a person along her path in life.

17. This was always a difficult point for Stoics. On the one hand, all men are kin and carry within them a spark of the rationality and goodness of the universe; on the other hand, some men are plainly farther than others from acting in accordance with that. Sometimes, as here, Marcus merely warns himself against them. Elsewhere he is more Stoic: "Either instruct them or put up with them" (8.59). Sometimes his misanthropy gets the better of him and he describes people in savage terms, as at 5.10 and 5.28. In theory, Marcus wanted to love his neighbors, but he found it hard to put it into practice.

public, and what kind of company they keep day and night.[18] So he also regards praise from such men as worthless, since it comes from those who find nothing pleasing even in themselves.

[5] Never act reluctantly, selfishly, thoughtlessly, or with conflicting motives. Don't embellish your thoughts with fancy language. Avoid garrulousness and officiousness. Also, let the god within you be the custodian of the creature that you are: a man, an elder, a statesman, a Roman, and a ruler who has taken up a post, but as one who's expecting to be recalled from life and is ready to be released from service, without needing to swear an oath or call a human witness.[19] Be joyful within and in need of no external assistance or peace provided by others. In other words, you must stand straight, not be straightened.

[6] If you find anything better in human life than justice, honesty, moderation, and courage[20]—if, to put it generally, you

---

18. This might seem to contradict the first sentence of the entry, but here he is not thinking about other people in the sense of trying to take them into consideration, but reminding himself how mean and base they are.

19. The military metaphor recurs at 5.31, 7.7, 7.45, 10.22, 11.10, 11.20. See also 2.17: "Life is war." The original source of the metaphor was Socrates in Plato's *Apology of Socrates* 28b–e, which is partially quoted by Marcus at 7.45.

20. The only true good for Stoics was virtue, and the primary virtues, from which the others were derived, were the four Marcus lists, except that "prudential wisdom" replaces Marcus's "honesty," as at 5.12. All other so-called goods, such as health, wealth, and popularity, are "indifferents."

find anything better than the self-sufficiency of your mind on those occasions when it ensures that your actions are compatible with right reason, as well as when something is allotted to you by fate without your having chosen it—if, I say, you're aware of anything better than this, turn to it with all your heart and enjoy the supreme good you've discovered. But if you find nothing better than the guardian spirit lodged within you, which has brought all your particular impulses under its control, which scrutinizes your thoughts, which, as Socrates used to say, has withdrawn itself from sensations,[21] which has put itself in the gods' hands, and which cares providentially for other people— if everything else turns out to be trivial and worthless by comparison, then make room for nothing else.

The point is that once you've turned your attention elsewhere and turned aside from your path, it will be impossible for you to give your undivided attention and the highest honor to the good that is peculiarly your own.[22] It's sacrilegious for what is rational and contributes to the common good to be rivaled by anything that is different in kind, such as popularity,[23] political

---

21. This is not a direct quotation, but a reflection of the kind of dualistic idea Plato put into Socrates's mouth at *Phaedo* 83a–b.

22. Compare Epictetus, *Discourses* 4.12.1: "When you relax your attention for a little while, don't imagine that you'll recover it whenever you choose, but bear in mind that because of the mistake you've made today you're bound to be worse off in everything you do in the future."

23. Popularity is condemned not just because it is an indifferent, but also because of the poor quality of the people who give it to one. Why should one seek to be liked by fools?

power, wealth, or sensual pleasure—all things that afford a brief illusion of happiness, but then suddenly overpower one and lead one astray. So, as I say, you must simply and freely choose the better course and stay with it. "But what is better is what does me good." If it does you good as a rational being, don't dispense with it; but if it does you good as an animal,[24] spurn it and keep to your original decision without preening yourself on it. Just make sure that you conduct your inquiry without coming to harm.

[7] Never count something to your advantage if it's ever going to force you to break a promise, relinquish your modesty, hate or suspect or curse anyone, dissemble, or desire something that needs to be concealed behind walls or curtains.[25] A man who gives pride of place to his own mind and guardian spirit, and to the worship of its goodness, doesn't make a drama out of his life or deplore his circumstances, and has no need of isolation or crowds. Most importantly, he'll live a life free from attraction and repulsion.[26] It makes not the slightest difference to him whether his soul is to be encased in his body for a longer or shorter time, because even if today is the time for him to depart, he's so ready to be released that he leaves as though this were just another action to be performed in a conscientious and orderly manner. His one

---

24. Marcus here condemns the seeking of pleasure and avoidance of pain, which are due to our animal nature and therefore cannot fulfill us as human beings.

25. That is, strange sexual practices.

26. Free from pleasure (which attracts us) and pain (which we try to avoid).

concern throughout his life is that his mind should never be in a state that is inappropriate to a rational and social being.[27]

[8] In the mind of someone who's been chastened and purified you'll find no suppuration, nothing putrid or festering.[28] Nor does the day of his death catch him with his life incomplete, so that you might say that the actor is leaving the stage before the drama is over, before it's run its course.[29] You'll also find no trace of slavishness or affectation, neither dependency nor disengagement, nothing suspicious and nothing lurking unseen.

[9] Revere your faculty of judgment. Insofar as your command center is now free of judgments that are not in accord with nature and the constitution of a rational being, this is entirely its doing. And it's this faculty that holds out the promise of

---

27. The first, famously, to say "Man is a social being" was Aristotle, at *Politics* 1253a. To Marcus, being socially minded is the same as being focused on promoting the common good.

28. Medical analogies came naturally to Marcus, because he held that philosophy was a kind of therapy of the soul.

29. The image of actors on a stage recurs at 10.27, 11.1, and especially 12.36. Epictetus also made powerful use of the image, at *Handbook* 17.

freedom from hasty assent,[30] of affinity with your fellow men, and of conformity with the will of the gods.

[10] Throw everything away and retain only these few truths. Remember also that each of us lives only in the fleeting present moment, and that all the rest of our lives has either already been lived or is undisclosed. Each person's life is but a small thing, and small is the little corner of the earth where he lives.[31] Small too is even the longest-lasting posthumous fame, and it depends on a sequence of little men who will die very soon, and who aren't aware even of themselves, let alone someone who died long ago.

[11] There's one point yet to add to the above reminders. Always define or describe to yourself every impression that occurs to your mind, so that you can clearly see what the thing

---

30. "Assent" was a technical term in Stoicism. We assent to impressions, whether internally or externally generated; or, more strictly, we assent to the propositional content of impressions. See the Introduction, xlviii–xlix. Marcus here worries about hasty assent because it leads one to make wrong judgments about what things are and their value, and thus leads one to do or go wrong. As Epictetus says (*Discourses* 2.18.24): "Hold on a moment, impression. Let me see what you are and what you are an impression of. Let me put you to the test." One can see why truthfulness was such an important virtue for Marcus, because to lie is to perpetuate a false judgment.

31. Compare Julian of Norwich's beautiful description of the earth in her *Revelations of Divine Love* (early fifteenth century): "A little thing, the quantity of a hazelnut." Marcus's tone is similarly detached, here and commonly elsewhere, especially when he tells himself to take a view "from on high."

is like in its entirety, stripped to its essence, and tell yourself its proper name and the names of the elements of which it consists and into which it will be resolved.[32] Nothing is more conducive to objectivity than the ability methodically and honestly to test everything that you come across in life, and always to look at things in such a way that you consider what kind of part each of them plays in what kind of universe, and what value it has for the universe as a whole and for a man who is a citizen of the highest state, the state of which all other states are, so to speak, mere households.[33]

This thing that is now causing an impression in my mind: What is it? What is it made of? How long will it last, given what it is? What virtue is called for in its case? Not that this is a complete list, but is it calmness, perhaps, or courage, honesty,

---

32. For this exercise in objectivity (putting things under a microscope, as we might express it), see also 2.12, 6.13, 9.34, 9.36, 10.11, 11.2, 11.16, 11.17, 12.2, 12.8.

33. Or, as some Stoics put it: since all human beings have affinity, or are *oikeioi*, with one another, they belong to a common household (*oikos*). When we are born, we have a natural affinity with ourselves (which throughout our lives leads us to value self-preservation); this sense of affinity gradually expands, from self to mother to family to friends (as contributing to our survival), until by the time one is an adult human being, with a developed rational faculty, one sees that one has affinity with all other human beings (which should bring with it a sense of obligation toward others) and sees that the life of the mind and virtue is where the good must lie, not in mere physical preservation. We move from "appropriate actions" to "right actions."

fidelity, unaffectedness, self-sufficiency? In each case, then, here's what you must say: "This has come from God," or "This is an accidental result of the web woven by fate and a fortuitous coincidence of some kind," or "This has come from one of my own kind, someone who is kin and a member of the same society, but who's ignorant of what's in accord with his nature." But I *do* know, and so I treat him with kindness and justice, in accordance with the natural laws of human intercourse,[34] but at the same time I aim for equity, dealing with him as he deserves, when it comes to things that are morally neutral.[35]

[12] If you carry out every present task by following right reason assiduously, resolutely, and with kindness; if, rather than getting distracted by irrelevancies, you keep your guardian spirit unspoiled and steady, as though you had to surrender it at any moment; if you engage with the task not with expectations or evasions, but satisfied if your current performance is in accord with nature and if what you say and express is spoken with true

---

34. They are "natural" laws because the Stoics held that, as human beings, we are naturally endowed with the resources for virtue.

35. As a Stoically inclined emperor, Marcus would see his job as promoting virtue, but he did of course have to live in the real world, not the ideal Stoic world where virtue is recognized as the only good and vice as the only bad. He had to praise or condemn people for matters that, to a Stoic, were merely indifferent. See also 5.36, 6.45, and 9.11.

Roman honesty, you'll be living the good life.[36] And there's no one who can stop you doing so!

[13] Just as doctors always keep their instruments and implements ready to hand for emergency procedures, so you should keep your principles ready for understanding the divine and human realms, and everything you do, however trivial, should be done with consciousness of the bond that unites the two realms, in the sense that you won't succeed on the human level without simultaneously aiming at the divine, or vice versa.

[14] Don't be sidetracked anymore! You're not going to read your notebooks, or your accounts of ancient Roman and Greek history, or the commonplace books you were saving for your old age.[37] Head straight for your final goal and be your own savior,

---

36. "The good life" was shorthand in Greek philosophy for the ideal human condition, however conceived.

37. It is possible that some of the extracts that Marcus included in *Meditations*, especially in Notebooks 7 and 11, were originally written for his commonplace book. This entry gives us a fascinating insight into Marcus's other literary activities. It seems that none of them was intended for publication; even the notes on history were likely intended for the instruction of Marcus's son, the future emperor Commodus. It is not clear what the "notebooks" are to which he refers; perhaps earlier in his life he had tried to jot down the kinds of thoughts and reflections that make up our twelve notebooks, but in a less sustained fashion. If so, some of the entries in these earlier notebooks might well have been incorporated into the ones we have.

if you care for yourself, by abandoning vain hopes for the future while you still can.

[15] They do not know the full significance of terms such as thieving, sowing, buying, keeping the peace, and seeing what needs to be done. The significance is not apparent to the eyes, but to a different kind of vision.

[16] Body, soul,[38] mind. To the body belong sense perceptions, to the soul, impulses, and to the mind, principles. Being stamped with impressions is an attribute also of cattle; being tugged here and there by impulses is an attribute also of wild beasts, queers, Phalaris, and Nero; having the mind as a guide to what appears to be appropriate action is an attribute also of atheists, traitors, and people who behave with depravity behind closed doors.[39] So, if everything else is shared with the animal kingdom and the kinds of people I've just mentioned, what remains is what's peculiar to a good man. This is embracing and welcoming every experience that comes his way and is woven for him by fate, and

---

38. Marcus here uses the Greek word *psykhē* (see Notebook 2, note 20) in a restricted sense, as the animating force that we share with animals (but not with plants), ignoring for the moment that the *psykhē* also contains a person's guardian spirit, the command center. He is working with a tripartite division of psychic faculties: rationality (peculiar to humans and gods), "soul" (shared with animals), and natural growth (shared with plants).

39. We meet again the intellectualist conception of virtue. Everyone, even a traitor or a sexual pervert, does what he thinks best; it is just that he is acting on a mistaken belief as to what is truly good for him.

not defiling or disturbing the calm of the guardian spirit lodged in his breast with a horde of impressions, but making sure that it remains serene by following God in a decorous fashion, and by never saying anything untrue or doing anything unjust. Suppose everyone else in the world refuses to believe that he lives a simple, moral, contented life: he doesn't get angry with any of them, and he doesn't deviate from the path that leads him to the end of life, which he must reach in a state of purity and peace, ready to be released, and in willing harmony with his fate.[40]

40. The use of the third person in this entry is striking. It is Marcus's way of not claiming that degree of enlightenment for himself.

NOTEBOOK 4[1]

[1] In its natural state, the situation of the ruler within us as regards the events of the world is such that it readily adapts itself to what's feasible. It isn't wedded to any particular material that's proper specifically to it, but sets out with reservation to

———

1. Notebooks 4–11 are on the whole less personal in tone than Notebooks 2, 3, and 12, and more concerned with doctrine and theory. Hence, for instance, references to the inner god, the guardian spirit, are replaced by references to the "universal nature" that directs all things and to our intelligence as a splinter of universal nature. It is as though Marcus's personal worries and concerns pale into insignificance compared with the vast cosmic forces he touches on in these notebooks; death, for instance, is treated in them as a natural phenomenon rather than as something that should trigger personal reform, as in Notebooks 2–3.

achieve its objectives,[2] and converts everything that it encounters into material for itself. It's like a bonfire overpowering the objects that are thrown onto it; a small fire would be extinguished by them, but a good blaze very quickly appropriates to itself all the objects that are piled on it, consumes them, and uses them to grow greater.[3]

---

2. "Reservation" is a technical term within Stoicism. It refers to the fact that future-directed impulses, even rational impulses, should always be accompanied by a conditional, because it is always possible for things to go wrong. You might have an impulse to eat to preserve your health, but you add the reservation "If God wills it" or something similar. In this way, a wise man's impulses are never thwarted, because he was already expecting impediments. He recasts his impulses in response to the realities he faces so that all reality is material for him—every event an opportunity to try to act with virtue (5.20, 6.50, 8.32, 8.35, 8.41, and 11.37)—literally making a virtue out of necessity. It might seem weak to let your original intention be deflected like this, but what was important to the Stoics was not what we do but the moral attitude with which we do it. As Epictetus puts it at *Handbook* 4: "This [the thwarted action I originally set out to do] wasn't the only thing I wanted; I also wanted to keep my will in accord with nature." The Roman Stoics emphasized reservation, especially in the political sphere, because they were concerned about remaining engaged with the world, but they appreciated that the world was going to throw up obstacles.

3. So our rational faculty grows more powerful the more use is made of it, the more it is allowed to do its job of dealing rationally with the world.

[2] Never act without purpose; make sure that all your actions conform to the philosophical principles that constitute the art of living.[4]

[3] People try to find retreats for themselves in the countryside, by the sea, and in the mountains. A marked longing for such a haven has been a habit of yours too. But nothing could be more unphilosophical, given that you may retreat into yourself whenever you want. There's no retreat more peaceful and untroubled than a man's own mind, and this is especially true of a man who has inner resources which are such that he has only to dip into them to be entirely untroubled (and by "untroubled" I mean "composed"), so never stop allowing yourself to retreat there and be renewed.[5] Make sure that these inner resources are concise and fundamental so that, when they present themselves to you, they are immediately sufficient to wash away every vexation

---

4. To live virtuously, in agreement with nature, is to follow natural law, the rules laid down by nature as discerned by one's command center; but knowing rules and acting accordingly is what artists and craftsmen do; therefore, the Stoics concluded in Socratic fashion, virtue was an art or craft, the art of living.

5. In true Stoic fashion, Marcus often calls the psychological benefit of philosophy calmness, imperturbability, or tranquility, perhaps most strikingly at 7.68.

once more and to send you back without resenting whatever it is that you're returning to.[6]

After all, what is it that you resent? The fact that people aren't virtuous? Recall the notions that rational beings are on this earth to help one another, that tolerance is an aspect of justice, and that people don't deliberately do wrong.[7] Remember also how many people spent their lives seeing others as their enemies, suspecting them, hating them, battling with them, only to be laid out for burial and burned to ashes—and put an end to your resentment. Do you also resent the lot that has been assigned you by the universe? Refresh in your mind the disjunction

6. On retreat within oneself, see also 6.12, 7.28, 7.59, and 8.48. The world is manifestly corrupt: would it not be wise, then, to retreat from it? Marcus's reply is that such retreat must be only temporary, a means of refreshing oneself, by consulting one's basic precepts (his "resources"), in order to return to the fray. He is not a mystic but a dutiful emperor, and the practice he recommends of consulting basic precepts is not at all like the practice of meditation in mystical systems.

7. The intellectualist view of virtue again. People do not mean to do wrong because they always think they are acting in their own best interests and do not realize that wrongdoing is against their own interests.

"Either providence or atoms"[8] and the arguments proving that the universe is a kind of community.[9] But bodily things will still have a hold on you, won't they? Remember that once the mind has become detached and knows its own power, it stops mingling with any spirit that's in a disturbed state, whether the motions are

---

8. That is, things either happen because they have been predetermined by providence (the Stoic view), or they are a completely random coincidence of atoms (the Epicurean view). Marcus was fond of posing this dichotomy, or drawing on its terms: 4.27, 6.4, 6.10, 6.24, 7.32, 8.17, 9.28, 9.39, 10.6, 11.18, 12.14. But in no case does this represent any uncertainty on his part about the correctness of the Stoic view. He generally uses the dichotomy either to point out the objectionable consequences of the Epicurean view or as a way of saying, "Whatever your worldview, such-and-such is the case." Here, the former is implied, because on the Stoic view that the universe has been providentially designed, he should not resent the lot that has been assigned him.

9. The Great City, of which all rational beings are citizens. Marcus argues for the reality of this city in the next entry.

smooth or rough,[10] and then remember all the ideas about pain and pleasure that you've heard and to which you've assented.[11]

Will you be diverted by fame? Focus on the speed with which everything and everyone is forgotten, the infinite temporal gulf that stretches before and after a lifetime, the hollowness of applause, the haphazard fickleness of those who appear to speak well of you, and the narrowness of the place where fame is confined. The whole earth is just a speck. How tiny is the little corner of it where you reside? How many people are there here to praise you? What kind of men will they be?

So then, remember that you already have a little estate into which you can retreat, and make it your priority not to get agitated or tense. Better to be your own master and look on the world as a man, a human being, a citizen, and a creature doomed to die. Make sure that among the truths into which you'll be dipping you have the following two perfectly available for reference: first, that the things of the world cannot affect the soul; they lie

---

10. Spirit (*pneuma*) was for the Stoics the vital principle that organizes not just an individual but also the whole universe; hence it is also called God. Here Marcus is saying that the pure *pneuma* that is the rational human soul remains detached, or rather should stay detached, from bodily *pneuma* and its constant motions, which may be either smooth or rough—smooth motions being pleasant sensations and rough ones, unpleasant. The same description of bodily pleasure and pain, which is derived from Epicurus, recurs at 5.26 and 10.8.

11. Specifically, that one should master pleasure and pain, and not be their servant.

inert outside it, and only internal beliefs can disturb it.[12] Second, that everything you see will shortly change and before long will cease to exist; and bear constantly in mind how many changes you personally have gone through in the past. "The universe is change, and life a supposition."[13]

[4] If intelligence is something we have in common, then reason too, which makes us rational beings, is something we have in common. If so, then the reason that dictates what we should and shouldn't do is also something we have in common. If so, then law too is something we have in common. If so, then

---

12. Things are "inert" in the sense that if you suspend judgment about them, they cannot generate the passions that disturb your peace of mind, because all such disturbances stem from your opinion or judgment about things, not from the things themselves. See also 5.19, 6.52, 7.14, 9.15, 11.11, 11.16. The Stoics held that a passion was the product of a belief formed by assent to an impression presented to the mind in propositional form. Distress, for instance, is triggered by the idea that something bad is present. To correct a passion, you had to correct your beliefs. This point of Stoic dogma is frequently repeated in the notebooks. In practical terms, it meant that a Stoic had constantly to be aware of what he was thinking and feeling in order to make corrections if necessary. Passions are a kind of impulse, and all impulses lead to action, so that correcting passions should lead one to act more rationally and more in accord with nature.

13. This saying, along with dozens of other such saws, is attributed in our sources to an otherwise unknown Democrates. Many scholars think that "Democrates" is a mistake for "Democritus," an important thinker of the fifth century BCE (mentioned by Marcus at 3.3). It serves as the kind of concise and fundamental truth that Marcus was urging himself, earlier in this entry, to have at his command.

we're fellow citizens. If so, then we have some form of society in common. If so, then the universe is a kind of community, since the universe is the only shared society that anyone could describe as common to the entire human race.[14] And it's from there, from this shared community, in fact, that we get intelligence, reason, and law.[15] I mean, where else could they come from? After all, just as the earthy part of me is a fragment of some earth, and the watery part of me is a fragment of another element, and the airy part has come from some source, and the hot, fiery part has come from *its* own specific source—for nothing comes from nothing,

---

14. It should go without saying that Marcus's conception of the "universe" was considerably different from ours. He is not here envisaging the possibility of rational beings on other planets, but a "cosmopolitan" community of rational beings, gods and humans, in a single world. See, for example, Epictetus, *Discourses* 2.5.26. Marcus deploys two arguments to justify his thinking of himself, and every rational creature, as a citizen of the universe. In addition to the argument here, there is also the frequent assertion that humans are social creatures (e.g., 5.16, 7.55) and bonded by their rationality (12.26).

15. Compare Heraclitus, fragment 114 Diels/Kranz: "All human laws are in the keeping of the one divine law." The Stoics too believed in natural law—that the fundamental moral principles that form or should form the basis of man-made legal codes are dictated to us by nature. This is a large part of what Marcus means by "living in accord with nature," and he uses the term "law" for it also at 3.11, 7.9, 8.2, 10.11, 10.25, 10.33, and 12.1. See also the distinction between (natural) equity and (man-made) justice at 11.20. Socrates (as in Xenophon, *Memorabilia* 4.4) was an influence on the Stoics in this respect, as was Heraclitus.

just as nothing returns to nothing[16]—so our intelligence too has come from somewhere.[17]

[5] Death is like birth, a mystery of nature—the compounding and disintegration of the same elements—and there's nothing at all shameful in it, because there's nothing about it that's unsuitable for an intelligent being or contravenes the principle of his constitution.[18]

[6] Given the character of the person in question, this outcome was inevitable. To want it not to be the case is to want a fig tree not to have sap.[19] In any case, remember this: in no time at

---

16. Since for the Stoics there can be no creation ex nihilo, they posited an eternally existing substance (4.40) out of which each iteration of the universe arises and back into which it is dissolved.

17. Marcus is drawing on a traditional Stoic argument for the rationality and perfection of the universe. The argument derives ultimately from Socrates (in Xenophon, *Memorabilia* 1.4) and is expressed in a particularly clear fashion by Cicero, at *On the Nature of the Gods* 2.18–22.

18. I take "the principle of his constitution" to mean that he is made of the four elements. Since the four elements came together at some point to make him, they will fall apart again at some point. This is the principle of our human constitution, and it is why death is a natural and inevitable process.

19. See also 12.16. At 8.15, 10.8 (end), and 11.33, Marcus again uses the fig tree as an example of something that cannot be other than what it is. Fig-tree sap had various medical and culinary functions, but what Marcus is thinking of here is the fact that the sap makes your skin sting and can even cause burns. There are unpleasant things in the world just as there are unpleasant people in the world.

all both you and he will be dead, and shortly after that not even our names will remain.[20]

[7] Remove the belief and "I've been harmed" goes as well; remove "I've been harmed" and the harm goes as well.[21]

[8] Anything that doesn't make a person worse in himself doesn't make his life worse either, and does him no harm, external or internal.[22]

———

20. Marcus usually deals with his impatience with other people by reminding himself that they too are rational beings and hence his kin. Here he adopts a more objective view. In any case, he is attempting to find the right attitude to adopt toward the existence of evil and stupid people: their existence is necessary; they do not deliberately do wrong; they are rational beings and therefore kin (and therefore also open to correction); and they cannot harm us. All four of these precepts are recurrent themes in the book.

21. In other words, no one hurts you unless you choose to be hurt—a common motif in the notebooks. There is clearly very little difference between forming a belief and framing it as a sentence or proposition, whether in thought or speech, but Marcus here separates them for the sake of clarity.

22. The only truly bad thing is moral vice; nothing else is truly harmful.

[9] This was inevitable, given the nature of the force for good.[23]

[10] "Whatever happens, it's right that it should happen." If you observe things carefully, you'll find this to be the case. When I say that it's right, I don't mean merely that it plays its part in the universal sequence of cause and effect, but that it's consistent with justice—as though there were someone rewarding things as they deserved. So carry on observing with the same care with which you started, and accompany every one of your actions with being a good man, following your specific understanding of what it is to be a good man.[24] Hang on to this in everything you do.

[11] Don't align your thinking with that of the man who's dishonoring you. Don't think as he wants you to think, but see things as they truly are.

––––––––––

23. That is, providence. In a sense, of course, providence and determinism make everything "inevitable." But in Marcus's and the Stoic universe, volition, dependent on a person's character, not his destiny, was still a potent factor. We exercise it in choosing at every moment to welcome everything that happens to us, however horrible; we exercise it in approaching the world "with reservation" (see Notebook 4, note 2); and we exercise it in trying at every moment to be self-reliant moral agents. Determinists who claim that there is no point in deliberating or doing anything are falling into the trap the ancients called the "lazy argument" (see Brennan, *Stoic Life*, 270–287). We are bound to die, for instance, but how we die (and to an extent when we die) is up to us. On determinism and human choice, see the Introduction, xlvi–xlviii.

24. A good man in the Stoic sense is aligned with and thereby assists the providence that ensures that everything that happens is just.

[12] You should be ever ready in two respects. First, to act only as the reason embodied in the arts of kingship and lawmaking proposes, for the benefit of humanity. Second, to change your mind if there happens to be someone around to correct you and steer you away from any form of presumption.[25] But the change must always be founded on a conviction that the outcome will be just, or will enhance the welfare of the state, and you must only ever act in ways that contribute to such outcomes, without taking pleasure or popularity into account.

[13] "Are you endowed with reason?" Yes, I am. "Why don't you use it, then? I mean, if it's doing its job, what else can you want?"

[14] You came into existence as a part within a whole, and you will disappear into that which caused your birth—or rather,

---

25. There is a tension in Marcus's thinking between his desire to be independent of others' opinions (e.g., 2.17, 5.3, 5.19) and his readiness to accept advice (e.g., 6.21, 8.16). The following entry contains an example of the kind of advice Marcus would be happy to accept.

through a process of transformation, you'll be received back into its seminal principle.[26]

[**15**] Many beads of incense on a single fire altar, one tossed on earlier than another, but all equal.[27]

[**16**] In ten days' time or less, if you return to your principles and your devotion to reason, you'll be regarded as a god by them, the men who now regard you as an animal, an ape.[28]

---

26. One is "received back into" the seminal principle (or principles: 6.24) of the universe in the sense that, on death, the four elements separate and go their ways, to be available for reuse and the perpetuation of the universe. In man, the seminal principle was regarded as a natural faculty under the control of the command center or as a function of the command center; the same goes for the universe at large (and so Stoics equated the seminal principle with God, the command center of the universe). Macrocosm and microcosm are subject to the same laws: both the universe and a person are born, live for an allotted amount of time, and die; both reproduce themselves.

27. Our lives are like offerings to the universe, from which we came and back into which we will be reabsorbed. The entry has been well compared to a Japanese haiku (Rutherford, *Meditations*, 138).

28. Marcus has in mind a saying of Heraclitus (fragments 82–83 Diels/Kranz): "The wisest man is an ape compared to God, just as the most beautiful ape is ugly compared to man." So he is saying that it would not take long for an undeviating adherence to his principles and his devotion to reason to make others judge him wise. This is a poignant entry: Marcus will never be able to devote even ten whole days entirely to the study and practice of philosophy without being distracted by his duties as emperor.

[**17**] Don't act as though you were going to live for ten thousand years. Fate is hanging over your head. While you live—while you can—be a good man.

[**18**] How much freedom is gained if a man ignores what his neighbor said or did or intended and considers only what he himself is doing and how to make his actions just and right, the kinds of things a good man would do! Don't let your attention be caught by the darkness of others' humors; just run straight on the line, with no ungainly movements.

[**19**] Anyone who gets excited by the prospect of posthumous fame[29] is failing to realize that all the people who remember him will very shortly be dead themselves, and that the same goes for the next generation in its turn, until the memory is totally extinguished as it progresses from person to person, each of whom is lit and then snuffed out.[30] Even if we posit immortality for the people who are to remember you, and hence for their memories of you, what's that to you? I don't mean just that being remembered is nothing to the dead; I'm asking what good praise does someone while he's alive, unless it serves some further

---

29. Fame as a topic (here and in the next entry) naturally follows from the previous entry, because to desire fame is to be concerned with what other people think of you.

30. Relay races, in which the baton was a lighted brand, were popular in the ancient world. The application of the image to the succession of human lives originated with Plato (*Laws* 776b).

purpose.[31] The point is that, as things are, by being dependent on others' thinking, you're throwing away the opportunity to gain nature's gift.[32]

[20] So then, anything that's fine, in any sense of the word, owes this to itself and is complete in itself, and praise forms no part of it.[33] At any rate, praise has no effect for better or worse on anything that's fine, and I mean this to apply also to entities that are commonly called fine in the sense of beautiful,[34] such as material objects or works of art. So does what is truly fine need anything apart from itself? No more than law does, or truth, or benevolence, or modesty. Is the fineness of any of these things preserved by its being praised or destroyed by its being

---

31. Fame and praise were of course for Marcus indifferents, in that they have no bearing on one's attempt to live a virtuous life. Marcus can accept that if people like what he does as emperor, it makes his life easier, without committing himself to thinking such praise at all important.

32. By "nature's gift," Marcus means the ability to live as an independent moral agent.

33. Marcus quite often disparages praise, and this entry gives us one of his reasons: it makes no difference to the essential quality of anything; at best, it is icing on the cake.

34. The Greek word *kalos*, "fine," covered a range of commendable qualities, from physical beauty to moral fineness.

disparaged? Does an emerald's beauty fade if it isn't praised? And what about gold, ivory, purple,[35] a lyre, a knife, a flower, a bush?

[21] If souls survive death, how does the air accommodate them, since this has been going on for all eternity?[36] You may as well ask how the earth accommodates the bodies of people buried over the same vast period of time. Just as here on earth it's the transformation and decomposition of these bodies that makes room for more corpses, so it is with souls that have migrated to the air. After remaining there for a while, transformation and disintegration occur, and then they're turned to fire when they're received back into the seminal principle of the universe.[37] In this way they make room for the newly arriving immigrants. That's how to respond to the question, on the assumption that souls do survive death. And one should bear in mind not only the

---

35. Various shades of red and purple dye were extracted, with immense labor, from the murex shellfish. A deep purple dye, sometimes called "royal purple," was the rarest and most expensive of these dyes and was highly prized. It was used in Rome to dye the hems of the togas of the most senior officials, and emperors wore togas that were entirely purple.

36. Most Stoics seem to have believed in the continued existence of the soul after death, while falling short of talking of *personal* survival in any form. The objection implicit in Marcus's opening question is based on a superficial understanding (as he in effect goes on to say) of the Stoic view that even our souls are material.

37. The seminal principle (see Notebook 4, note 26) was equated by some Stoics with the primary fire, the source and underlying matter of the entire universe.

number of human bodies buried in this way, but also the number of animals that are eaten every day by us and by other animals. Look at all the animals that are being consumed, and so in a sense are being buried inside the bodies of those they once fed. But there's still room for them because they change into blood and are transformed into an airy and then a fiery state.[38] How does one search for the truth in this case? By distinguishing the matter and the cause of things.[39]

[22] Don't stray, but do what's right whenever you're moved to act, and stick with what's clear and certain whenever you think.

[23] Universe, whatever is consonant with you is consonant with me; if something is timely for you, it's neither too early nor too late for me. Nature, everything is fruit to me that your seasons

---

38. So something material and solid (earthy) is turned into the other elements. In contemporary medical thinking, all food turns into blood (water); its animating or cohesive force returns to air; and its heat (fire) returns to the seminal principle of the universe, to be reused for fresh creation.

39. For this method of investigation, see also 5.13, 7.29, 8.3, 8.11, 9.25, 9.37, 12.10, 12.18, 12.29. It is perfectly in keeping with Stoicism, for which everything in the universe was either active or passive. The body, for instance, is matter, inert and passive in itself, and the soul or mind a cause, because it is the active source of movement and life; this is the relevant distinction in this entry. Earth and water are passive elements, air and fire active; God or reason is an active craftsman and the matter he works on is passive. Essentially, Marcus is saying that we can encapsulate the most important aspects of a thing by considering its matter and its cause: a shoe is an object made out of leather (its matter) for a particular purpose (its cause).

bring; everything comes from you, everything is contained in you, everything returns to you. "Beloved city of Cecrops," says the poet;[40] won't you say "Beloved city of Zeus"?[41]

[24] "Do little," he says, "if you want to be content."[42] But wouldn't it be better to do what's necessary—everything the reason of a naturally social being requires, and in the manner in which it requires it? The upshot will be not only the contentment that comes from doing the right thing but also the contentment that comes from doing little. After all, most of our words and actions are unnecessary, and dispensing with them gives one more freedom and greater peace of mind. It follows that you should prod yourself every time by asking: Is this really necessary? And

---

40. That is, Athens. The phrase is preserved in fragment 112 Kassel-Austin of the great comic poet Aristophanes (c. 455–386 BCE).

41. For the universe as a great city, here the city of Zeus, see especially 2.16 (end). This is a rare mention of one of the traditional gods. Marcus certainly believed in the compatibility of Stoicism with the traditional gods, but the dominant religion of the book is philosophical; he encourages himself to revere the mind that governs the universe and universal nature, not to sacrifice or pray more often to Diana and Mercury. He speaks of "God" and "the gods" somewhat indiscriminately.

42. These are the first words of Democritus, fragment 3 Diels/ Kranz. The saying was also taken up by the Epicureans. The extent to which a philosopher should engage with the world was a major bone of contention between the two schools, with the Epicureans recommending withdrawal, and the Stoics engagement, basing their view, as Marcus does here, on the fact that we are by nature "social beings."

it's important to dispense with not only unnecessary actions but unnecessary thoughts as well, because that will ensure that no redundant actions follow either.

[25] Try living the life of a good man and see how it too suits you—a man who's gratified by the lot he's been assigned by the universe and satisfied with the justice of his acts and the kindness of his character.[43]

[26] You've looked at things from that perspective, haven't you? Now look at them from this. Don't upset yourself; don't complicate your life. Is someone treating you badly? He's doing it to himself.[44] Has something happened to you? Good: every one of your experiences has been ordained and fated for you from the beginning by the universe. In a word, life is short. You must profit from the present moment with right reason and justice. Stay sober in your hours of leisure.

[27] The universe has either been put into order, or it's a cocktail the ingredients of which have been jumbled together but

---

43. This entry follows naturally from the previous one, both being about how to find contentment. The assonance between "gratified" and "satisfied" corresponds to Marcus's Greek.

44. The recurrent idea that wrongdoing harms the agent herself.

which still form an ordered universe.[45] Can there be order within you, but disorder in the universe at large?[46] Especially seeing that all things are distinct, interblended, and interactive.[47]

[28] A dark-hued character, an unmanly character, a stubborn character, bestial, brutish, childish, devious, coarse, mercenary, tyrannical.[48]

[29] If a stranger to the universe is someone who's unfamiliar with the things in it, no less so is someone who's unfamiliar with

---

45. The universe has order, but has that come about as a result of intelligent design (Stoicism) or by chance (Epicureanism)? In this entry, Marcus leaves both options open, while clearly inclining toward the Stoic view, according to which the universe is as thoroughly ordered as a human person. "Cocktail" translates *kukeōn*, which was a drink made of various ingredients (typically barley meal, grated cheese, wine, and honey), which did not blend together. It was stirred before drinking to prevent the settling of the ingredients. Heraclitus too (fragment 125 Diels/Kranz) put *kukeōn* to metaphorical use (things do not cohere without movement), and at 6.10 Marcus uses it again as an image of the Epicurean universe.

46. This is one possible answer to the question why one should believe that the universe is orderly. Other answers are given or implied at 6.10, 9.39. 11.18, and 12.14.

47. In Stoic physics (i.e., their attempt to explain how the universe works), each thing has its own specific properties but is also "blended" with everything else, because it is made up of the same four elements and is created and maintained by the same indwelling spirit.

48. Who is Marcus thinking of? We cannot know, but he is certainly reminding himself of qualities that he personally wanted to eliminate from himself. "Childish" here means "passionate and irrational," since children were held to be not fully rational.

the processes that affect those things. He has no home here if he shuns the social principle;[49] he's blind if he closes the eye of the mind; a beggar if he's dependent on others and can't rely on himself for all his life's needs; a tumor on the universe if he stands apart and separates himself from the principle of our common nature just because his experiences have soured him (after all, this thing, experience, is no less a product of nature than you are); a fragment cut off from civilization if he cuts his own mind off from that of rational beings, when in reality mind is single.

[30] One philosopher has no tunic, another no book. Another of them,[50] half-naked, says: "I have no bread and I remain true to reason." But as for me, I gain no sustenance from my studies and fail to remain true to them.

[31] Treat the art that you've learned as a friend and lean on it for rest.[51] Go through what remains of your life as one who has wholeheartedly entrusted his entire self to the gods and has made himself neither a tyrant nor a slave to any man.[52]

---

49. The principle that we are all kin and that people should act for the common good.

50. Marcus has Cynic philosophers in mind, the most authentic of whom shunned all social conventions and lived like tramps.

51. The art of living (4.2 and 11.5).

52. Since every human being shares in divine reason, they should treat one another as equals. "The idea of universal respect for the dignity of humanity in each and every person, regardless of class, gender, race, and nation . . . is, in origin, a Stoic idea" (Nussbaum, *Therapy*, 12).

[**32**] Take the time of Vespasian,[53] for example, and you'll see the same old things: people marrying, raising a family, getting sick, dying, making war, celebrating festivals, trading, farming, flattering, acting in their own interests, being mistrustful, scheming, praying for their enemies to die, grumbling at their circumstances, falling in love, storing up wealth, longing for the consulship or sole rule.[54] And now not a trace remains of that life of theirs. Then turn to the time of Trajan and it's the same all over again; that life too has died. Likewise, if you consider the histories of other periods and peoples in their entirety, you'll see how all those men sweated and toiled, and then died a short while later and were resolved into their elements. But, above all, recall those whom you once knew yourself, and see how, agitated by vain projects, each of them failed to act in harmony with his own nature, to abide by it and be satisfied with it. It's essential to use this case to remind yourself that the attention given to anything one does has its own value and proportion, because then you won't wear yourself out spending more time than you should on less important matters.

[**33**] Words familiar long ago are now archaisms; so also names that were on everyone's lips long ago are now the equivalent of archaisms: Camillus, Caeso, Volesus, Dentatus, a little later Scipio and Cato, then Augustus, then Hadrian and

---

53. Marcus quite often encourages himself to dwell on the past like this: 4.50, 6.24, 7.19, 8.25, 8.31, 8.37, 9.30, 12.27.

54. There are similar lists of human activities/life on earth at 7.3 and 7.48; see also 9.30.

Antoninus. Everything is transient; everything quickly becomes the stuff of stories, and then is quickly buried by complete oblivion. I'm talking here about men who shone, in one way or another, with wonderful brilliance; everyone else no sooner breathes his last than he is "out of sight and out of mind."[55] In any case, what is it to be remembered forever? Nothing but vanity. So what should one take seriously? Only the following: a just mind, socially useful actions, speech that only ever tells the truth, and the ability to welcome everything that happens as necessary, as comprehensible by reason, and as flowing from an equally rational original source.[56]

[34] Willingly surrender yourself to Clotho[57] and let her spin a web for you out of whatever events she wishes.

[35] Everything is ephemeral—not just the rememberer but the remembered as well.

[36] Observe at every moment how change is responsible for everything that comes to pass, and familiarize yourself with the idea that there's nothing the universe loves so much as changing

---

55. A reference to Homer, *Odyssey* 1.242. In the 1989 film *Dead Poets Society*, the inspiring teacher (played by Robin Williams) gets his pupils to contemplate photographs of former students at the school to communicate the same lesson that Marcus wants to learn: life is fleeting.

56. Entry 5.8 is Marcus's longest elaboration of the recurrent theme that a good man welcomes whatever comes his way; see also 6.44, 10.1, 10.6.

57. One of the three Fates, and so a stand-in here for "destiny."

things and creating similar new things.[58] The point being that everything that exists is in a sense a seed for what takes its place, but to your way of thinking the only seeds are those that are sown in the ground or the womb, which is distinctly unphilosophical.[59]

[37] Your death is imminent, and you haven't yet achieved simplicity,[60] imperturbability, the conviction that nothing external can make you a worse person, or the ability to deal serenely with everyone, nor do you dedicate your intelligence solely to right action.

[38] Carefully consider their command centers: what are their likes and dislikes?

[39] What's detrimental to you doesn't depend on someone else's command center, and certainly not on some worsening or alteration of surrounding conditions. On what, then? On that part of you that takes things to be bad.[61] If it believes no such thing, all is well. Even if what is closest to it, the body, undergoes surgery or cautery, or is left to suppurate or putrefy, you should still get the part of you that forms beliefs to keep quiet—that is,

---

58. On global change, see also 2.17 (end), 4.3 (end), 6.15, 7.25, 7.47, 8.50, 12.23.

59. Marcus is reflecting the Stoic idea that the "seminal principle" (4.14, 4.21), otherwise known as God, pervades everything.

60. Simplicity is being integrated, focused, undisturbed by passions, and capable of dealing with others without artifice and without compromising one's principles.

61. Compare Hamlet's remark in Shakespeare's play: "There is nothing either good or bad, but thinking makes it so."

to judge that nothing that can happen equally to bad and good people is either bad or good. After all, anything that happens equally to people whether their lives are dissonant or consonant with nature is itself neither consonant nor dissonant with nature.

[40] Never stop regarding the universe as a single living being, with one substance and one soul,[62] and pondering how everything is taken in by the single consciousness of this living being, how by a single impulse it does everything, how all things are jointly responsible for all that comes to pass, and what sort of interlacing and interconnection this implies.[63]

[41] You're a pathetic little soul sustaining a corpse, as Epictetus used to say.[64]

[42] Going through change isn't bad for things in any respect, just as coming into existence as a result of change isn't good for them either.[65]

[43] Time is a river of events and its current is strong: no sooner does something heave into view than it's swept away

---

62. A striking statement of pantheism.

63. A magnificent description of the Stoic view of the universe and its interlocking chains of causation.

64. This saying does not occur in the surviving works of Epictetus (it is fragment 26 Schenkl), although he is given to claiming that the body is in itself inanimate and lifeless, a carcass or a corpse. Marcus repeats the saying in a slightly different form at 9.24.

65. Change is the subject of the next few entries as well.

and something else is being carried past instead, only to be swept away.[66]

[44] Everything that happens is as ordinary and familiar as a rose in spring or fruit in summer. That goes also for sickness, death, slander, intrigue, and everything else that makes foolish people happy or miserable.[67]

[45] What comes next is always related by affinity to what went before. It's not a matter of mere enumeration of discrete units in a mechanically inevitable sequence, but of a rational connection. Just as existing things are arrayed in harmonious relation to one another, so things in the process of coming into existence don't exhibit mere succession but a wonderful affinity.

[46] Always remember Heraclitus's words: "The death of earth is the birth of water, the death of water is the birth of air, the death of air is fire," and the same in the reverse direction. Remember also his saying about the person who forgets where his path is leading. And "They pull away from that with which they are in the most continuous contact," the reason that directs the universe, "and their daily experiences strike them as strange." And we shouldn't act and speak "as though we were asleep" (for even when asleep we do think we're acting and speaking).

---

66. Marcus liked the river image and employs it again at 2.17, 5.23, 6.15, 7.19, and 9.29.

67. They are foolish to treat things that are indifferent as in any way important. The sameness of things is a recurrent theme. Here Marcus seems to imply that it helps him to be objective about the minimal value of most things.

Nor should we behave "like children with their parents," that is, simply accepting things as they've been passed down to us.[68]

[47] If a god informed you that you were going to die tomorrow, or the day after at the latest, you'd hardly think it mattered whether it was tomorrow or the day after, at any rate unless you were hopelessly small-minded. It's not as if there were much difference in time involved. By the same token, you should consider it an utterly trivial matter whether your life lasts for years or comes to an end tomorrow.[69]

[48] Continually call to mind how many doctors have died, after knitting their brows time and again over patients; how many astrologers, after foretelling others' deaths as though death were something important; how many philosophers, after racking their brains about death and immortality; how many great warriors, after having taken numerous other lives; how many tyrants, after exercising the power of life and death with terrible high-handedness, thinking themselves immortal; how many whole towns have died, so to speak—Helice, Pompeii,

---

68. It is not easy to disentangle Heraclitus's actual words from Marcus's paraphrases, but these citations of Heraclitus are, in the standard Diels/Kranz edition, fragment 76, and then fragments 71–74. Leaning on Heraclitus, Marcus stresses the universal flux of things, people's lack of awareness of reality, and his desire to be independent of others.

69. Length of life is less important than quality of life, a life lived virtuously and in accordance with the will of the universe; see also 6.23 and 11.1.

Herculaneum, and countless others.[70] Recall also people you've personally known, the sequence of them: A saw to B's funeral and was then laid out for his own funeral, which was seen to by C—and it all happened so quickly. In short, always look on human life as transient and worthless; yesterday a bit of slime,[71] tomorrow a mummy or ashes. So spend this fleeting moment of time living in accord with nature, and take your leave with serenity, as a ripe olive might fall, blessing the earth that bore it and grateful to the tree that gave it growth.[72]

[49] Be like a headland:[73] the waves beat against it continuously, but it stands fast and around it the boiling water dies down. "It's my rotten luck that this has happened to me." On the

---

70. The destruction of Pompeii and Herculaneum in the eruption of Vesuvius in 79 CE is well known. Helice was a Greek town on the south coast of the Gulf of Corinth, which was swamped, along with neighboring Bura, by a tsunami following an earthquake in 373 BCE. Seneca made the conclusion explicit (*Natural Questions* 6.32): "The sea swallowed Helice and Bura whole: shall I fear for one poor body?"

71. Seminal fluid: see 6.13.

72. It is one of the recurrent pleasures of the book that Marcus takes the shortness of human life not to license nihilism, the view that everything is ultimately pointless, but to make it urgent to become a virtuous person as quickly as possible.

73. Marcus is thinking of a famous Homeric simile, at *Iliad* 15.615–622—or, rather, of its adaptation by Seneca to the constancy of a Stoic sage (*On the Constancy of the Wise Person* 3.5): "Just as certain rocks projecting upward break the sea and yet show no traces of its ferocity despite being assaulted through the ages, just so solid is the wise person's mind" (translated by James Ker).

contrary: "It's my good luck that, although this has happened to me, I still feel no distress, since I'm unbruised by the present and unconcerned about the future." What happened could have happened to anyone, but not everyone could have carried on without letting it distress him. So why regard the incident as a piece of bad luck rather than seeing your avoidance of distress as a piece of good luck? Do you generally describe a person as unlucky when his nature worked well? Or do you count it as a malfunction of a person's nature when it succeeds in securing the outcome it wanted? Well, you know from your studies what it is that human nature wants. Can what happened to you stop you from being fair, high-minded, moderate, conscientious, unhasty, honest, moral, self-reliant, and so on—from possessing all the qualities that, when present, enable a man's nature to be fulfilled? So then, whenever something happens that might cause you distress, remember to rely on this principle: this is not bad luck, but bearing it valiantly is good luck.

[50] An unphilosophical but still effective method for helping you to scorn death is to run over a list of people who clung tenaciously to life, asking yourself what they gained over those who died young. One way or another, they're all in their graves now: Caedicianus, Fabius, Julianus, Lepidus, and all the others like them who saw to many funerals and were then buried themselves. The span of one's life is altogether insignificant— and look at the experiences, the kinds of people, and the poor body one has to endure while seeing out the time! Don't regard your life as in any way important, then. Look behind you at the yawning gulf of time and see the other immeasurable stretch

ahead. From this point of view, what's the difference between a baby who lives for three days and someone who lives three times as long as Nestor?[74]

[51] Always run the short road, and the short road is the one that's in accord with nature.[75] Say and do everything, then, in the most sound way possible. With that kind of purpose, one is freed from fatigue, hesitation, ulterior motives, and affectation.

---

74. "Someone who lives three times as long as Nestor" is a single word in Greek, made up by Marcus: it is literally "triple-Gerenian," Nestor being from Gerenia in southwest Greece. Three days and three hundred years are indeed both specks in infinite time, but from a subjective point of view it makes a great deal of difference whether one lives a shorter or longer life. In Stoic terms, a three-day-old baby has not even had a chance to develop rationality and thereby the chance of being virtuous.

75. Marcus liked the image of "nature's road": 4.18, 5.3, 5.4, 5.34, 10.11 (end), 11.9, 12.23 (end).

NOTEBOOK 5[1]

---

1. This fifth notebook generally avoids Stoic technicalities in favor of simplicity of presentation and repeated emphasis on familiar moral themes. It is largely positive, with even gloomy entries such as 5.10 and 5.33 ending on more constructive notes. It makes a very good introduction to Marcus's recurrent ideas.

[1] At dawn, when you're reluctant to get up,[2] have this thought readily available:[3] I have work to do as a human being, and that's why I'm getting up. Do I still resent it if I'm on my way to do the work for which I was born and for the sake of which I was brought into the world?[4] Or is this what I was made for, to lie in bed and keep myself warm? "But it's really nice." So is pleasure what you were born for? And, in general, was it for feeling, not for doing? Can't you see plants, sparrows, ants, spiders, and bees all doing their own work and playing their part

---

2. For extended periods, Marcus daily took a compound medicine called "theriac," which was considered a kind of universal panacea, partly as an antidote against being poisoned by his enemies (Galen, *On Antidotes*, Kühn vol. 14.3–5, 201). The medicine contained a small amount of opium or mandragora. Finding that it made him drowsy, he cut out the soporific, but then could not sleep, so he reintroduced it. At 8.12, he also expresses reluctance to get up. He was also fundamentally insomniac: Galen (who was Marcus's personal physician) mentions this in the passage just cited, and so does Cassius Dio at *Roman History* 72.24.4.

3. Marcus quite often urges himself to keep this or that thought "readily available" or "to hand" and he meant it quite literally. As Epictetus said: "Have these thoughts readily available day and night; write them down, read them" (*Discourses* 3.24.103). See further the Introduction, xxxi–xxxii, on this exercise.

4. That is, to do good, do his natural work, act with virtue, align himself with the will of nature/God/providence/the universal Reason (*logos*)—all synonyms.

in the world's order?[5] And are you then reluctant to do human work? Why aren't you eager to do what comes naturally to you? "But rest is important too." Yes, I agree. Nature has set limits on rest, however, as it has on eating and drinking as well; but aren't you overstepping those limits and taking more than suffices for your needs? It's only when it comes to action that you haven't yet reached the limits of your abilities. And the reason is that you don't love yourself. If you did, you'd love your nature and its purpose. Other people who are devoted to their areas of expertise wear themselves out over them, forgetting to wash or eat. Do you value your own nature less than an artisan does his metalwork, a dancer his dancing, a miser his money, a celebrity his moment of fame? In their obsession, they're willing to give up food and sleep in favor of spending more time over the objects of their passion. Does state business seem less important to you, worth less effort than they put in?

[2] How easy it is to banish and erase every upsetting or un-welcome thought and gain immediate and complete tranquility!

[3] Judge yourself entitled to say or do anything that's in accord with nature, and don't let yourself be talked out of it by any criticism or argument that may follow as a consequence. If it was the right thing to do or say, don't put yourself down. Other

---

5. There are more lessons from the natural world at 5.6, 6.54, 9.9, 10.10, 11.18. "Go to the ant, you sluggard; consider her ways and be wise" (Proverbs 6:6). Here the thought is that if every creature in the world simply did its proper work, the world would be an orderly and happy place.

people have their own command centers and their own impulses, and you shouldn't let your attention be caught by them, but carry straight on,[6] following your own nature and universal nature, two things that share a single path.

[4] I make my way on nature's road until the time comes for me to fall and take my rest, sending my final breath into the air I daily breathe, and falling on the earth from which my father garnered his seed, my mother her blood, and my nurse her milk[7]—the earth which has supplied my food and drink day after day for so many years—the earth which bears me as I trample it and abuse it in so many ways.

[5] They can't admire you for perspicacity, but that's all right: there are many other qualities for which "I wasn't made that way" doesn't provide you with an excuse. The qualities you can offer, then, are those that are entirely up to you: candor, dignity, endurance, indifference to pleasure, acceptance of your lot, frugality, kindness, self-reliance, unaffectedness, discretion,

----

6. The recurrent metaphor of life and the Stoic art of life as a path, and one that is to be followed without deviation.

7. It was usual in the ancient world for upper-class women not to feed their babies themselves but to hire a wet-nurse, often a woman whose own baby had died (a very common occurrence in antiquity), leaving her with full breasts. In contemporary embryology, based on Aristotle's work, the father's seed, once planted in the womb, was formed into an embryo, and then nourished and fostered, by the mother's blood. The umbilical cord provided the embryo with air to breathe.

stateliness.[8] Do you see how many you're able to offer right now, without excusing yourself on the grounds of ineptitude and incompetence? And yet you persist, of your own free will, in doing worse than your best. Or is it innate ineptitude that compels you to grumble, to be stingy, to flatter, to blame your body, to be obsequious, to brag, to change your mind so often? No, most certainly not! You could have eliminated these faults a long time ago and been convicted, if at all, only of being rather slow and dull-witted. Yet even this can be worked on—as long as a person doesn't disregard or even relish his stupidity.

[6] One kind of person, when he does someone a good turn, is also ready to calculate the monetary value of the thanks owed to him. Another may not go so far, but he still privately thinks of the other person as in his debt and is conscious of what he's done. Yet another, however, is in a sense not even conscious of what he's done, but resembles a vine that, after bearing grapes, doesn't immediately go in search of something else to do, once it has borne the fruit that's proper to it. Or you could say he resembles a horse after a gallop, a hound after a hunt, a bee that has made its honey. A man who's done good doesn't shout it from the rooftops, but goes on to the next good deed, as a vine goes on to bear grapes again in its season. That's the goal to aim for, to be one of these men oneself, who do good without

---

8. In short, virtue is up to us, whereas something like lack of intelligence is innate and there is nothing or almost nothing one can do about it. Nor does virtue depend on intellectual perspicacity.

noticing it, in a way.[9] "Yes, but that kind of action is exactly what one is required to pay attention to, since, we're told, it's typical of the socially minded man to be aware of the actions he takes for the good of society—and, by Zeus, to want others in his society to be aware of them as well."[10] You're right, but you're not understanding the point I'm trying to make at the moment, and that's why you'll belong among the first kinds of people I mentioned, who are also misled by a kind of plausible logic. But, if you choose to get the point, don't be afraid: it won't make you neglect any socially useful act.

[7] An Athenian prayer: "Rain, Zeus, please. Rain on the farmland and the fields of the Athenians." That's how to pray,

---

9. Doing good is its own reward; see also 7.73 and 9.42.

10. The social man is aware of the good he does because he does it deliberately; if he wants others to be aware of it too, that is perhaps so that his action can serve as a model for their future actions. It is not surprising that Marcus immediately accepts this point; it is presumably exactly why he added the qualification "in a way" just above. He differs from the objector only because he is repudiating a different kind of awareness—that is, patting oneself on the back for what one has done and expecting recognition for it. Otherwise, the objector's stress on the importance of intentions for judging the value of an act is fully in line with orthodox Stoicism.

simply and in a spirit of self-reliance; otherwise, one shouldn't pray at all.[11]

[8] There's no real difference between saying, "Asclepius prescribed horse riding for him, or cold baths, or walking barefoot"[12] and, "The universe prescribed illness for him, or mutilation, or wasting, or some other affliction."[13] In the first sentence, "prescribed" means something like "instructed him to do such-and-such as conducive to his health," and in the second sentence the meaning is that a person's experiences have somehow been

---

11. See also 9.40 on prayer, where Marcus finds a reason to pray even for things that, to a strict Stoic, are indifferents. Here he seems to reject petitionary prayer altogether in favor of prayer that is simple (asking for good, but not good for oneself alone) and self-reliant (not courting the gods' favor). Strictly, petitionary prayer was blasphemous in Stoic terms, since it was asking for the world to be different when it is perfect as it is.

12. Asclepius (the god of healing) may be shorthand here for "doctors," but it is also worth remembering that the god was also thought to dictate or adumbrate remedies in dreams. It is not clear what ailments the specific prescriptions mentioned by Marcus were meant to cure, but there was a large element of faith healing involved in ancient medicine, so that even walking barefoot might serve to cure an ailment if you believed it might.

13. It was a particularly acute problem for a Stoic that, in a world that was supposed to be providentially organized by good gods, there existed suffering and moral evil. Marcus's reply is that, if we had the big picture, we would see how what we think of as bad is actually good, if not for me personally, then at least for the world as a whole.

ordained for him as conducive to his destiny. By the same token, when we say that we meet with these experiences, we mean it in the sense in which builders say that bricks "meet" in walls or pyramids, because they connect and form a certain specific structure. For in the universe at large everything is interconnected, and just as all bodies together make up the specific body that is the universe, so all causes together make up the specific cause that is fate.

Even people who have never touched on philosophy in their lives understand what I'm saying; at any rate, they say, "He had it coming," when to say that is to say that the experience was prescribed for him. So we should accept our experiences just as we accept what Asclepius prescribes. After all, not a few of his prescriptions too are harsh, but we welcome them in the hope that they'll improve our health. So you should treat the realization and fulfillment of the decrees of universal nature as you do your health. That is, you should welcome every experience even when it seems rather harsh, because it contributes to the health of the universe and to the advancement and success of Zeus's activity. He wouldn't have allotted the experience to anyone unless it was good for the universe as a whole, any more than any nature at all allows anything to happen that is inappropriate for what is under the direction of that nature.

There are two reasons, then, why you should gladly accept whatever happens to you. First, because the experience happened to you, was prescribed for you, and was the product of a web somehow woven just for you way back in time, out of the most ancient causes.[14] Second, because, for the directing principle of the universe, even what happens to each of us as individuals plays a part in its advancement, perfection, and, by Zeus, its very preservation. After all, any whole is impaired if you cut the connection and continuity of its parts to any extent at all, and the same goes if you cut the chain of its causes. But this is what you do, insofar as it's in your power, whenever you're dissatisfied with your lot. In a sense, this is an act of destruction.

[9] Don't give up in disgust or weariness if your ability to act consistently on the basis of right principles doesn't consolidate into a permanent habit. After every repulse, go back, and be happy if the majority of your actions are worthy of a human being. And hold it dear, what you're going back to. Don't return to philosophy as a child to a teacher, but as someone with an eye inflammation turns to the swab and the eyecup, or as another turns to his bandage and poultice.[15] Then you'll be showing that compliance with reason is no burden, but a relief. Remember that philosophy wants only what your nature wants, and that it was you who were wanting something else

---

14. Because there is an unending chain of cause and effect since time began, what happens to you today has been ordained since the beginning of time.

15. On philosophy as therapy, see the Introduction, xxxvii–xxxviii. Here the image is triggered by the mention of Asclepius in the previous entry.

that was not in accord with nature.[16] And what could be more delightful than satisfying your nature's wants? After all, isn't that how pleasure beguiles us? But it may be that you'll find high-mindedness, self-reliance, simplicity, courtesy, and piety more delightful.[17] And what could be more delightful than wisdom itself, when you consider how consistently infallible and fluent the faculty of understanding and knowledge is?

[10] Things are so veiled, as one might put it, that quite a few philosophers, and not the least eminent ones at that, claim that it's impossible for us to achieve the slightest degree of

---

16. Notice the split between "you" and "your nature"—between ego and essence, as we might put it nowadays. The true self is in a sense impersonal, because it is reason, and reason is shared with every other rational being.

17. There are different categories of pleasure. The wise man feels pleasure and pain, naturally, but he does not feel the kinds of pleasure and pain that are the result of mistaken judgments. Base pleasures should not be allowed to distract us from the work, but the exercise of virtue has its own pleasure—which, Marcus argues here, is partly the pleasure of relief from pain. In fact, the life of virtue is the most pleasant life, even if the pleasures involved are not intense, because there is no admixture of pain, since one is forever living in accord with nature. In the next sentence, Marcus implies that all the virtues he mentioned (and, implicitly, all the virtues there are) are aspects of wisdom. The idea stems from Zeno of Citium, the founder of the school, and before him from Socrates.

cognitive certainty about them,[18] while even the Stoics[19] regard things as hard to grasp with certainty. Every assent we give to our perceptions is liable to change;[20] after all, there's no such thing as a man who isn't liable to change. And then what about the actual objects of the world, which underlie our impressions? See how transient and worthless they are, and how they can belong to perverts, prostitutes, and thieves. And then what about your acquaintances, character-wise? See how even the most refined of them are hard to tolerate—not to mention how difficult it is to endure even oneself. Given all this gloom and grime, given the great flux of being and time, of movement and moving things, I cannot begin to comprehend what there is to value or take at

---

18. The Skeptics in particular denied the possibility of knowledge.

19. This is Marcus's only explicit mention of the Stoics. Too much has been made of it. In saying "the Stoics" like this, he is not implying that he is not a Stoic himself, just as a Christian can say "Christians believe X" without distancing himself from them. Alternatively, Marcus may just mean "Stoic teachers."

20. In Stoic epistemology, we have to "assent" to an incoming impression (or, rather, to the proposition embedded in it) to actually form a clear perception or thought and be impelled to act on it. However, contrary to what Marcus says here, Stoics held that some impressions truly correspond to the object that is providing the impression: the impression I have of a pomegranate really is an impression of a pomegranate and not of a wax model of a pomegranate. Under these circumstances, true belief and even knowledge are possible (though in fact, for Stoics, knowledge requires another condition, "strong assent," which is available only to a Stoic sage), which will inevitably lead to right action.

all seriously. On the contrary, one should console oneself with the prospect of natural release, without being impatient at its delay, but finding solace only in the following thoughts. First, that nothing will happen to me that isn't in accord with universal nature; second, that it's impossible for me to do anything that goes against my inner god, my guardian spirit, because no one can compel me to contravene its will.

[11] To what use am I now putting my soul? That's the question to ask yourself all the time. And you should interrogate yourself: At this moment, what is occupying that part of me they call the command center? What kind of a soul do I actually have at the moment? Is it the soul of a child? A teenager? A woman? A tyrant? A farm animal?[21] A wild animal?

[12] What follows is a way of understanding the kinds of things that are taken to be good by ordinary people. If one were thinking of the possession of things that are truly good (such as wisdom, moderation, justice, and courage),[22] with those on his mind he wouldn't be able to make sense of the saying about being "crowded by good things," because it wouldn't apply. However, if he were thinking of the things ordinary people take to be good,

---

21. See also Marcus's somewhat contemptuous references to "herds [of people]" at 6.16, 7.8, 9.30, 9.39.

22. These are the four primary virtues in Stoicism, separated out because they were held to be the only ones that were consistently good for the agent.

he'll get the playwright's point and see its appropriateness.[23] So even ordinary people glimpse the difference between the two sets of goods, because otherwise the saying wouldn't cause offense and attract criticism, while we accept it as a pointed and humorous comment on wealth and the blessings associated with luxury or prestige. Then next you need to ask whether it's right for one to value and regard as good things of which, when we have them on our minds, it can appropriately be said that their possessor is so well off "that he has no place to shit."[24]

[**13**] I consist of cause and matter.[25] Neither of these will perish into nothingness, just as they didn't arise out of nothingness.[26] It follows that every part of me will simply undergo change and be assigned to some part of the universe, and then later that part will

---

23. First, because they are material goods, many of which take up space, and second because there are many of them, whereas the virtues are few. The playwright is Menander of Athens (c. 345–292 BCE), the brilliant leading poet of Athenian New Comedy.

24. So (after a fairly dense entry) the full saying is "Being so crowded by good things that he has no place to shit." It comes from a largely lost play by Menander called *The Ghost* and is part of fragment 42 Sandbach.

25. The soul is a cause, the body matter. Everyone is a part of the great cosmic web of causes operating on matter; the ubiquity and impersonality of this takes away fear of death.

26. "Nothing comes from nothing, just as nothing returns to nothing" (4.4). The universe always has exactly the same amount of matter, which is endlessly recycled into different creations (7.23, 7.25, 10.1). Thus the universe is the only thing that is completely self-sufficient, because it takes from nowhere but itself.

be changed to form another part of the universe, and so on ad infinitum. It was a similar process of change that was responsible both for my existence and for that of my parents, and so on back in another infinite sequence. It's legitimate to talk like this, even if the universe is in fact organized as a sequence of finite cycles.[27]

[14] Reason and the art of reasoning form a closed system between themselves and their results. They set out from their own proper starting point and make their way to the designated goal.[28] That's why rational actions are called "right actions," as a way of indicating that they keep us on the right path.

[15] A human being should pay no attention to things that aren't proper to him qua human.[29] Such things make no demands of him as a human being, nor are they guaranteed by his nature as a human being, nor do they fulfill human nature. So the end of human life isn't located in them either, nor are they good, because goodness is what the end of human life is all about. Moreover, if any of them were proper to him as a human being, it wouldn't be proper for him to scorn and resist them, nor would we find it

---

27. Even if the universe is periodically destroyed by fire, as the Stoics believed, so that time periodically starts again, it is still legitimate to talk of infinite time, because these periodic conflagrations also form an infinite sequence.

28. This is meant to apply to every little act of reason—say, reasoning through a syllogism to a conclusion—and to the action of reason overall in our lives, which leads us toward the goal of wisdom or sagehood.

29. Presumably, these improper things are "indifferents," things that are neither good nor bad, since only goodness is proper to human nature, which is essentially good.

commendable to have no need of them, nor, if they were good, would someone who was without any of them be a good person. But, in fact, the more someone deprives himself of them or other similar things, or even allows himself to be deprived of them, the better a person he is.

[16] Your mind will come to resemble your frequently repeated thoughts, because it takes on the hue of its thoughts.[30] Dye your mind, then, with a succession of ideas such as the following: Wherever it's possible to live, it's possible to live well; it's possible to live in a palace; therefore, it's possible to live well in a palace.[31] Or here's another: Everything is drawn to that for which it has been made and to which its constitution responds; what it's drawn to is or entails its goal in life; its goal in life is coextensive with what is beneficial and good for it; therefore the good for a rational being is community. It was established long ago that we were born for community.[32] Or is it not clear that, while lower beings are made to serve higher beings, higher

30. Marcus repeats the thought at 6.30. Hence the frequent repetitiousness of the notebooks: Marcus is attempting to dye his mind with valuable precepts.

31. See 1.17. But Marcus entertains the idea that the palace is an impediment to goodness at 6.12 and 8.9.

32. Starting with Aristotle at *Politics* 1253a. But, judging by what follows, Marcus has a different approach in mind, dating perhaps from the early Stoics of the third century BCE.

beings are made to serve one another?[33] Animate creatures are superior to inanimate objects, and rational creatures are superior to merely animate ones.[34]

[17] To pursue impossibilities is madness, and it's impossible for bad men not to behave like that.[35]

[18] Nothing happens to anyone that he's not equipped by nature to bear.[36] Another person has the same experience as you, and either out of ignorance of what has happened, or because he's putting on a show of detachment, he remains calm and unbowed. It's frightening, then, that ignorance and obsequiousness are stronger than wisdom.

[19] In themselves, the things of the world have no effect on the mind; they can't get through to it, they can't sway it, and they can't stir it. The only thing that changes and stirs the mind is the mind, and when external objects are presented to it, it has them

---

33. So only superior—that is, rational—creatures are naturally made to be social; the rest play a support role. See also 5.30: the model of society that Marcus assumes is one in which the lower classes support the upper.

34. This scale, from inanimate to animate to rational, recurs in various forms throughout the book. It was considered to be a commonsensical notion and was taken over as such by Stoics.

35. Marcus is again commenting on something one of his acquaintances had done that is unknowable to us. The sentiment is the same as at 4.6.

36. Marcus returns to the thought at 8.46 and 10.3.

conform to the judgments that it deems itself justified in making about them.[37]

[20] From one point of view, nothing is more proper to me than a human being, insofar as it's my job to do people good and tolerate them. But insofar as some people threaten my proper work, I count a human being as just another indifferent, no less than the sun or the wind or a wild animal. These things may impede some of my activities, but they can't impede my impulses or my state of mind, because I have the powers of reservation and adaptation. The mind can adapt and alter every impediment to action to serve its purpose; something that might have hindered a task contributes to it instead, and something that was an obstacle on the road helps you on your way.[38]

---

37. The ideal independence of the mind is a recurrent theme in Marcus: see, for example, 2.15, 4.3, 7.16. Here his meaning seems to be that it is up to us (up to our minds) to judge things. We are back to the idea that things are only good or bad if we think them so: compare 2.15 and 4.39. At every moment, we choose to make the world we live in fair or foul. The trick is to catch the moment before you have judged it foul and, by accepting that all is done by the will of God, turn it fair. Compare Epictetus, *Discourses* 2.18.24: "But the first thing is not to be carried away by the intensity of an impression. You should say: 'Hold on a moment, impression. Let me see what you are and what you are an impression of. Let me put you to the test.'"

38. Again, Marcus stresses the independence of the mind and the possibility of seeing the world in a positive light. If the previous entry was the theory, this one focuses on the practice. On "reservation and adaptation," see 4.1 and 6.50. On "indifferents," see the Introduction, xl–xli.

[21] Honor the greatest power in the universe; everything and everyone are its instruments and subjects. By the same token, honor the greatest power in yourself as well. It's the same in kind as that universal power,[39] since the same goes for you too: all your parts are its instruments and your life is under its direction.

[22] Anything that does the state no harm does no harm to its citizens either. Whenever you think you've been harmed, apply this criterion: if it leaves the state unharmed, it does me no harm either.[40] On the other hand, in any case of actual harm to the state, one shouldn't get angry with the person who's responsible for it, but show him what he's overlooking.[41]

[23] Remind yourself at frequent intervals how quickly things and events are carried past and swept away. Reality is like an endlessly flowing river, its activities constantly changing, its causes variable beyond counting. It's hardly an exaggeration to say

---

39. "Two things that share a single path" (5.3).

40. The interests of the whole take priority over the interests of any of its parts, so first we must align ourselves with the interests of the whole. Then we will see personal harm as less important.

41. Marcus is clearly thinking of Rome; the Great City "of which all other states are mere households" (3.11) cannot be harmed by any means imaginable in Marcus's time. But for the emperor of Rome to show such leniency toward someone who has harmed the state seems extraordinary, and I doubt Marcus was able in real life to put it into practice. See also Notebook 11, note 37, attached to another entry with penological implications.

that nothing is stable, even what is close to us in time.[42] Past time is infinite and the future a yawning gulf in which everything is swallowed up. In these circumstances, isn't it just sheer stupidity for a man to get angry, agitated, or aggrieved, as though anything lasted any amount of time and could irritate him for long?

[24] Call to mind the whole of existence—and the minuteness of your portion of it. Call to mind the whole of time—and the brief and fleeting stretch of it that has been allocated to you. Call to mind fate—and how exiguous a part of it you are.

[25] Is someone treating me badly? That's his concern. He's his own man and his actions are his own. I currently have what universal nature wants me to have, and I'm acting as my nature currently wants me to act.[43]

[26] The command center, the ruling part of the soul, should not be swayed by any smooth or rough motions in the body.[44] Make sure, then, that it doesn't get caught up with them, but isolates itself and restricts those feelings to the bodily parts. But

---

42. It is fairly obvious, when you look over a long stretch of time, that even slowly changing things are changing, but things "close to us in time" can seem to be unchanging.

43. That is, the events he experiences and his actions do not depend on other people; and these events and actions were predestined anyway, so at any moment he has and does exactly what he's supposed to. But then, so does the other person—which is precisely Marcus's point: he has to work out his destiny, just as Marcus does his. The difference is that the other person is doing wrong because he has not attuned his command center to the will of universal nature.

44. That is, pleasant and unpleasant bodily feelings.

when these feelings are transmitted to the mind (since, as is bound to happen in a unified organism, the two interact), there's no point in trying to resist the sensation, which is involuntary, but the command center should not add, as its own contribution, any belief about the goodness or badness of the feeling.

[27] "Live with the gods." The man who lives with the gods is the one whose soul is constantly on display to them as content with its lot and obedient to the will of the guardian spirit, the fragment of himself that Zeus has granted every person to act as his custodian and command center. And in each of us this is mind and reason.[45]

[28] Surely you're not angry with a man because of his foul stench or stinking breath, are you? What good will that do you? That's the way his mouth is, that's the way his armpits are, so they're bound to give off foul odors. "But, as a human being, he's been equipped with the faculty of reason and has the ability, if he applies his mind, to realize what's making him so offensive." Fine, but it follows that you have the faculty of reason too. Use rationality to activate rationality: explain things to him, bring

---

45. So a person "lives with the gods" if she accepts her lot and acts rationally.

the matter up with him.[46] If he gets the point, you'll cure him and there'll be no need for anger. Be neither an actor nor a whore.[47]

[29] Your life here has the potential to be no different from the life you intend to live after you've passed away.[48] If that ever proves impossible here, take your leave of life then, but not as though death were a bad experience for you. "Smoke? Then I'm leaving."[49] Why make a big deal out of it? But as long as there's no pressing reason to go, I remain self-reliant; no one can stop me

---

46. On relying on explanation rather than anger, see also 5.22 and 9.42.

47. I think that with these enigmatic last words Marcus is advising himself not to dissimulate in his dealings with his smelly friend, and not to sell himself cheap (i.e., by failing to use his rational faculty).

48. Marcus probably means "You can live with the gods here on earth, as you will live with the gods after your death." The Stoics saw human death as the separation of the soul from the body; and most of them held that the soul, or at least the ruling part of the soul, the command center, then carries on existing for some time—a short time for immoral people, but for enlightened people right up until the final conflagration of this universe. The idea of personal survival tempted Marcus: see 3.3 ("If it takes you to another life . . ."), 4.21 (the soul survives "for a while"), 8.58, 12.5, and in general his entertainment of the possibility of survival/change of place as the third postmortem possibility along with dispersal or extinction.

49. These are reminders for Marcus of some famous words of Epictetus: "Has someone made the house smoky? If it's not too bad, I'll stay; if it's too much, I leave" (*Discourses* 1.25.18). On suicide, see Notebook 3, note 3.

from acting as I want. And what I want is to act as a rational and social being would naturally act.

[30] The mind of the universe takes thought for society.[50] At any rate, it has made lower beings serve higher ones[51] and has harmonized the higher beings with one another. It's easy to see what it has done by way of subordination, coordination, and the allocation of everything to the station it deserves, and how it has brought superior creatures into harmony with one another.

[31] How have you behaved up until now toward gods, parents, siblings,[52] wife, children, teachers, tutors, friends, family, and slaves? Check whether toward all of them so far your principle has been "Do no evil and speak no evil."[53] Remind yourself what you've been through and what you've had the strength to endure,

---

50. 5.29–31 seem to form a kind of unit. The mention of the ideal "rational and social being" in the previous entry triggers the thought of this entry. Then, after outlining how the "mind of the universe" creates harmony, Marcus checks in the next entry whether he has done the same in his personal life.

51. In the first instance, Marcus means that inferior beings such as plants and animals serve superior beings such as humans and gods. But (see also 5.16) there is also a political implication, that some people are destined by their natures to belong to the lower orders.

52. Marcus had only one natural sibling, his sister Annia Cornificia Faustina, but he always spoke of his brother by adoption, Lucius Verus, as though he were a sibling.

53. A close paraphrase from memory of Homer, *Odyssey* 4.690.

and that the story of your life is now coming to an end,[54] your service completed. Remind yourself of all the admirable deeds you've witnessed, how many times you've overcome pleasure and pain,[55] how many distinctions you've disdained, and how many discourteous people you've treated with courtesy.

[32] Why do uninformed and ignorant minds confound an informed and knowledgeable man? Well, what is an informed and knowledgeable mind? It's one that knows the beginning and the end, and knows the reason that permeates all existence and administers the universe in regular cycles throughout all eternity.[56]

[33] Before long, either ashes or a skeleton, and either just a name or not even that—and what's a name but noise and a fading echo? The things that are valued in life are vain, rotten, and trivial: puppies bite one another; children squabble, laugh, and then cry a moment later. Fidelity, modesty, justice, honesty—"gone to

---

54. "Story" is not just a nice metaphor, but perfectly suited to Marcus, who, as emperor, could be sure that his reign would be written up by historians.

55. That is, exhibited strength of will in not being tempted by a pleasant prospect or put off by an unpleasant one.

56. And so it is stupefied by the pettiness of most people's concerns. The "regular cycles" are the identical stretches of time between the universal conflagrations that renew the world. God survives the conflagration by withdrawing into himself (finding his own "inner retreat": 4.3) so that he is able to initiate the next sequence; but the gods in the plural will perish, along with everything else, at the time of the conflagration: see Epictetus, *Discourses* 3.13.4.

Olympus from the wide-pathed earth."[57] What is it that still keeps you here, since sensible objects are changeable and uncertain, the senses dull and easily duped, the soul itself just a vapor given off by blood,[58] and fame in a world like this nothing more than delusion? What to do, then? Why don't you wait peacefully for whatever it may be, either extinction or a change of place?[59] "And until that time comes, what do I need to do?" Just worship the gods and sing their praises, do good to men, and "bear and forbear."[60] As for anything that falls outside the compass of your lump of flesh and your bit of spirit, remember that it's nothing to do with you and isn't subject to your will.

[34] You can always be content if you continue to make good progress, which is to say if your beliefs and actions keep you on

---

57. A quotation from Hesiod, *Works and Days* 197—an apt quotation, since Hesiod (c. 650 BCE) was talking about the disappearance from earth of qualities similar to those listed by Marcus.

58. Actually, the Stoics claimed that the soul, being air or breath, was formed and nourished/replenished partly by evaporation from the blood (which is replenished by the food we eat) and partly by the air we draw in when we breathe. Marcus here stresses the vapor because he wants to stress the evanescence of things. The Stoics claimed that the idea that soul was evaporation from blood was another idea they got from Heraclitus.

59. These are the two afterlife possibilities that are compatible with Stoicism. They were famously postulated by Socrates in Plato's *Apology of Socrates*, at 40c–41c.

60. This neat tag comes from Epictetus (from the very end of fragment 10 Schenkl); it was his mnemonic for the two essential keys to peace of mind: bear your ills and abstain from pleasures.

the path of reason. There are two features that are common to the minds of gods, men, and any other rational beings there may be: they are immune to external obstruction, and what they count as good is right thinking and right action, which they make the limit of their desire.

[35] If it's neither my wrongdoing nor the outcome of something I did, and if the state is no worse for it, why am I troubled by it? And is the state being harmed?

[36] Don't get completely carried away by their thoughts, but give as much help as you can and as the situation deserves, even if the loss they're suffering involves nothing of moral significance.[61] But don't think that they're really being harmed; that would be a bad habit to get into. You should behave like the old man who went off to demand the return of his foster child's whirligig, even though he was well aware that it was only a whirligig.[62] That's also how you should act on the Rostra.[63] Have you forgotten, my friend, how little these things are worth? "Yes, but they're of

---

61. Marcus is undoubtedly thinking of Epictetus, *Handbook* 16: "When you see someone weeping from grief at the loss of a child or of some property of theirs, take care that his thoughts don't carry you away."

62. This sounds like a reference to a scene from a play, but if so, we cannot identify it.

63. The Rostra was the speaker's platform in the Roman forum. Marcus is saying that, although much of politics is concerned with things that are, in Stoic terms, morally neutral, he should still play his part, like the old man in the play. See also 3.11, 6.45, and 9.11.

great importance to these people." Well, is that any reason for you to behave like an idiot as well?[64]

[37] "Once I was a lucky man, wherever I was to be found." But a lucky man is one who makes his own good fortune,[65] and good fortune consists in good uses of the mind, good impulses, and good deeds.

64. So Marcus should act in public as though he were dealing with important issues, but without getting idiotically carried away and caught up in others' views of what is and is not important.

65. See 4.49. The idea originated with Plato's Socrates, at *Euthydemus* 279c–280b.

NOTEBOOK 6

[1] The physical substance of the universe is compliant and plastic, but there's nothing inherent in the reason that directs the universe that could cause it to do wrong.[1] Badness isn't one of its qualities, nor does it do things badly, nor is anything made worse by it. Everything comes into existence and runs its course in accordance with its will.

[2] It should make no difference to you, as long as you're acting appropriately, whether you're cold or warm, drowsy or refreshed by a good night's rest, unpopular or popular, dying or otherwise engaged. For even dying is an action taken in life,

---

1. Since matter is passively compliant to the active will of the rational principle of the universe, and the rational principle can do no wrong, it follows that there is nothing bad in the universe. If there is a common thread to this sixth notebook, it is the nature of the universe and the consequences for human beings.

so there too it's a matter of making the best use of the present moment.[2]

[3] Look under the surface. Don't let either the specific quality or the value of anything pass you by.

[4] Everything that exists will very soon change, and will either be vaporized, if substance is single, or dispersed.[3]

[5] The reason that directs the universe knows its own disposition; it knows what it does and the material with which it has to work.

[6] The best form of defense is not to become like one's enemy.[4]

---

2. See 2.14: life is a succession of present moments, right up to the end. 12.3 is Marcus's most sustained meditation on the importance of the present moment. Focusing on the present is a good way to train the attention (this is perhaps implicit in 12.3), and it reduces distress, because an instant has no qualities, pleasant or unpleasant (8.36, 11.2).

3. As elsewhere in the book, the choice is between a Stoic and an Epicurean view. According to the Stoics, the universe undergoes periodic conflagration (the "vaporization" of its substance); according to Epicureanism, the atoms of which all things are made will be dispersed or scattered. Here Marcus does not choose between the two alternatives (though we may guess that he preferred the orderliness and meaningfulness of the Stoic picture), because his point is that, in either case, everything is ephemeral.

4. See also 4.11. Compare Diogenes of Sinope, the founder of Cynicism, as quoted by Plutarch, *How to Profit by One's Enemies* 88b: "How shall I defend myself against my enemy? By proving myself good and honorable."

[7] Find joy and rest in one thing alone: in moving from one socially useful act to another, while remaining mindful of God.

[8] The command center is self-motivated and versatile; it not only makes itself what it wants to be, but also makes everything that happens appear as it wants it to appear.[5]

[9] Everything is accomplished in accordance with universal nature. After all, there is, of course, no other universe that could do this, whether it contained this universe or was contained by it, or existed as a discrete entity outside.[6]

[10] Either (a) a cocktail of ingredients that interlock and disperse, or (b) unity, order, and providence. If (a), why would I even want to spend time in a world like that, a random compound and a confused jumble?[7] Why would I care about anything except how at some point to "turn into earth"?[8] And why should that even trouble me? I'll end up being dispersed whatever I do. If (b),

---

5. This is the idea we meet elsewhere, that everything is as we—our command centers—judge it to be. See, for example, 2.15 and 4.39. In a sense, human reason here treats its experiences as "plastic" in the same way that divine reason does the matter of the world at 6.1.

6. Marcus intends these to exhaust the possibilities. The entry is a forceful way of saying that, by definition, the universe is single. The universe is complete and perfect as it is, so there cannot be another such, however or wherever we conceive of its existence.

7. The Epicurean universe is not a teleological universe: there is no overall plan, just the random separation and recombination of atoms. Marcus prefers an ordered universe.

8. The quoted phrase is either a vague reminiscence of Homer, *Iliad* 7.99, or from an unknown poet.

however, my response is reverential awe, I have a stable place to stand, and I place my trust in the power that directs the universe.[9]

[11] When the pressure of circumstances somewhat disturbs your peace of mind, recover quickly and don't lose your rhythm for longer than necessary. In any case, you'll master the measure all the better by constantly returning to it.

[12] If you had both a stepmother and a mother, you'd do your duty by your stepmother, and yet you'd constantly return to your mother. That's how you stand today in relation to the imperial court and philosophy. Return, then, at frequent intervals to philosophy and lean on it for rest. With its help, even court business seems tolerable to you, and you become tolerable while attending to it.

[13] How useful it is, when you're served roast meat and similar dishes, to think to yourself: this is the corpse of a fish, this is the corpse of a bird or a pig! Or again, to see Falernian wine as mere grape juice,[10] your purple-hemmed cloak as sheep's wool dyed

---

9. Some scholars maintain that Marcus was somewhat undecided between the Epicurean and Stoic views of the makeup of the universe, but it is hard to imagine that the man who wrote this entry would ever be attracted to the Epicurean view. Whenever he raises the Epicurean possibility, it is either explicitly or implicitly rejected.

10. Falernian wine, from Campania, was widely considered to be the best of the Italian wines.

with shellfish blood,[11] and sexual intercourse as just the rubbing of an organ and the spasm-induced emission of a little slime.[12] How good these thoughts are at reaching and getting to the heart of things! They enable you to see things for what they are. This should be a lifelong exercise:[13] whenever things particularly seem to deserve your acceptance, strip them bare so that you can see how worthless they are and dispense with the descriptions that make them seem more significant than they are. Vanity is terrifyingly good at derailing rational thought, and it's when you think you're engaged on important matters that you're most under its spell. At any rate, consider what Crates said about Xenocrates.[14]

[14] Most of the things that are admired by the masses belong to the very capacious category of things that are sustained by cohesion (stones and timber, for example) or by nature (figs,

---

11. See Notebook 4, note 35. Actually, the dye did not come from the blood of the murex but from a fluid extracted from its hypobranchial gland.

12. Similar outspoken realism at 2.2, 5.28, 8.24, 8.37, 9.36.

13. This is the same stripping exercise as at 3.11, but with a different purpose: at 3.11 it was to remove fear of death.

14. We have no idea what Crates said about Xenocrates. They both lived in Athens, where they were respected enough to be chosen for diplomatic missions, despite not being citizens.

vines, olives).[15] Those that are admired by people of the middling sort belong to the category of things that are sustained by animal soul, such as flocks and herds, or merely the ownership of a large number of slaves. Those that are admired by more refined people belong to the category of things that are sustained by a rational soul—not qua rational, however, but qua possessing artistic or intellectual expertise. But anyone who values the rational and social soul no longer finds anything else deserving of his attention; his priority is the maintenance of his own soul in a rational and sociable condition, and ensuring that it keeps moving along these channels, and to this end he cooperates with others who are like him.[16]

[15] Some things are rushing toward existence, others rushing to have done with existence, and in a certain respect anything that comes into existence is already extinguished.[17] The world is continuously being renewed by flux and alteration, just

---

15. The word translated "cohesion" is *hexis*, a technical term in Stoic physics. Cohesion is one of the principal modes of *pneuma*, the divine life-force in everything. Inanimate things have *pneuma* as cohesion; things that are capable of growth (i.e., plants) have *pneuma* as *physis*, "nature"; things that have the powers of perception, movement, and reproduction have *pneuma* as *psykhē*, "soul"; and the top of the scale is occupied by beings that are capable of rational thought, who have *pneuma* as *logikē psykhē*, "rational soul," which has the highest rate of tension. Rational beings have *pneuma* in all four modes.

16. The question of the relative value of things is also addressed in the next two entries; the three entries form a kind of unit.

17. Because it is not what it was before, perhaps; compare 7.40, 9.19.

as infinite time is forever being renewed by the uninterrupted flow of time. In this torrent of instability, which of the things that are flying past might one value? It's as if one were to begin to feel affection for a certain sparrow as it flew past—but it's already gone from sight. In fact, life itself, the life of every individual, is no different from the vapor that's given off by blood or a breath drawn from the outside air,[18] in the sense that there's no real difference between our momentary drawing in and releasing of air, and releasing the ability to breathe as a whole—an ability you acquired at birth yesterday or the day before—back to the place from where you first drew it.

[16] There's nothing of value in transpiration (which plants do),[19] or respiration (which cattle and wild animals do), or being stamped by impressions, or being tugged here and there by impulses, or gathering in herds, or feeding ourselves. In fact, feeding ourselves is equivalent to the evacuation of food waste. So what is valuable?[20] Applause? No. And therefore the same goes for verbal plaudits, seeing that the praise of the multitude is just

---

18. It was commonly held that the soul was sustained by vapor given off by blood and by the air we breathe.

19. The ancients believed that plants and all creatures, including humans, took in at least a portion of their air through pores in the skin, and they called this "transpiration."

20. The previous entry raised this question but left it unanswered. Of course, it is illogical of Marcus to reject out of hand the idea that there can be value in qualities we share with plants and animals; he is assuming, or allowing the *scala naturae* to dictate, what perhaps needs proving.

the clapping of tongues. So you've rejected so-called fame. What's left to value? This, in my opinion: acting or refraining from action as dictated by the way we're made. And here our occupations and crafts show the way, since it's the aim of every craft that what it makes should fit the purpose for which it was made.[21] This is the aim of the farmer tending his vines, as it is of the horse-breaker and the dog-trainer. And what else is it that tutors and teachers strive for?

So that's where value lies. And if just this one thing goes well, you won't be interested in procuring any of the other so-called goods for yourself. So won't you stop finding all sorts of other things valuable as well? Otherwise, you won't be self-reliant or self-sufficient or impassive, because you're bound to suffer from envy and jealousy, to mistrust those who are able to deprive you of the things you prize, and to intrigue against those who have them. All in all, anyone who needs any of those things is bound to find himself in emotional turmoil, and also to find fault frequently with the gods.[22] But a modest respect for your own mind won't only make you happy with yourself, but also congenial to others and in harmony with the gods—which is to

---

21. So we too have been made, or are constituted, for a certain purpose, to act or refrain from acting in certain ways—that is, with virtue as our constant goal. There are echoes of the doctrine espoused by Socrates in some of Plato's dialogues that virtue is a kind of craft knowledge.

22. Blaming the gods for his lack of what he covets.

say that you'll have nothing but praise for all that they assign you and have arranged for you.

[17] The elements move up and down, and in cycles,[23] but such movements don't apply to virtue. Something more divine is involved in its case; it advances on a path that's hard to fathom.

[18] What a way to behave! They're reluctant to praise any of their contemporaries, who are actually here with them, but they attach considerable importance to being praised by future generations, whom they've never seen and never will see. This is pretty much the same as being upset because earlier generations didn't compose eulogies for you!

[19] If you personally find something hard to achieve, you shouldn't suppose that it isn't humanly possible. Think rather that, if something is humanly possible and is proper to a human being, it's attainable by you too.[24]

[20] If, while taking exercise, someone scratches us with his nails or butts us with his head as he breaks out of a hold, we don't blame him or take offense or suspect him subsequently of wishing us ill. True, we exercise caution and try to avoid being hurt again, but in a kindly fashion, not because we regard him as malicious

---

23. On the recycling of the elements, see also 2.17 (end), 4.3 (end), 7.23, 7.25, 7.47, 8.50, 12.23. For their upward and downward motion, see 9.9.

24. He is probably thinking above all of virtue. The Stoic assumption was that it was possible to be fully virtuous, and so Marcus urges himself to keep trying. But there was considerable argument about whether perfection in this respect was humanly possible; Marcus urges himself to think that it was.

or suspect him of anything. That's how we should behave in the rest of our lives as well. We should overlook much of what those whom we could call our wrestling partners do. After all, as I said, one may avoid trouble without being suspicious or hostile.

[21] If someone can prove me wrong and show me that something I thought or did was mistaken, I'll gladly change, because my goal is the truth and the truth has never harmed anyone. The man who's harmed is the one who persists in his own self-deception and ignorance.[25]

[22] I carry out the tasks that are proper to me without letting other things distract me; they're either inanimate or irrational, or they've gone astray and lost their way.[26]

[23] Treat irrational animals, and things and objects in general, in a detached and generous manner, since you have the faculty of reason and they don't. Treat human beings, who do have the faculty of reason, in a sociable manner. And in all things call on the gods for help, and never worry how much time you will have to act in this way; even three hours of such a life is enough.[27]

---

25. Or, as Socrates famously said: "The unexamined life is not worth living" (Plato, *Apology of Socrates* 38a).

26. It is arguable that this entry and the next should be made into a single unit. They both assume a tripartite division of entities into inanimate objects, irrational creatures, and rational creatures.

27. Quality of life is more important than quantity. See also 4.47 and 11.1.

[24] Alexander of Macedon and the man who tended his mules were made equal by death, either because they were received back into the same seminal principles of the universe or because they were both equally dispersed into atoms.[28]

[25] Bear in mind how much is going on simultaneously in each of us, taking our bodies and minds together, at any given instant, and then you won't be surprised at the far greater number of events—in fact, the totality of events—that exist simultaneously in the single, comprehensive entity that we call the universe.

[26] If someone were to ask you how to spell "Antoninus,"[29] would you enunciate each letter through gritted teeth? And if that makes them angry, would you get angry in return? Wouldn't you just gently itemize each letter, one after another? You need to remember that here on earth too appropriate action is always made up of a certain number of stages, which you have to observe—without getting worked up or responding with anger when others get angry—so that you can complete the task at hand in a methodical fashion.

---

28. The point of this entry is pretty much the same as that of 6.4. As usual when Marcus offers himself the choice between Epicurean and Stoic doctrine, he prefers the Stoic, although he does not spell that out here, because his point is just that death is a leveler, whatever your view of the constitution of the universe.

29. This was Marcus's name. When he became emperor, as an act of homage to his predecessor on the imperial throne, Antoninus Pius, he added "Antoninus" to his name, so that he was Marcus Aurelius Antoninus.

[27] How cruel it is to thwart people's attempts to get what they think is proper to them and expedient for them! And yet, in a sense, you act as just such an obstacle when you get cross with them for their flaws. I mean, they're bound in any case to be drawn to what they take to be proper to them and to their advantage.[30] "But they're wrong!" So instruct them and explain things to them, without getting angry.[31]

[28] Death brings relief from reacting to sense impressions, from being tugged here and there by one's impulses, from associative thinking, and from service to the body.

[29] It's horrible that in this life, while your body keeps going, your mind gives up first.[32]

[30] Beware of becoming Caesarified, dyed in purple.[33] It does happen. Keep yourself simple, good, guileless, dignified, unpretentious, devoted to justice, pious, kind, affectionate to

---

30. This is, again, the Socratic and Stoic idea that everyone wants what they take to be good for themselves. Weakness of will is actually false belief about what is good for oneself.

31. The previous entry stated that anger was not an appropriate response; now Marcus explains why.

32. See 3.1, where this thought is treated at greater length. Seneca wrote similarly about old age at *Letters* 58.32–36.

33. Marcus coined a new word "to become Caesarified." He is probably referring to Julius Caesar, and he means "Don't become a dictator." At the same time, since he also warns himself against being "dyed in purple," what he wants to avoid is becoming so identified with his role as emperor that he forgets his common humanity. On purple, see Notebook 4, note 35.

others, and resolute in carrying out your proper tasks. Strive to be and remain the kind of person philosophy would have you be. Revere the gods and keep men safe. Life is short. There's only one crop to be reaped from your time on earth, and that is a reverential disposition and socially useful actions.[34]

In all you do, be a disciple of Antoninus:[35] his energetic approach to rational action, his constant equability, his piety, the composure of his features, his kindness, his lack of vain self-importance, and his determination to get to the heart of matters. Then there was the way he'd refuse to let anything go until thorough examination had led him to understand it perfectly; how he put up with unfair criticism without being critical in return; how he never rushed things; and how he refused to listen to malicious gossip. He was an accurate judge of character and what people did, without being disparaging, timid, distrustful, or sophistic. He was easily satisfied when it came to things like lodgings, bedding, clothes, food, and attendants. He was industrious, patient, and able to stay in place until evening because, thanks to his frugal diet, he didn't need to evacuate waste except at his habitual time. He was a reliable and consistent friend. He was tolerant of frank criticism of his plans and happy if

---

34. Two things that form a single "crop": one is the inner and the other the outer manifestation of being a philosopher.

35. For the eulogy that follows, compare 1.16. Since the "first" notebook was probably written last, it was passages such as this eulogy that inspired Marcus to write it and commemorate his various teachers; see also 6.48.

someone could show him a better way. He was religious without being superstitious. If in all these respects you're his disciple, the hour of your death will find you with as clear a conscience as his.

[31] Sober up,[36] come back to yourself, and once you've aroused yourself again from sleep and understood that what was bothering you was no more than a dream, regard what you see now that you're awake again as no different from what you were seeing in your dream.[37]

[32] I consist of body and soul. To the body, everything is indifferent, because it's incapable of making distinctions. To the mind, everything is indifferent unless it's one of its own activities, from the set of those that are within its power. But even as regards these activities, it's concerned only with the one that it's currently engaged on; its future and past activities are themselves matters of indifference at that moment.

---

36. Marcus might mean this literally. It was not uncommon for Romans to get through quite a lot of wine in a day, and wine was a major component in every soldier's rations. Plus, in Marcus's case, opium may have contributed to a groggy feeling the morning after (see Notebook 5, note 2). I take this entry to be evidence that Marcus kept his notebooks by the side of his bed at night, because he clearly wrote this after waking up in the middle of the night from a bad dream.

37. If the things of this world are as illusory as what he was seeing in his dreams, there is equally no reason to let them disturb his equilibrium. This is not a very good argument, because it is only after waking up that you realize the dream was an illusion; when asleep, dreams can certainly disturb one's equilibrium.

[33] No form of toil is unnatural for the hand or the foot, as long as the foot is doing the work of a foot and the hand the work of a hand. By the same token, no form of toil is unnatural for a human being either, qua human being, as long as he's doing human work. And if it's not unnatural for him, it's not bad for him either.

[34] How intense are the pleasures enjoyed by thieves, perverts, parricides, and tyrants![38]

[35] Don't you see how common artisans adjust their work to a certain extent to suit nonspecialists but still stay just as true as ever to the rational principle of their art and hate to abandon it?[39] Isn't it shocking, then, for the builder and the doctor to respect the rational principle of their crafts more than a person respects his own rational principle, which is common to him and the gods?

---

38. Marcus does not mean that a parricide feels intense pleasure actually while killing his father, but just that such a person is capable of feeling intense pleasure. For Marcus, all pleasures are matters of indifference, and the fact that rotten people are motivated by pleasure proves its valuelessness (see also 3.16). As 5.10 shows, this principle applies, in his view, even to possessions, not just pleasures. In the background is a passage of Plato's *Gorgias* (493d–495a), where Socrates too condemns the pleasures of, among others, "perverts."

39. If Marcus means this to be analogous to his own situation, the "adjustment" he makes is that he rewards his officers with indifferents even though he knows they are worthless: see 3.11 (end) and 5.36 (beginning).

[36] Asia, Europe: mere corners of the universe. Every ocean: a droplet in the universe. Mount Athos:[40] a clod of earth in the universe. The entirety of present time: an instant in eternity. Everything is petty, changeable, vanishing. Everything comes from heaven, either springing directly from the universal command center or as a consequence. The lion's gaping jaw, poison, and all forms of criminal behavior are, like thorns or mud, no more than by-products of those sublime and beautiful sources.[41] You shouldn't think of them as having nothing to do with the object of your reverence, but take into account the common source of all things.

[37] Anyone who has seen all there is to see now has seen everything that has existed in the infinite past and everything that will exist in the infinite future. Everything is homogeneous and uniform.[42]

[38] Meditate often on the concatenation of all things in the universe and their relationship to one another. You could almost say, since all things are intertwined with one another, that they're in a loving relationship. They cohere one with another thanks to

---

40. A spectacular mountainous promontory in northern Greece, now famously the isolated site of a number of Greek Orthodox monasteries.

41. Marcus deploys the same argument for seeing the beauty in everything at 3.2 and 8.50.

42. A recurrent thought in *Meditations* (e.g., 2.14, 4.32, and 6.46), which often induces expressions of boredom in Marcus.

tensional movement, the breath that permeates them all, and the unity of all substance.[43]

[39] You've been allotted certain events by destiny and you should adapt yourself to them; as for the people you've been allotted, hold them dear, but do so genuinely.[44]

[40] A good instrument, tool, or utensil is one that does the job for which it was made. In their case, however, the person who made them is no longer in the picture. But natural products are different: the power that fashioned them is inside them and

---

43. In Stoic physics, spirit (*pneuma*) is central. There is no void in the world (whatever the Epicureans may say); reality is a single continuum of spirit-permeated substance. Matter itself being totally inert, the qualities of things are determined by the different tensional movements (a kind of inner vibration) of the *pneuma* within them. Relatively inert things have low tension and the *pneuma* in them acts merely to keep them cohesive (see 6.14, with the note); active things have high tension and the *pneuma* in them is soul (*pneuma* in general is identical with divine reason); and every individual thing has its own individual tension. The Stoic view, reflected here by Marcus, was that there was mutual compatibility or sympathy between the tensional vibrations of things, so that this aspect of the universe too was a unifying force.

44. This is something Marcus found personally difficult, as his frequent outbursts of disdain for others demonstrate. So he also frequently reminds himself of the community of all rational beings, and that all other human beings are his kin. Here he suggests that the solution is simply to submit to the will of the universe, and this is a theme in the following entries as well.

remains there.[45] It follows that you should revere it all the more, and believe that if your disposition and your conduct are in compliance with its will, everything will go well, as you would want it to go. The same goes for the universe as well: its affairs proceed as it wants.

[41] If you treat things that aren't subject to your volition as good or bad,[46] it's inevitable that, when you meet one of these "bad" things or fail to gain one of these "good" things, you'll blame the gods and hate the men who are responsible for what happened or who you suspect may be responsible for such a thing in the future. In fact, many of the wrongs we commit are a consequence of our assigning value to these things. But if we judge only things that are up to us to be good and bad, you'll be left with no reason to criticize the gods or adopt a hostile attitude toward other men.

[42] We're all working together toward a single end, some consciously and knowingly, others in ignorance—like Heraclitus's sleepers, I think, whom he described as laborers, working together at what happens in the universe.[47] Everyone makes a different

---

45. Unlike inanimate and man-made objects, animate things have an inner drive to fulfill their function.

46. Only things that are "up to us," within our power, are good or bad. Everything else—all the things that just happen to us—are neither good nor bad in themselves, but we can make good or bad use of them. This entry is reminiscent of Epictetus; see, for instance, *Handbook* 1.

47. This is Heraclitus, fragment 75 Diels/Kranz. The original was perhaps cast in the form of one of Heraclitus's famous paradoxes, starting "Though asleep, they are at work."

contribution; there's room even for the man who doesn't like what's happening, and tries to resist it and make it not happen. The universe needs him too.[48] So all you need to do is determine which camp you'll join. The director of the universe will make good use of you in either case and will incorporate you in his workforce, but you need to make sure that the part you play doesn't resemble the worthless and ridiculous verse in the comedy, which Chrysippus mentions.[49]

[43] Does the sun take on the work of the rain? Does Asclepius take on the work of the Lady of the Harvest?[50] What about the heavenly bodies? Each of them is different, but they still work together toward the same end.[51]

[44] If the gods deliberated about me and the lot they had in store for me, they came to the right decisions. After all, it isn't easy to conceive of a god who's a poor decision maker, and

---

48. Because everything it has us do, whether positive or negative, fulfills part of its predetermined plan.

49. "Just as comedies contain ridiculous lines, which, though inferior in themselves, add a certain charm to the play as a whole, so, although if you took vice on its own you might censure it, the universe as a whole does not find it useless" (Chrysippus, quoted by Plutarch, *On Common Conceptions* 1065d).

50. The Lady of the Harvest is Demeter (or Ceres to the Romans); Asclepius was the healer god.

51. So Marcus continues the theme of the previous entry: each thing plays a different part, all contributing to the end determined by God or the Reason that providentially directs the universe. On the sympathetic unity of the heavenly bodies, see 9.9.

why would they intend to do me harm? What would that gain either them or the common good, which is the chief concern of their providence? Even if I personally wasn't the object of their deliberations, they certainly took thought for the common good,[52] and, since what happens to me is a concomitant of that, I'm bound to welcome and embrace these experiences too. On the other hand, if we suppose that they take no thought for anyone or anything—it would be sacrilege to believe this, or at least we'd have to do away with sacrifices, prayers, oaths, and all the other things we do on the assumption that the gods are a presence in our lives. Still, if it were true that they have no interest in us or our affairs, I'm still at liberty to take thought for myself and consider what's good for me. And what's good for anyone is what's consonant with his own constitution and nature; and my nature is rational and social. As Antoninus,[53] my social community and my country is Rome, but as a human

52. This is a perennial debate, as alive today as when Marcus was writing. Do the gods care for us individually, or only for humankind in general? The broader debate to which Marcus next alludes is whether the gods take thought even for humankind in general. The Epicureans held that they did not, and the Stoics—or some Stoics, at least—that they did, not just generally, but that they saw us and cared for us as individuals (see further Epictetus, *Discourses* 1.12). As usual, Marcus sides with the Stoics.

53. Marcus's full name as emperor was Marcus Aurelius Antoninus.

being it's the universe.[54] So it's only things that benefit these communities that are good for me.

[45] All of a person's experiences are beneficial to the universe. That's enough on its own. But a little observation will generally show you also that what's beneficial for one person is beneficial for others as well[55]—though in this case "benefit" is to be understood in the vulgar sense, referring to things that are in fact neither good nor bad.

[46] Just as the productions that are put on in the amphitheater and such places exasperate you because it's merely the same show over and over again, and the lack of variety makes them boring, so is your experience of life as a whole: look

54. "Let's embrace the idea that there are two commonwealths. The one is vast and truly common to all, and includes the gods as well as mankind; within it, we look neither to this mere corner nor to that, but we measure the boundaries of our state by the sun's course. The other is the one in which we are enrolled by the circumstances of our birth" (Seneca, *De Otio* 4.1, translation by G. Williams).

55. There are two ways to understand this. First (and rather trivially), if health, say, is something that is good for me, it is something that is good for others as well. Second, my personal health is good for others as well in the sense that, as a healthy person, I will treat others better.

where you will, everything is the same and consists of the same components. For how long, then?[56]

[47] You should bear in mind constantly that death has come to men of all kinds, men with varied occupations and various ethnicities, all the way down to Philistion, Phoebus, and Origanion.[57] And then what about other types of people? We too will inevitably end up where so many eloquent orators have gone, so many distinguished philosophers (Heraclitus, Pythagoras, Socrates), so many heroes of old, and so many generals and tyrants from more recent times. Add to these Eudoxus, Hipparchus, Archimedes, other brilliant intellectuals, high-minded men, hard workers, men of ingenuity, self-confident

---

56. In order to make his point (see especially 2.14), Marcus focuses here on the monotony of gladiatorial and wild animal shows. As heir apparent and then emperor, he was expected to be present at them when he was in Rome. Elsewhere he expresses some disgust at them (10.8), and Cassius Dio (*Roman History* 72.29) reports that Marcus ordered gladiators to fight with blunted swords. At 1.5, Marcus claims not to care who wins or loses such fights. This is probably true: in a letter written late in 147, Fronto lets slip that Marcus used the shows to catch up on his reading and letter writing. Entry 9.14 contains another expression of extreme ennui, as in the last words of this entry. Tedium was not enough on its own to make Marcus contemplate suicide, but it could make him contemplate death.

57. We have no idea who these people were, though they were presumably recently dead at the time of Marcus's writing. The names sound like slave names (hence perhaps Marcus's "various ethnicities"), so they might have been members of Marcus's household. Perhaps they had just died of the plague that was ravaging the camp.

men, men (like Menippus and his ilk) who mocked the very transience and impermanence of human life. Bear in mind, where all these men are concerned, that they are long dead and buried. Is there anything in this for them to fear? Or indeed for others, men whose very names are altogether lost? Only one thing is important: to behave throughout your life toward the liars and crooks around you with kindness, honesty, and justice.

[48] When you want to cheer yourself up, think of the positive qualities of your friends and acquaintances:[58] the efficiency of one, for instance, the moral sensibility of another, the generosity of a third, and so on. Nothing is more cheering than when the virtues are manifest in the characters of your friends and acquaintances, and especially when they occur all at once, insofar as that is feasible. So you should keep them in the forefront of you mind.

[49] Surely you don't resent the fact that you weigh only so many pounds and not three hundred? By the same token, there's no point in resenting the fact that you're going to live only so many years and not more. You're happy with the amount of substance that has been allocated to you, and by the same token you should be happy with the time allocated to you as well.

[50] Try to persuade them, by all means, but when it comes to action you should go ahead even if they demur, whenever the principle of justice directs you to do so. But if someone forcibly resists you, change course instead to a policy of grief-free

---

58. Marcus seems to be counteracting the cynicism of the last words of the previous entry—although cynicism is more usual for him.

acceptance. That is, use the setback as an opportunity to display another virtue,[59] remembering that you set out with reservation and that it was never your intention to go ahead if it proved impossible. What was your intention, then? To follow up your impulse, but in this conditional way. And you're proving successful at this. "This aim of ours is being fulfilled."

[51] To the glory-hunter's way of thinking, what's good for him is others' activity, while for the hedonist it's his own feelings. For an intelligent man, however, it's what he himself does.[60]

[52] You don't have to form an opinion about this and trouble your mind. Things themselves have no inherent power to form our opinions.[61]

---

59. Prudence, or wisdom, one of the four cardinal Stoic virtues. The overall point is connected to the idea of reservation (see Notebook 4, note 2). To use a Stoic image: whether or not an archer hits his mark is not entirely up to him, but he does have control over how well he shoots.

60. So he is an independent moral agent, doing only what is "up to him," while glory-hunters depend on others for their fame and hedonists depend on external stimuli. A strict Stoic would add "or, rather, how he does what he does."

61. As often elsewhere, we meet, in the first sentence, the Stoic idea that feelings are caused by opinions; remove the opinion, and no feeling follows. As independent moral agents, we should form our own opinions and judge their worth. See also 4.3 (end) and 5.19. In the second sentence, Marcus reintroduces the idea of the "inertness" of things (see Notebook 4, note 12).

[53] Get into the habit of listening attentively to anything that anyone says, and enter, as much as you can, into the mind of the speaker.

[54] Anything which isn't good for the hive isn't good for the bee either.

[55] If sailors criticized their helmsman or invalids their doctor, wouldn't their only concern be how he might ensure the safety of his crew or the health of his patients?[62]

[56] How many people, in whose company I came into the world, have already left it!

[57] People with jaundice find honey bitter,[63] those who've been bitten by a rabid dog have an aversion to water, and to little boys a ball is something to admire. So why am I angry? Do you think that false opinions have less influence than bile does on jaundice and poison on hydrophobics?[64]

---

62. Marcus seems to be consoling himself. Some people have criticized him, but he excuses it because of the validity of the underlying reason for their concern, to see that he does his job well. He chose his analogies carefully, because, by two common metaphors, as emperor he was the captain of the ship of state and the physician of the body politic. Moreover, Plato's Socrates had argued the same point: that the doctor and the ship's captain seek not their own advantage but that of their patients or passengers (*Republic* 342d–e).

63. Jaundice was held to be due to an excess of bitter bile in the body.

64. Marcus is urging himself not to get angry with someone who cannot, after all, help what he does: he is influenced by his false opinions no less than a hydrophobic is by the poison in his body.

[58] No one is going to stop your life being compatible with the rational aspect of your nature. Nothing is going to happen to you that isn't compatible with the rationality of universal nature.[65]

[59] Look at the kind of men they want to please! Look at the way they're going about it and what they're doing! See how quickly time will hide everything, and all the things it has already hidden!

---

65. Two familiar assertions here, the first of moral independence, the second of predestination and providence. The entry would have made a suitable envoi to the notebook as a whole. The next and final entry may be out of place, but since this is the case for many entries it is best not to embark on the game of rearranging them.

NOTEBOOK 7

[1] What is vice? Nothing you haven't often seen before. In fact, whatever happens in life you should keep readily available the thought that what you're seeing is nothing you haven't often seen before. As a general rule, look where you will, sameness is all you'll find: history books on ancient times, recent times, and the period in between are filled with the same things, and they are the same things with which states and households are fully occupied now. Nothing is new; everything is both familiar and temporary.[1]

---

1. This seventh notebook is one of the least unified, though the independence of the mind is a recurrent theme. It consists largely of reminders relevant to all the themes with which we are by now familiar. In this first entry, then, we meet again the eternal sameness of things, used as an easy way to deflect the shock that wrongdoing can generate: wrongdoing is not going to disappear; it is part of the fabric of life, so deal with it.

[2] The only way your principles can perish is if the thoughts that correspond to them are extinguished, and the rekindling of those thoughts is up to you, at every moment.[2] So if I'm able to form the appropriate opinion on any given matter, why should I be troubled? What lies outside my mind is of no concern to it. If only you could learn this lesson, you'd be standing straight. You can come back to life. See things once more as you used to see them in the past. That's how to come back to life.

[3] The vain pomp of a procession, plays on a stage, flocks, herds, skirmishes, a meager bone tossed to puppies, a scrap of bread tossed in a fish tank, the toiling of ants with their burdens, the scurrying of nervous mice, puppets tugged by their strings.[3] In the midst of all this, you should take a stand good-naturedly and without being bigheaded, but paying attention to the fact that the worth of every individual depends on the worth of what he values.

[4] In conversation, you should pay attention to what's being said; for every impulse, you should pay attention to what happens. In the latter case, try to see immediately what the objective is; in the former, try to determine the meaning.

————————

2. Here is a principle: "All rational creatures are created equal." The corresponding thought is applied in particular situations: "If all men are created equal, then I must treat so-and-so as an equal." Only by applying the principle in real life will it stay alive.

3. Compare 4.32, 7.48, and 9.30 for other lists signifying the totality of life. Here movement seems to be the dominant thought, and so Marcus urges himself to "take a stand."

[5] Is my mind capable of dealing with this or not? If it is, I put it to work as an instrument granted me by universal nature. If it isn't, I either cede the work to someone who's better equipped to carry it out,[4] or, if it's something that's not appropriate for another person, I do what I can, enlisting the help of someone who's able, by working with my command center, to do what's appropriate and good for the community at this moment in time. For whether I act on my own or with someone else's assistance, all my actions should be directed solely toward what is socially useful and fitting.

[6] How many people who were once world-famous have by now been consigned to oblivion! How many people who once sang their praises have long since departed!

[7] There's no shame in being helped, because you've got to do the job you've been set, like a soldier storming a city wall. Suppose you had a limp and were unable to scale the battlements on your own, but could do so with someone else's assistance.

[8] Don't be anxious about the future. You'll come to it (if you must), equipped with the same reason that you apply now to the present.

---

4. This commonsensical piece of advice was standard Stoic doctrine, in keeping with the notion of "reservation": see Notebook 4, note 2. The thought of this entry is continued in the entry after next, 7.7.

[9] All things are interwoven with one another. The bond that unites them is sacred,[5] and it's hardly an exaggeration to say that nothing is alien to anything else, because they've been formed into a collaborative system, and together they contribute to the orderliness of the same universe. After all, the universe, being made up of all there is, is one, and the God who permeates everything is one, and there's one reality, one law, one reason that's common to all intelligent creatures, and one truth—that is, if there's just one way in which beings that are related and share the same reason can be fulfilled.[6]

[10] It takes hardly any time for everything material to be lost in the substance of the universe, for every cause to be received back into the reason of the universe, and for every memory to be buried in eternity.

[11] For a rational creature, an action that's in accord with nature is also in accord with reason.

––––––––––

5. In Stoic physics, the bond that unites everything is *pneuma*, spirit, which permeates and steers all things. It can also, in a pantheistic way, be called God, so that everything that happens is in fact an activity of God. It permeates material things so thoroughly that it and they are separable only in thought, not in reality.

6. The one truth for all rational beings is the fulfillment they find in being aligned with the providence that guides them and the world as a whole. Lurking behind this entry is the idea that the world is a single community of rational beings. I take it that the "one law" is providence: "the divine law by which all events are regulated" (Seneca, *Letters* 76.23).

[12] Stand straight, not straightened.[7]

[13] Rational beings, in their separate bodies, have the same relationship to one another as limbs do in unified organisms, since they were made for a single cooperative purpose. The idea will strike you with greater force if you repeatedly tell yourself: "I am a limb of the composite whole made up of rational beings." On the other hand, if you substitute an *r* and say that you're a "part,"[8] you haven't got to the point of loving your fellow men with all your heart or of finding joy in doing good for its own sake.[9] You're still doing it as a mere duty, not yet in the knowledge that you're doing good to yourself.

[14] Anything external that so wishes may impact those parts that are capable of being affected by the impact. After all, the affected parts can complain, if they want. As for me, as long as

---

7. Standing straight seems to be a metaphor for being an independent moral agent rather than one who is straightened by others. See 3.5 and 7.2. But at the same time Marcus allows that some of his views might need correction: 4.12, 6.21, 8.16.

8. The Greek for "limb" is *melos*, and for "part" is *meros*.

9. I think the distinction Marcus is trying to make is that a "part" is still a distinct part, whereas a "limb" is an integrated part, in the sense that it has identified with the whole and aligned itself with the interests of the whole. A part may think it can go it alone, whereas a limb could not entertain such a thought. As limbs, we benefit when the organism benefits, and we avoid the self-conflict that is inevitable when a naturally social creature engages in antisocial acts. Elsewhere, however, Marcus is perfectly content to talk of "parts" without qualification, as if they were what he here calls "limbs."

I don't judge the experience bad, I'm immune from harm. And I don't have to make such judgments.[10]

[15] "Whatever anyone does or says, I must be good." This is no different from gold or emerald or purple repeating over and over: "Whatever anyone does or says, I must be emerald; I must stay this color."[11]

[16] The command center doesn't disturb itself, by which I mean that it doesn't alarm itself, distress itself, or give in to desire. If anyone else is able to alarm or distress it, that's up to him; the command center will not of its own accord cause any such worsening of itself. It's up to the body to ensure that it doesn't suffer, if it can, and it's up to the soul—the part that feels fear and distress—to speak out if it has such experiences. But the faculty that forms beliefs about these things won't be affected at all, because it won't make that kind of judgment as a concession to the soul.[12] In itself, the command center has no needs unless it creates one for itself, and it is therefore unperturbed and unhindered, unless it disturbs and hinders itself.

---

10. An assertion of the independence of the mind from the body, as also in 7.16. As in the previous entry, Marcus assumes that what happens to a "part" need not affect the whole. The whole, his body, can be regulated by having the mind form the correct beliefs.

11. We are innately good, and therefore to do good or be good is simply to express our own nature.

12. As we know from many other passages, it is only if the command center identifies a situation as frightening that one becomes afraid.

[**17**] Happiness is a good guardian spirit[13] or a good command center. So why, impression, are you acting like this?[14] Go away, for heaven's sake, back to where you came from. I have no need of you. It's only ingrained habit that has made it possible for you to come. I'm not angry with you, but just go away.[15]

[**18**] Is change something to fear? But can anything happen without change? Is there anything that's nearer and dearer to universal nature? What about you personally? Can you take a warm bath unless the firewood undergoes change? Can you be nourished unless your food undergoes change? Can anything else worthwhile take place without change? So don't you see that the changes that *you* experience are no different and are similarly necessary to universal nature?

[**19**] All bodies are carried along, as though by a torrent, through the substance of the universe, because they are of one nature with the universe and cooperate with it, as our limbs do

---

13. "Happiness is a good guardian spirit" is tautologous. "Happiness" translates *eudaimonia*, meaning, literally, having a good *daimōn*, and *daimōn* is Marcus's word for "guardian spirit." *Eudaimonia* had long been the standard term in Greek ethics for the good life—a happy and fulfilled life, however conceived.

14. As often, we can only guess what Marcus is referring to. Perhaps he is rebuking himself for being attracted to a different conception of happiness than the one he outlines here.

15. Note the deployment of an avuncular attitude toward one's failings, as a way to reduce their energy and defuse the hold they have over us. Getting angry and trying to eradicate them abruptly only feeds their energy.

with one another. How many Chrysippuses, Socrateses, and Epictetuses have already been swallowed up by eternity?[16] This is the thought that should strike you also about absolutely every person, and every thing too.

[20] Only one thing bothers me, and that's the possibility that I might do something that my human nature doesn't want done, or not in that way, or not at that moment.

[21] Soon you'll have forgotten everything; soon everyone will have forgotten you.

[22] It's typically human to feel affection even for people who make mistakes. The feeling is a response to the thoughts that they're your kin, that they're led astray against their will by their ignorance, that shortly both of you will be dead, and especially that he did you no harm, because he didn't make your command center worse than it was before.

[23] Universal nature molded universal substance, as if it were wax, and made, let's say, a horse; and then, after dissolving the horse, it reused its matter to make a tree, then a man, and then something else, with each of these things subsisting for only a very short time. But it's no more terrible for a box to be broken up than it was for it to be put together.[17]

[24] An excessively angry face is unnatural. When it occurs repeatedly, the decorousness of a person's features begins to perish

---

16. There is an implicit reference here to the doctrine of eternal recurrence (Notebook 2, note 42), according to which there have literally been a plurality of Chrysippuses and so on.

17. The entry after next, 7.25, continues the theme.

and in the end is so thoroughly extinguished that there's no way to revive it. What you need to note is that this happens without conscious thought. I mean, if our very awareness of doing wrong is lost, what reason is there left for living?

[25] In no time at all, everything you see will be changed by the nature that directs the universe. It will use their substance to create more things, and then it will use the substance of these things to create still more things, in order to keep the universe forever young.

[26] When someone mistreats you, the first question you should ask yourself is what conception of good and bad led him to do so. Understanding this will lead you to feel sorry for him,[18] and will dispel any shock or anger, once you see that your own conception of goodness is still either the same as his or closely related. And so you're bound to forgive him. On the other hand, if you've moved beyond this kind of conception of goodness and badness, it will be all the easier for you to be lenient toward him for not seeing things right.[19]

---

18. Marcus here slightly betrays his adherence to Stoicism, because a Stoic was not supposed to feel passions such as pity. But pity is better than anger, especially when anger is triggered, as here, by an "indifferent," such as being wronged by someone.

19. In this single short entry, we meet several of Marcus's most firmly held beliefs: the Socratic idea that wrongdoing is ignorance; the difference between how a wise man and an ordinary person conceive of good and bad; the obligations to tolerate one's neighbors and educate the unenlightened.

[27] Instead of imagining that you possess things you don't, select, from among those you *do* have, the ones you count yourself most fortunate to have, and remind yourself in their case how much you'd have wanted them if you didn't have them. But at the same time take care not to let your pleasure in them get you into the habit of valuing them too highly, to the extent that you'd be upset if you ever lost them.[20]

[28] Withdraw into yourself. It's natural for the command center to be content with the justice of its actions and with the tranquility it has as a result.

[29] Erase the imprint of the impression.[21] Put an end to being tugged here and there like a puppet. Restrict time to the present.[22] Recognize what's happening, whether it happens to you or someone else. Analyze and divide every object into cause

---

20. Marcus is here in an un-Stoical vein, because a Stoic would not want or find pleasure in any indifferents. Hence, perhaps, in the last sentence he somewhat qualifies his enthusiasm.

21. Every incoming impression impresses itself on the soul, like a seal in wax. So Marcus is telling himself not to hang on to whatever impression it is that has disturbed him.

22. Do not anticipate the future or regret the past; see also 8.36, 12.1, 12.3. Only the present moment is "up to us" and therefore offers scope for virtuous living.

and matter. Think about the hour of your death. Leave the wrong he did where it arose.[23]

[30] Apply your intelligence to what's being said. Get your mind to delve under the surface of what's happening and see what's making it happen.

[31] Find your bliss in simplicity, modesty, and indifference to the whole range of things between virtue and vice. Love humankind. Follow God's lead. The great man says: "Everything is subject to convention, but in reality there are only the elements,"[24] but it's enough to remember that everything is subject to convention and that very few things really are what they seem to be.

---

23. Comparison with 12.26 (see also 5.25, 7.16, and 9.20) suggests that what Marcus means is "Leave the wrong with the person who committed it, because it's nothing to you. He is only harming himself (9.4, 9.38)." The staccato first sentences of this entry are all individual or cumulative suggestions that will make possible the solution outlined in the final sentence.

24. This is a paraphrase of fragment 9 Diels/Kranz of Democritus (see also fragment 117 and fragment 125). He was saying that to describe something as "sweet," for instance, is a matter of convention or man-made agreement, whereas in reality there are only atoms and void. Marcus translates Democritus's "atoms" as "elements," a more congenial term for a Stoic. In the final sentence of the entry (where the Greek of the final clause is very uncertain), Marcus, as I understand him, is merely, and rather ham-fistedly, applying Democritus's saying. He is not talking metaphysics but Stoic common sense: almost everything that people take to be good, for instance, is indifferent.

[32] On death: If atoms, dispersal; if one substance, either extinction or a change of place.[25]

[33] On pain: Unendurable pain carries one off; chronic pain is endurable.[26] The mind preserves its tranquility by withdrawal, and the command center isn't impaired. As for the parts that are harmed by the pain, it is up to them to protest, if they can.[27]

[34] On fame: Look at the kinds of thoughts they entertain, and what they like or dislike.[28] Consider also that, just as sand dunes drift over other dunes and hide the earlier ones, so in life what went before is very soon covered up by what came later.

[35] "When a person is high-minded and contemplates all time and all existence, do you think he can place much importance on human life?—Impossible, he said.—So he won't find death terrifying either, will he?—Not at all."[29]

---

25. The usual choice between the (rejected) Epicurean notion of death as dispersal and the Stoic possibilities of extinction or survival.

26. Marcus borrowed this idea from Epicurus; see 7.64.

27. Their protest would presumably come in the form of pain, physical or mental.

28. The "they" of this sentence are those who award fame. Marcus's point is, as elsewhere, that anything that depends on such worthless people must be worthless itself.

29. Marcus embarks on a series of quotations (until 7.46, but interrupted by 7.37). Their relative accuracy suggests that he is not paraphrasing from memory, as he usually does, but copying extracts from his commonplace book (see 3.14). This one is from Plato, *Republic* 486a–b. Quite a few of the extracts here and in Notebook 11 were well known and used by other writers on moral issues.

[36] "A king's role is to do good and be reviled."[30]

[37] It's shameful that one's features do what they're told—that is, are shaped and composed at the bidding of the mind—but the mind isn't shaped and composed by itself.

[38] "It's pointless to let mere things make you angry, since they lack the ability to care."[31]

[39] "May you delight the immortal gods as well as us."[32]

[40] "Lives are harvested like ripe ears of wheat; one man lives, another dies."[33]

---

30. Antisthenes, fragment 86b Prince. Marcus obviously identified with this one! Antisthenes was a student of Socrates and lived in Athens from the middle of the fifth to the middle of the fourth century BCE. He was held by later Cynics to be the founder of their school, insofar as he taught Diogenes of Sinope. He is said to have come up with the quip after being criticized by Plato, another of Socrates's disciples. The saying is elsewhere attributed to Alexander the Great. Epictetus also preserves the saying, at *Discourses* 4.6.20, which is perhaps where Marcus got it from.

31. This is from Euripides's *Bellerephon*, of which only fragments remain. It is the first half of fragment 289 Nauck². Along with Aeschylus and Sophocles, Euripides was one of the triad of great Athenian tragic dramatists of the fifth century BCE.

32. Source unknown. The Greek is a perfect hexameter, which was the meter of epic poetry such as Homer's, so it may be from a lost epic.

33. This quotation, an extract from fragment 757 Nauck², is from Euripides's largely lost *Hypsipyle*. Marcus quotes it again in 11.6. It, and the following quotation in 7.41, counsel acceptance of one's fate.

[41] "If I and my sons are neglected by the gods, this too has its reason."[34]

[42] "Good is on my side and so is right."[35]

[43] "Don't join in the general lamentation; don't get all churned up."[36]

[44] "It would be fair for me to respond to him as follows: 'You're wrong, my friend, if you think that a man who's worth anything at all should weigh up his chances of living or dying. No, there's only one thing for him to consider whenever he acts, and that's whether what he's doing is just or unjust, and whether it's the act of a good man or a bad one.'"[37]

[45] "The truth of the matter is this, men of Athens: wherever a man posts himself, thinking it for the best, or wherever he's posted by his commander, there, in my opinion, he ought to stand

---

34. This is from Euripides's *Antiope*, of which we have quite a few fragments. This is part of fragment 207 Nauck². Marcus, of course, takes "reason" very literally here, because he believes that every event, even if negative, is part of the divine plan.

35. From an unknown play of Euripides, this is part of fragment 910 Nauck².

36. From an unknown source.

37. These stirring words form part of the defense speech Socrates delivered at his trial in 399 BCE, as written up by Plato in his *Apology of Socrates* at 28b.

his ground and face danger, taking neither death nor anything else into account apart from dishonor."[38]

[46] "No, my friend, you'd better consider the possibility that excellence and goodness don't consist merely in the preservation of life. Perhaps the mark of a real man is that he isn't worried about how long he lives, and isn't attached to life. What a real man should do is leave these matters in God's hands, believe his womenfolk when they tell him that no one can escape his fated end, and then consider best how to live however many years he still has to live."[39]

[47] Watch the stars in their courses as though you were accompanying them,[40] and reflect constantly on the changing of the elements into one another. A mind that is impressed in these ways is cleansed of the filth of life on earth.

[48] A good point of Plato's: Observing things on earth as if from on high is especially important for anyone who wants to discuss human life:[41] herds, armies, farms, weddings, divorces,

---

38. Plato, *Apology of Socrates* 28d. The theme of these three Platonic entries is that right action is more important than mere survival; it is no wonder that Marcus was attracted to them.

39. Plato, *Gorgias* 512d–e. One can see why the Stoics revered Socrates, Plato's spokesman here.

40. Probably (see 11.27), the idea is that our lives should be as regular and orderly as the courses of the fixed stars.

41. Talk of a view from on high is a natural way of expressing objectivity, but Marcus is thinking in the first instance of its use by Plato at *Theaetetus* 173e–174a.

births, deaths, the bustle of the lawcourts, deserts, all the various barbarian peoples, festivals, lamentations, markets—the intermixture of everything and the orderly interaction of opposites.[42]

[49] Look back at the past and all the changes that things went through in those days. You can also foresee the future, because it will be the same in all respects, incapable of deviating from the rhythm established by present events. It follows that, for observing human life, forty years is as good as ten thousand, since there's nothing more to be seen.[43]

[50] Also: "What is born from earth returns to earth, but the progeny of heaven returns to the celestial sphere."[44]

[51] Also: "Trying with food, drink, and magic charms to divert the stream and avoid death." "A wind sent by the gods weary mortals must endure without complaint."[45]

---

42. There was a long tradition in Greek philosophy for the world to be seen as the interplay of opposites. At a physiological level, for instance, animal life is made possible by the fact that the innate heat of the body is constantly being cooled by breathing in the surrounding air.

43. A familiar theme in *Meditations*; see especially 11.1.

44. Part of fragment 836 Nauck², from Euripides's lost *Chrysippus*. For Marcus's understanding of the lines, see 4.4 (end).

45. The first quotation is Euripides, *Suppliant Women* 1110–11, the second from an unknown poet. They might have formed separate entries in Marcus's original notebook.

[52] "A better wrestler,"[46] he may be, but not more concerned for the common good, or more moral, or more able to cope with events without getting flustered, or more kind in his treatment of those around him when they don't see things right.

[53] Where a task can be completed in accordance with the reason that's common to gods and men, there's nothing to fear, because no harm need be anticipated where one can benefit from activity that advances and makes progress in accordance with one's constitution.

[54] Wherever you find yourself, it's within your power, at every moment, to be reverently content with your present circumstances,[47] to behave with justice toward the people who are presently around you, and to manage your present impressions so that nothing slips into your mind that you haven't adequately grasped.

[55] Don't let your attention be caught by others' command centers, but look straight ahead to where nature is guiding you—both universal nature by means of what happens to you, and your own nature by means of the things you have to do. What every individual creature has to do is what follows from its constitution, and although all other beings have been created

---

46. Once, when a Spartan was defeated in the wrestling event at the Olympic games, someone said to him: "Your opponent proved himself the better man." "No," said the Spartan, "a better wrestler" (Plutarch, *Sayings of Spartans* 236e).

47. "Reverently" content, because it is the gods who have arranged your current circumstances.

to serve rational ones (and it's a universal principle that the lower serve the higher), rational beings are made to serve one another.[48] So the leading principle in the human constitution is concern for the common good, and the second is resistance to bodily feelings. For it's typical of rational and intelligent activity to be self-contained and never overcome by the activity of either the senses or the impulses.[49] The point is that sensations and impulses belong to our animal nature, while it's the aim of intelligent activity not to surrender its leadership and be overcome by them. And that's how it should be, because it's in its nature to make use of sensations and impulses for its own purposes. The third principle in the constitution of a rational being is to avoid being deceived by not rushing into assent.[50] So, if your command center remains true to these principles and proceeds straight ahead, it will be fulfilled.

[56] Imagine that you've actually been dead and that you haven't lived your life up to the present moment, and then treat what remains of your life as a bonus and live in accord with nature.

---

48. Repeated from 5.16. See also 11.18 (start).

49. Compare the "retreat" of 4.3.

50. The soul receives impressions (sense impressions or thoughts), and if it "assents" to them, it identifies them as such-and-such. Overhasty assent leads to being deceived, either as to the nature of the impression or as to its worth.

[57] All you have to do is embrace your experiences, or in other words the destiny that's been woven for you. After all, what could be more perfectly suited to you?

[58] For every experience that you have, imagine the people to whom the same thing happened in the past, and their subsequent annoyance, surprise, or indignation. Where are they now? Nowhere. Well, do you want to be like them? Why not leave others' moods to the modifiers and the modified, while you focus solely on how to make use of your experiences? You'll get the best out of them that way, and they'll act as the raw material of your life.[51] Just pay attention and make sure that what you want for yourself is for all of your actions to be those of an honorable person. And bear in mind the following two points: that your actions are important, and that the context of those actions is a matter of indifference.[52]

[59] Dig inside yourself. Inside you, there's a wellspring of goodness, which is capable of gushing all the time, as long as you keep digging.[53]

---

51. The "material for [the exercise of] rational and social virtue," as Marcus puts it at 7.68. Somewhat paradoxically, the Stoics claimed that virtue was sufficient unto itself, and yet needed raw materials, which are the indifferents one meets with minute by minute.

52. There is a gap of uncertain length in the Greek, after "the following two points," making this last sentence a matter of guesswork.

53. Some springs need constant attention or they become blocked. For the image of the spring, see also 8.51.

[60] The body too should be firm and not ungainly, whether it's in motion or at rest.[54] The kind of provisions the mind makes for the face in order to maintain an intelligent and decorous expression are required for the body as a whole as well. But all this must be attended to in a matter-of-fact manner.

[61] Living is more like wrestling than dancing: one should stand ready for every contingency and avoid being thrown even by unforeseen developments.[55]

[62] Never stop checking out the people whose endorsement you want—that is, their command centers. If you look into where their beliefs and impulses are coming from, not only will you not criticize them when they make involuntary mistakes[56] but you won't require their endorsement either.[57]

[63] "No soul," he says, "is willingly deprived of the truth."[58] The same goes, then, for justice, moderation, kindness, and so

---

54. A good body expresses a good character: see also 7.24 and 11.15.

55. See also 12.9.

56. This is shorthand for "when they make mistakes, all mistakes being involuntary"—the Stoic view.

57. Just recently, at 7.55, Marcus reminded himself not to think about other people, but here he is saying that he has to keep checking them out. There is no contradiction: see Notebook 3, note 18.

58. The "he" in "he says" is Plato, but the sentence does not occur in any of his published works, though the sentiment occurs at *Republic* 413a and *Sophist* 228c–d. Marcus took the saying from Epictetus, *Discourses* 1.28.4 or 2.22.36. It recurs at 11.18 (third point).

on and so forth. It's absolutely essential to keep this constantly in mind, because then you'll be gentler with everyone.[59]

[64] Whenever you're in pain, have this thought readily available: it isn't a shameful thing, nor does it impair the mind that holds the helm. Pain has no deleterious effect on the mind qua rational, nor qua concerned for the common good. As far as most instances of pain are concerned, there's a useful saying of Epicurus:[60] "Pain is either not unendurable or not everlasting"— as long as you remember that it has limits and as long as you don't judge it further.[61] And remember this too, that there are plenty of disagreeable feelings that are the same as pain, even if we might not realize it, such as drowsiness, heat exhaustion, and loss of appetite. So when one of these is making you miserable, tell yourself that you're giving in to pain.[62]

---

59. Marcus, as we know, is often cynical about people, seeing them as rotten and stupid. Here, as elsewhere, he counsels himself to be more tolerant, by recognizing that they do not intend to be rotten and stupid.

60. The quotation is Epicurus, fragment 447 Usener; it was also paraphrased at 7.33.

61. Especially by adding the judgment that it is bad.

62. Succumbing to pain, or pleasure, was the definition of weakness of the will. For a Stoic, pain was an "indifferent," and therefore to be risen above.

[65] Be sure not to behave toward antisocial people as people behave toward other people.[63]

[66] How do we know that Telauges wasn't a better person than Socrates?[64] It's not enough that Socrates died a more glorious death, or that he dealt more skillfully with the sophists in his discussions with them, or that he displayed supreme endurance by spending all night outside in the freezing cold,[65] or that, when ordered to arrest the man from Salamis, he decided it was more

---

63. A cynical entry, since Marcus is assuming that people generally behave badly toward one another, and he urges himself not to behave so badly even toward antisocial people.

64. Marcus is referring to one of the dialogues written by Aeschines of Sphettus, a follower of Socrates, which was named after Socrates's chief interlocutor in the dialogue, a certain Telauges, but we know nothing of the content of the work.

65. A famous episode in Socrates's life, told by Plato at *Symposium* 220a–d. While serving in the Athenian army in northern Greece, he spent the best part of twenty-four hours outside in the winter, standing motionless, barefoot and wearing only thin clothes. Why he did so is uncertain.

honorable for him to refuse,[66] or that he used to swagger in the streets (though there are excellent grounds for doubting the truth of this story).[67] No, what one ought to look into is the quality of Socrates's soul—whether he was capable of being satisfied with treating his fellow men with justice and the gods with reverence,

---

66. Leon of Salamis (the island was Athenian territory) was a prominent democrat in Athens toward the end of the fifth century. After the Athenians lost the Peloponnesian War (431–404 BCE), a narrow oligarchy of thirty men (the notorious "Thirty Tyrants") was imposed on the city by the victorious Spartans. The Thirty set about killing their opponents and at one point ordered Socrates (whose relationship with the Thirty was ambiguous at best) to join the detachment that was to arrest Leon. Socrates refused to obey the order, while the others carried out the arrest, and Leon was duly killed. Socrates avoided arrest himself perhaps only because the regime of the Thirty soon collapsed. The story is told by Plato, at *Apology of Socrates* 32c–d, and is mentioned by another contemporary source (Andocides, *On the Mysteries* 94), and then, as a famous story, by many later writers.

67. Aristophanes, *Clouds* 362. Aristophanes was a playwright specializing in satirical or farcical comedies at the end of the fifth century BCE in Athens (hence Marcus's grounds for doubting the story). Prominent Athenians were often his targets, and in *Clouds*, produced in 423 BCE, it was Socrates's turn. The line is referred to by Plato at *Symposium* 221b. Swaggering on the streets is scarcely on a par with the two previous examples, but the point Marcus is making is that Socrates's superiority to Telauges did not lie in his external practices but in his inner morality. For Stoics, even the way one walked was indicative of one's character, though quite what trait Socrates's swagger indicated is unclear. Self-assurance, perhaps.

without getting angry at men's iniquity, or meekly accepting someone's ignorance, or regarding anything that was allotted to him by the universe as alien to himself or an unbearable burden that had to be suffered, or allowing his mind to be affected by bodily feelings.

[67] The way in which nature blended you with the compound whole leaves open the possibility of your being self-contained and having what is proper to you under your control.[68] After all, it's distinctly possible for someone to be a godlike man and yet be unrecognized as such by anyone.[69] Never forget this, or the fact that it takes very little to live a fulfilled and happy life. You may have resigned yourself to never being good at logic or physics,[70] but don't on that account despair of being self-reliant, modest, focused on the common good, and obedient to God.

[68] Live your whole life unswayed by outside forces and with a wholly joyful heart, even if everyone else is crying out against you and wild beasts are tearing limb from limb this lump of paste that has been caked around you. After all, is there

---

68. What is proper to us as humans is rationality and virtuous conduct. This is, as usual, "up to us."

69. A somewhat caustic comment on the fact that many holy men flaunt their charisma and magical powers. Insofar as Marcus aspired to be a godlike man—that is, one who always acts rationally—he still did not want to be like that.

70. Marcus's acknowledgment that, of the three disciplines of philosophy, he could claim expertise only in ethics. See the Introduction, xxxv–xxxvii, and 1.17 (end).

anything in all this that makes it impossible for the mind to maintain its tranquility, or its ability to judge situations correctly, or its facility at making good use of the circumstances with which it is presented? In effect, then, Judgment says to Situation: "This is what you really are, even if opinion makes you seem otherwise." And Good Use says to Circumstance: "I've been looking for you! As far as I'm concerned, the present is always material for rational and social virtue, and in general for the application of human or divine skill." The point being that everything in the world is suitable material for God or man. And nothing is new or unmanageable, but familiar and easy to work with.[71]

[69] Perfection of character lies in this: to live each day as though it were your last, without turmoil, without listlessness, and without pretense.

[70] The gods, who are immortal, don't resent the fact that for all eternity they'll inevitably and always be obliged to tolerate so many despicable creatures. In fact, they even take care of them in all sorts of ways.[72] So won't you, who have only the shortest time to live, renounce resentment, especially since you're one of the despicable creatures?

---

71. Here Marcus implies a more positive attitude toward the endless sameness of things. He encourages himself to think of familiarity not as inducing tedium but as making it easier to make skillful use of one's circumstances.

72. See, for example, Xenophon, *Memorabilia* 1.4.5–18 and 4.3, which list examples of the gods' providence and kindness to human beings and argue for a rationally ordered universe.

[71] It's absurd not to try to escape from one's own iniquity, which is possible, and just as absurd to try to escape from the iniquity of others, which is impossible.[73]

[72] Whatever the rational and social faculty finds to be neither intelligent nor socially useful it reasonably judges to be inferior to itself.[74]

[73] When you've done a good deed, and someone else has benefited, why do you still look for a third gain over and above these two? It's sheer foolishness to desire recognition for having done good or to want something back in return.[75]

[74] No one tires of being benefited, and benefiting others is in accord with your nature. So you shouldn't tire of being benefited while benefiting others.[76]

---

73. Virtuous behavior is entirely up to oneself, but the actions of others are not.

74. This seems to be an answer to the question: "But what makes something inferior, and therefore (see 5.16 and 5.30) obliged to serve the superior?"

75. See 9.42 (end). As we say, "Virtue is its own reward." But Marcus also wants not to take any possible reward into account: 5.6.

76. The missing premise is that acting in accordance with nature is beneficial. So, in a sense, there is a "third gain," despite its denial in the previous entry—the gain of being benefited oneself even as one benefits others (also at 11.4). A related principle is that what is good for the whole is good for the part (10.6). This is how Marcus reconciled the usual Stoic focus on oneself (starting with the basic instinct for self-preservation and ending with the goal of complete self-reliance) with his concern, especially as emperor, for the good of others: they are identical.

[**75**] Universal nature set out to create a world. As things stand at present, either everything that comes to pass is a consequence of that, or even the most important things to which the universal command center directs its impulse are devoid of reason.[77] Remembering this will enable you to approach many situations with tranquility.[78]

---

77. This second, Epicurean alternative, is, of course, a nonstarter as far as Marcus is concerned.

78. Secure in the knowledge that the universe is proceeding according to a rational plan.

NOTEBOOK 8

[1] Another thing that will help you curb your tendency toward self-importance is the fact that you no longer have the opportunity to live your whole life, or at least your adult life, as a philosopher.[1] In fact, it's obvious to a great many people, not just yourself, that you're a long way off being a philosopher. You're neither one thing nor the other, and consequently not only has the time passed when it was feasible for you to win the glory of being a philosopher, but also your role militates against its ever

---

1. The personal tone of this entry is a recurrent thread in this notebook and the next. Hence there are more implicit references to Marcus's life as an emperor in Notebook 8 than in any other.

happening.[2] So, if this is a true assessment of the situation, leave off worrying about what people will think of you, and be content if you live the rest of your life in compliance with your nature. Just consider, then, how your nature wants you to live, and don't be sidetracked by anything else. You know from personal experience that in all your detours the good life was nowhere to be found: not in logic, or wealth, or prestige, or sensual pleasure—nowhere. So where is it to be found? In doing what your human nature requires. And how is one to do this? By adhering to principles that guide your impulses and actions. What principles? Those that are concerned with good and bad, and state that nothing is good for a human being except what makes him honest,

---

2. An admission that it is hard to be both a successful philosopher and a successful man of the world. "You cannot serve both God and Mammon." Any kind of spiritual discipline has to be a full-time occupation, and single-minded as well, because one cannot "ride two horses at once," so as to be, say, both a Buddhist and a Christian. Epictetus says as much, too, at *Handbook* 1.4: "But if you want not only these things [the benefits of Stoicism], but also public offices and wealth, the chances are that, in aiming at the former, you won't get even the latter; and you'll certainly fail to get the former." However, Marcus seems to be forgetting that he can always withdraw and refresh himself (4.3, 6.12), and his remarks on the incompatibility of emperorship and philosophy are contradicted at 8.9 and 11.7.

moderate, courageous, and self-reliant, and that nothing is bad except what inculcates the opposite qualities in him.[3]

[2] Every time you do something, ask yourself: "Do I find this acceptable? Might I not come to regret it?" Before long, I shall be dead and then "away with everything." If the work I'm currently engaged in is proper to an intelligent and social being, one who lives under the same laws as God, what more could I want?

[3] Alexander, Caesar, Pompey—how do they compare to Diogenes, Heraclitus, and Socrates?[4] The philosophers saw the things of the world for what they are—that is, they saw things

----

3. This is a curious, slightly self-contradictory entry. On the one hand, Marcus says that he is not a philosopher and never will be. That is, he cannot satisfy the strict criteria for being a philosopher, as outlined in 2.17 (and perhaps also because he is not strong on two branches of philosophy, physics and logic: 7.67). On the other hand, he thinks he can spend the rest of his life living in accord with nature and being virtuous, but that is the philosophic life as he understands it, because it is based on philosophical principles. So perhaps we should read his self-reproach at the beginning of the entry as regretting that he will never be an all-round philosopher, not that he is not some kind of philosopher.

4. The relative worth of generals compared to philosophers was a common debating topic. Plutarch, for instance, wrote an essay titled "Whether Military or Intellectual Exploits Have Brought Athens More Fame." Marcus is still reflecting on the incompatibility of engagement with the world and philosophy, as in 8.1; 8.8 is also relevant to the theme.

in terms of their causes and their matter[5]—and their command centers were autonomous. As for the others, look at the kinds of worries they had and how little freedom they had!

[4] It won't make any difference: they won't stop even if you explode with rage.

[5] First, don't be upset. Nothing happens that isn't in accord with universal nature, and before long you won't exist at all, just like Hadrian and Augustus. Second, fix your gaze on the matter in hand and see it for what it is, and then, keeping in mind your obligation to be a good man and the demands of your humanity, go right ahead and do it, in the way that seems to you to be most just. But do it with kindness and modesty, and without dissembling.

[6] The job of universal nature is to change things from one state to another, to transform them, to pick them up from where they are and carry them elsewhere.[6] Change is ubiquitous, but this needn't make you worry that something unusual will occur:

---

5. Everything in the universe is material, and everything happens as the result of some cause, and everything animate has its own causative principle embedded within it, so to analyze things as cause and matter is a simple way of understanding something important about them. But the division between causal and material components was Stoic, and none of the thinkers Marcus names here were Stoics. He seems to be treating the division more as a commonsensical way of looking at things than as an aspect of Stoic physics. The division occurs or is implied at 5.13, 7.29, 8.3, 8.11, 9.25, 9.37, 12.10, 12.18, 12.29.

6. See, for example, 7.23. This seems to be just an emphatic description of change, not a strict attempt to classify three kinds of change.

everything is familiar—but also the destinies allotted to things are equal.[7]

[7] Every nature is content when it makes good progress, and a rational nature makes good progress by withholding assent from false or unclear impressions,[8] by steering its impulses only toward socially beneficial works, by restricting its desires and aversions to things that it's possible for human beings to attain or avoid, and by welcoming everything that's allotted to it by universal nature. For it is part of universal nature, just as a leaf's nature is part of a plant's nature. Except that a leaf's nature is part of a nature that isn't equipped for perception or rational thought, and is capable of being obstructed, whereas human nature is part of a nature that's unimpeded, intelligent, and just, seeing that it gives each and every thing equal shares, according to their

---

7. This final clause is hard to understand, and some editors omit it. I think it is explained in the next entry, where what is here called "destiny" is spelled out in terms of five essential properties (time, substance, cause, activity, and experience). I think the clause was scribbled down by Marcus in elliptical haste, as he was being called elsewhere, to act as a reminder. When duly reminded, he wrote the next entry, but forgot to erase the reminder.

8. On assent, see the Introduction, xlviii–xlix.

deserts,[9] of time, substance, cause, activity, and experience. But don't expect to find every individual entity equal to every other in each of these respects; you'll find, rather, that the sum total allotted to one thing has an overall equivalence to the totality allotted to another.

[8] There may be no time for reading, but you can still curb arrogance, prevail over pleasure and pain, and scorn fame.[10] You can still refuse to get angry with people for their stupidity and ingratitude. What's more, you can still care for them.

[9] Don't let anyone, even you yourself, ever again hear you finding fault with palace life.[11]

[10] Regret is a kind of censure of oneself for having missed a favorable opportunity. Anything favorable is bound to be good and should be of interest to every upright and good man. But

---

9. Marcus is explaining the justice of universal nature. A common definition of justice was "giving everyone and everything its due, what it deserves." So the type of "equality" that Marcus has in mind is what the ancients called "geometrical" or "proportional equality." "Arithmetical equality" is democratic, in that everything gets exactly the same; "geometrical equality" is meritocratic, in that everything gets what it is perceived to deserve or need.

10. Virtue takes no time because it accompanies whatever one is doing anyway.

11. A continuation of the thought of the previous entry. External circumstances should not be allowed to make one's life better or worse; that is entirely up to you. But out on campaign, Marcus may also simply be missing the comforts of home.

no such man would regret having missed an opportunity for pleasure. It follows that pleasure is neither favorable nor good.

[11] What is this thing in itself, in terms of its own constitution? What is its substantial and material component? What is its causal component? What is its function in the universe? For how long does it exist?[12]

[12] Whenever you find it difficult to wake up, remind yourself that doing socially useful work is proper to your constitution and your humanity, while sleeping is something you share with irrational animals as well. And anything that's proper to an individual's nature has greater affinity to him and is second nature to him—and, moreover, is more refreshing.

[13] Every moment and whenever an impression arises, do your best to be a scientist, a psychologist, and a logician.[13]

[14] The first question to ask yourself when you meet someone is "Where does he stand on goodness and badness?"[14] For if he believes such-and-such about pleasure and pain and

---

12. Marcus here subordinates analysis by matter and cause (as at 4.21 [end]) to analysis by probing (as in 3.11 and 10.9). The questions here are reminiscent of the five properties of 8.7. The point of the exercise is to make sure that one does not give one's assent to something too hastily, because sound judgment is the foundation of sound moral living.

13. The Stoics divided philosophy into physics (studied by natural scientists), ethics (here psychology, my translation of "expertise in the passions"), and logic.

14. This way of assessing people is common in Marcus's writings: see especially 7.26. Correct knowledge of good and bad is, of course, the mainstay of a good man's life.

what gives rise to them, about fame and obscurity, and about death and life, I won't be surprised or taken aback if he acts in such-and-such a way, and I'll remember that he has no choice but to act in that way.[15]

[15] Remember that, just as it would be shameful to be surprised if a fig tree bears figs, it would be equally shameful to be surprised if the universe produces things, like this, that are its natural products. It would also be shameful if a doctor was surprised by a patient's fever or a helmsman by a contrary wind.[16]

[16] Remember that neither changing your mind nor being guided by someone who's setting you straight impairs your self-reliance. It's your own doing, the outcome of your own impulse and judgment, and of your own mind.

[17] If it's up to you: why are you doing what you're doing? If it's not up to you: who or what do you hold responsible? Atoms? Gods? Blaming either of these is crazy. There's no point in assigning blame, because either you can set the person straight, in which case you should do that, or, if you can't do that, you

---

15. Socratic and Stoic intellectualism again: your behavior depends on your opinions. Correct behavior therefore depends on correct opinions, and the therapy that results in virtue and virtuous action is the correction of opinions. Hence the importance for Marcus of writing down correct ideas and fixing them in his consciousness by doing so and by repeating them.

16. The doctor and the helmsman recur at 6.55. Marcus adds these last two examples, I think, because the comparison with the fig tree did not explain why he spoke of "shame." It would help to know what he was referring to with "like this."

should straighten out the business itself. And if you can't do that, what's to be gained by assigning blame? There's no point in doing something pointless.

[18] When something dies, it doesn't fall out of the universe.[17] But if the universe is where it remains, the universe is also where it's changed and broken down into its constituents, which are the elements not only of the universe but of yourself. And those elements change without grumbling.

[19] Everything—a horse, for instance, or a vine—has come into existence for some purpose.[18] Is there anything surprising in that? Even the sun would say, "I was born to do a certain job," and so would the other gods. So what's *your* purpose in life? To experience pleasure? Is that a sustainable idea, do you think?

[20] The ending of each thing is intended by nature no less than its beginning and its trajectory in between, just like someone tossing a ball. For the ball, is there anything good in its upward motion or bad in its downward motion, or even in its having struck the ground? Is there anything good for a bubble in its formation or bad in its bursting? A lamp is another case in point.

[21] Turn it inside out and see what it's like, and what becomes of it when it's aged, or diseased, or in pain. Nothing lives for long, neither praiser nor praised, neither rememberer

---

17. The Stoic universe was surrounded by infinite void. Void being the absence of matter, by definition there can be nothing there.

18. See also 5.6 for this matter of faith. The Stoics justified it by pointing to the rationality of the universe and the overall divine plan.

nor remembered. What's more, even in a tiny corner of this zone of the earth not only is there no unanimity, but individuals don't agree even with themselves either.[19] In any case, the whole earth is no more than a speck.

[22] Pay attention to something: the object, the activity, the principle, the meaning. It's right that you should be feeling like this, since you'd prefer to become good tomorrow than to be good today.

[23] When I act, I do so with reference to the good of mankind. When something happens to me, I accept it by attributing it to the gods and the universal source which ensures that everything that happens is interconnected with everything else.[20]

[24] The way you regard all the filth involved in bathing— the grease, sweat, grime, and scum—should also be the way you regard every aspect of life and everything you encounter.[21]

---

19. So praise can never be unanimous or wholehearted.

20. Marcus reflects further on which attitudes are correct when one is active or passive at 9.31, 10.11, and 12.32.

21. The contemptibility of the world is a recurrent theme, but this is one of its most vivid expressions. Romans were in fact regular bathers, but we should remember that Marcus was writing this while on campaign. From a philosophical perspective, there is a recurrent tension in the book between Marcus's urging himself to welcome everything that the gods put his way, and his disgust with people and things.

[25] Lucilla saw to Verus, and then it was Lucilla's turn.[22] Secunda saw to Maximus, and then it was Secunda's turn. Epitynchanus saw to Diotimus, and then it was Epitynchanus's turn. Antoninus saw to Faustina, and then it was Antoninus's turn. That's how it always goes. Celer saw to Hadrian, and then it was Celer's turn. These people, all of them clever or prescient or proud—where are they? People like Charax, for example, and Demetrius the Platonist and Eudaemon and so on.[23] All creatures of a day, all long dead. Some of them weren't even remembered for very long, while others were turned into stories, and some have by now faded even from stories. You need to remember, then, that either the compound that is you is inevitably going to be dispersed, or your spirit will be extinguished or change place and be assigned another posting.[24]

[26] Happiness for a human being lies in doing what's proper to a human being. And what's proper to a human being is benevolence to his own kind, disdain for the activity of the

---

22. Seeing to their funeral is presumably what each of them did to the other (see 4.48, 4.50), though there is no verb in the original Greek, in Marcus's shorthand.

23. We do not know who all the people mentioned in this entry were; see "The People and Gods of *Meditations*," 293–310.

24. He offers himself the full range of postmortem possibilities this time. Dispersal is the Epicurean option, while the other two are compatible with Stoicism.

senses, discernment of reliable impressions,[25] and contemplation of universal nature and all its works.

[27] Three relationships: first, with the vessel that encases you;[26] second, with the divine cause, the source of everything that anyone ever experiences; third, with the people you encounter in life.[27]

[28] Pain is a negative experience that is either physical (in which case the body is entitled to protest) or mental. But the mind can preserve its own clarity and tranquility by refusing to take pain to be bad. For every judgment, impulse, desire, and aversion is internal, and nothing bad intrudes there.[28]

[29] Never stop erasing impressions by saying to yourself, "At this moment it's up to me whether or not this soul of mine is harmed or in need, or in fact is disturbed in any way. By

---

25. See Notebook 5, note 20, for the importance of this for right action.

26. The body: see also 10.38. A Stoic was on this earth, so he had to have a relationship with his body, but he did not have to count any of its functions and needs as important or let it distract his mind with its "rough or smooth movements" (5.26).

27. Marcus probably means this tripartition to exhaust all the significant relationships that affect a person's life. You have a duty to yourself, to rely only on reason and not on passions and bodily sensations; you have a duty to the gods, to perpetuate their work; you have a duty to other people, to be good to them. Marcus is asking how successful he is at handling the three relationships.

28. Provided one has practiced withdrawal: 7.28, 7.33. The next entry is a continuation of this one.

seeing all things as they truly are, I deal with each of them on its merits." Remember that you have this possibility, granted to you by your nature.

[30] When you speak, whether you're addressing the Senate or just anyone, do so decorously and lucidly. Employ speech in a sound way.

[31] The court of Augustus—wife, daughter, grandsons, stepsons, sister, Agrippa, relatives, household, friends, Arius, Maecenas, doctors, sacrificers: the death of an entire court.[29] And what about other courts? What about the death not just of individuals but of entire families, such as the Pompeys?[30] Think of that familiar inscription on tombstones, "the last of his line," and of the frenzied lengths to which the predecessors of these men went to leave behind an heir, but then in the end someone was inevitably the last. Yet again, then, the death of an entire family.

[32] Your life must be constructed one action at a time, and if each action is performed as successfully as may be, you can be content. And no one can prevent you from carrying them out successfully. "But something external will get in the way." Nothing, at any rate, that can stop you acting with justice, moderation, and sound judgment. "But I may be stopped from being effective in other ways." Yes, but by cheerfully accepting the

---

29. See "The People and Gods of *Meditations*," 293–310.

30. Pompey the Great himself, and all the members of his immediate family, died in the course of the Roman civil wars that led, ultimately, to Augustus's sole rule in the first century BCE.

obstacle itself and by turning, in a spirit of compromise, to what's feasible instead, another action takes the place of the hindered one, and will contribute to the construction of your life, which is what I'm talking about.[31]

[33] Accept graciously, let go easily.

[34] If you've ever seen a dismembered hand or foot, or a head hacked off and lying somewhere apart from the rest of the body—well, a man does his best to make himself like that if he refuses to accept his lot and cuts himself off from society or behaves selfishly. At some point, you've made yourself an outcast from the unity that's natural to you by virtue of the fact that you became a part of it at birth. At the moment, then, you've cut yourself off, but the brilliant thing is that you can unite yourself with it again. No other part has been granted this right by God, to rejoin the unity after having become disjoined and disconnected. Consider what this tells us about the goodness of God, that he has privileged humankind in this way. He has made it up to each individual whether or not he's broken off in the first place from the whole of which he's a part, and if he is broken off he's given him the power to return, to be grafted back on again, and to resume his status as a part.

[35] Along with all the other powers that every rational creature has, here's another ability we've been granted by uni-

---

31. So a Stoic remains unperturbed because he only ever acts with reservation, accepting that obstacles may well arise, and if they do, he calmly changes direction and undertakes what is feasible. See Notebook 4, note 2.

versal nature. Just as universal nature turns every hindrance and impediment to its own purposes, assigns it to its destined place, and makes it a part of itself, so it's possible for a rational creature to make every obstacle material for itself and use it for the end it set out to attain.[32]

[36] Beware of the disquiet that can follow from picturing your life as a whole. Don't dwell on all the various kinds of troubles that have happened and are likely to happen in the future as well. No, focus on the present, and ask yourself whether there's anything about the task before you that's unbearable and insupportable, because it would be shameful to admit that there is. And then remind yourself that neither the future nor the past can weigh on you, but only the present,[33] and that the present

---

32. See 4.1 and 7.58. We meet again (as just now in 8.32) the recurrent theme of how to deal with obstacles and turn them to one's own advantage. Marcus undoubtedly met many obstacles every day, since he was at war and had to be constantly negotiating with others.

33. Marcus is not interested in philosophical theories about time. He emphasizes the present moment (a) to avoid the negative emotions that follow from remembering the past or looking ahead to the future, and (b) because the present is the only time we have in which to act. The present, not the past or the future, is the only time that is under our control. The present is all one has (2.14, 3.10, 12.26 end), and we tend to make it worse for ourselves by burdening it with our memories of the past and expectations of the future.

becomes easier to bear if you take it on its own; and rebuke your mind if it's too feeble to endure something that's so uncluttered.[34]

[37] Is Verus's coffin still attended by Panthea or Pergamus? Or Hadrian's by Chabrias or Diotimus? Ridiculous! And even if they were still sitting there, were Verus or Hadrian going to notice it? And even if they noticed it, were they going to be pleased? And even if it did please them, were the mourners going to live forever? Aren't they too fated first to grow old and then to die? So what were the dead going to do after their mourners had died?[35]

[38] Nothing here but a foul stench and a sack of blood. If you have sharp sight, use it!

[39] "In keeping," as the poet says, "with the judgment of the truly wise," I see in the constitution of a rational being no virtue that's likely to resist justice, but I do see the virtue that's capable of resisting pleasure: self-control.[36]

---

34. In this entry, Marcus outlines an exercise that is an aspect of the recurrent stripping exercise, in that here what is being stripped away is any relation between the present and the past or future.

35. I take it that the point is the oft-repeated one, that the dead depend on the living for their survival as memories, but even those who are still alive and holding the memories are soon going to die. But Marcus expresses the idea oddly here, with his counterfactual talk about the dead feeling pleasure.

36. If you make justice your goal, all the virtues will support your aim; if you make pleasure your goal, they will not. The author of the quotation is unknown.

[40] If you get rid of the belief about what seems to be hurting you, you stand in an absolutely hurt-free place. "Which 'you'?" Reason. "But I'm not reason." All right. So reason won't cause itself pain, and any other part of you that's suffering is welcome to believe that about itself.

[41] Obstruction of the senses is bad for animal nature, as is obstruction of impulse. Something else is similarly obstructive of and bad for the constitution of plants. By the same token, then, obstruction of intelligence is bad for a rational nature.[37] Apply all this to yourself. Are you affected by pain and pleasure? That's the concern of your senses. Did something thwart an impulse of yours? Well, if you set about it without reservation, it's no wonder that it's detrimental to you as a rational being. But if you anticipate the obstacle, it has done you no harm and you haven't even been obstructed.[38] And functions that are specific to the mind can't be hindered by an external agent, because it's immune

---

37. The usual *scala naturae*, from plants to animals to humans.

38. See Notebook 4, note 2, on the Stoic doctrine of "reservation." You are not obstructed because you change direction.

to fire, steel, tyranny, abuse, or anything.[39] When it has become "a rounded sphere,"[40] it remains so.

[42] I don't deserve to hurt myself, because I've never deliberately hurt anyone else.

[43] Different things make different people happy. I'm happy if my command center is in a healthy condition—which is to say, if it doesn't shun any human being or any human experience, but regards everyone with kindly eyes, and accepts and deals with everything on its merits.

[44] Come on, make yourself a gift of this time. People who are overinterested in posthumous fame fail to take into consideration the fact that those who come after them will be no different from those they currently find objectionable, and just as

---

39. See 4.39 and 8.51 for similarly vehement expressions of the same point. Hence the famous Stoic paradox, that it is possible to be content even on the rack.

40. Part of either fragment 27 or fragment 28 Diels/Kranz of Empedocles, quoted again in 12.3. Marcus quotes the fragment out of context but correctly, as an image of perfect self-sufficiency and impregnability. It resonates with his occasional call for "simplicity" and with the Stoic notion of the universe as complete in itself with nothing outside it, and is in effect another metaphor for what Marcus elsewhere calls the "inner citadel" (4.3, 8.48).

mortal as well. In short, what is it to you what opinions they voice about you or what conception they have of you?[41]

[45] Pick me up and throw me where you will. Wherever it is, I shall preserve the serenity of my guardian spirit, or in other words its contentment with its condition and its activity, given their compatibility with its own constitution. Is there anything about the present situation that justifies my soul's being in a bad way and out of sorts—depressed, yearning, constrained, scared? In fact, do you think there's any situation which would justify that?

[46] Nothing can happen to any human being that isn't a proper incident for a human being; nothing can happen to a cow that isn't proper to a cow, or to a vine that isn't proper to a vine, or to a stone that isn't proper to a stone.[42] So, if whatever happens to anything is normal and natural for it, why should you complain? Universal nature wasn't bringing you anything you couldn't endure.

[47] If something external is causing you distress, it's not the thing itself that's troubling you but your judgment about it, and it's within your power to erase that right now. And if it's something internal to yourself, is anyone stopping you from

---

41. This entry is the closest Marcus comes to admitting that he is tempted by the prospect of posthumous fame himself. When he says, "People who..." he means to include himself. He can improve the quality of his life—make himself a gift of the time he has been allotted—by not worrying about such things.

42. Marcus lists entities from each stage of the *scala naturae*: human, animal, plant, inanimate stone.

looking at it in a more positive way? Likewise, if you're distressed because you're failing to do something that strikes you as sound, why not do it rather than indulge in distress? "But the obstacle is too strong for me." In that case, there's no need for distress, because you're not responsible for your inability to act. "But my life isn't worth living unless I get this thing done." You'd better take your leave from this life, then, as kind in death as one who is still active, and at peace with those who stood in your way.[43]

[48] Remember that the command center becomes invincible when it withdraws into itself and is self-sufficient, doing nothing that isn't in conformity with its will, even if its stance is unreasonable.[44] How much more secure it is, then, when it reaches a rational decision about something after due consideration. That's why an impassive mind is a citadel. A man can have no better stronghold where he can take refuge and remain unassailable. To be unaware of this is ignorance, but to be aware of it and not to make it his place of refuge is a real misfortune.

[49] Don't elaborate on what your immediate impressions report.[45] Suppose the report is that so-and-so is maligning you. End of report; nothing in it about your having been harmed. I see

---

43. On suicide, see Notebook 3, note 3.

44. Unreasonableness is a sign not of no command center but of a malfunctioning one; see also 10.13.

45. This is a very important idea and introduces an important Stoic exercise: seeing things for what they are *before* any response to them has arisen in you in the form of a value judgment. This is how the Stoics tried to deal with their passions.

that my child is ill; that's what I see, but I don't see that he's in any danger. So always go with your first impressions, adding no extra commentary of your own from within, and you're not affected. Or rather, add "As one who is acquainted with everything that happens in the world."[46]

[50] Is the cucumber bitter? Throw it away. Are there brambles on the path? Avoid them. That's enough, without going on to ask, "Why are there such things in the world?"[47] A scientist would mock you for the question, just as you'd be mocked by a joiner or a cobbler if you saw in their workshops the shavings and trimmings of the things they were working on and condemned them for it. Of course, they have somewhere to dispose of these things, whereas universal nature has nothing outside itself, but that's precisely what's astonishing about its skill: self-contained as it is, it changes into itself any of its components that are clearly perishing, aging, and no longer of any use and uses them as material to create more new things. Hence universal nature

---

46. In other words, it is not as if you are the only person ever to have lost a child. The apparent callousness of Stoicism in this respect should be understood in the light of the extreme frequency of infant and childhood death in antiquity.

47. But elsewhere Marcus does answer this question: 3.2, 6.36. The Stoics came up with various reasons why there are "bad" or useless things in the world, such as that good cannot exist without bad, or that if we saw things better, we would understand that what we think is bad is actually good. Notice that a question that for us might be religious ("Why on earth did God make mosquitoes?") is for Marcus a matter for a scientist or philosopher.

requires no substance outside itself and has no need of somewhere to dump rubbish; it has its own place, its own matter, and its own skill, and they are all it needs.

[51] When doing something, don't be sluggish; when talking to people, don't be muddled; when thinking, don't be vague. Don't ever let your soul contract or leap.[48] Don't fill your life with busyness. "They kill you, butcher you, hound you with curses."[49] But does this in any way stop you preserving the purity, lucidity, moderation, and justice of your mind? Suppose someone standing by a clear, sweet spring were to curse it: it just keeps right on bringing drinkable water bubbling up to the surface. Even if he throws mud or dung in it, before long the spring disperses the dirt and washes it out, leaving no stain. So how are you to have the equivalent of an ever-flowing spring? If you preserve your self-reliance at every hour, and your kindness, simplicity, and morality.

[52] Anyone who doesn't know what the universe is doesn't know where he is.[50] Anyone who doesn't know for what purpose it was made doesn't know who he is or what the universe is. Anyone who's wanting in any one of these respects couldn't even say what the purpose of his own existence is. So what do you think of someone who courts the approval of, or noise generated

---

48. In pain or in pleasure.

49. This sounds more like a quotation than Marcus's alter ego, but if so we do not know its source.

50. He is a stranger in the world (and not in a good way): see 4.29.

by, people who applaud while having no idea where they are or who they are?[51]

[53] Do you want to be praised by a man who curses himself three times an hour? Do you want to be liked by a man who doesn't like himself? If a man regrets almost everything he does, can he be said to like himself?

[54] As well as partaking of the surrounding air when you breathe, from now on, when you think, partake also of the all-encompassing intelligence. After all, intelligence is spread throughout the entire universe, permeating everything, so it's just as much there for anyone who's able to draw on it as air is for anyone who's able to breathe.[52]

[55] Iniquity in general does no harm to the universe, and individual iniquity harms not the person at the receiving end, but only the perpetrator, and he has the possibility of ridding himself of it. He only has to make that choice.

[56] To my will, my neighbor's will is just as much a matter of indifference as his spirit and his flesh. For even though we

---

51. Marcus frequently feels the need to remind himself of the unworthiness of most people who are quick to praise others. His other recurrent insight into praise is that both it and the praisers are short-lived. It might seem odd for Marcus to spend so much time on praise, but, first, it was in the nature of his job that everything he did was available for public scrutiny and, second, personal glory and the ability thereby to enhance future generations of one's family were important to upper-class Romans, to an extent that is hard for us to imagine.

52. Intelligence permeates everything in the universe in the form of *pneuma*, the vital spirit that sustains everything.

exist first and foremost to help one another, nevertheless, where our command centers are concerned, each of them has its own particular sphere of authority. Otherwise, my neighbor's iniquity would be bad for me, but it was not God's intention that my misfortune should be determined by anyone else.

[57] Sunlight seems to pour down, and even though it spreads everywhere, it doesn't get poured away, because this apparent pouring is in fact an extension. (At any rate, the term "rays" for its beams is derived from "extension.")[53] You can see what the nature of a ray is if you watch sunlight entering a darkened room through a narrow opening. It extends in a straight line and, so to speak, impacts any solid object that encounters it and cuts off the air from the other side of the object.[54] It settles there, without sliding off and falling away to the ground. That's what the outpouring and diffusion of thought should be like—an extension rather than a draining of itself. Its impact on obstacles that encounter it should never be violent or forceful, and it certainly shouldn't fall away, but should settle, and illuminate any object that accepts it. Anything that repels it will deprive itself of its light.

[58] To be afraid of death is to be afraid of either unconsciousness or a different kind of consciousness. But if death is the end of consciousness, you won't be conscious of anything bad

---

53. Marcus (falsely) derives *aktines* (rays) from *ekteinesthai* (to be extended).

54. Air is here seen as the conveyor of the sunbeam. The solid object cuts off the air so that the light cannot extend beyond it.

either.[55] And if you gain a different kind of consciousness, you'll be a different kind of creature, which is to say that you'll still be alive.[56]

[59] If human beings exist to help one another, you must either instruct them or put up with them.

[60] An arrow moves in one way, the mind in another. But even when the mind exercises caution and circles around an object of investigation, it's still moving straight for its target.

[61] Get through to everyone's command center,[57] and make it possible for everyone to get through to yours.[58]

---

55. This argument was also used by Epicureans to remove fear of death.

56. So, if you are still alive, there is no reason to fear death. We have already several times met Marcus's attraction to the idea of some kind of survival after death. It could be justified in Stoic terms by the argument that, since the soul is *pneuma* at a higher rate of tension than the body, it takes longer to fall apart than the body. But Marcus here seems to be talking about survival even of consciousness and personality.

57. The instruction is similar to that of 4.38, 6.53, 7.62, 9.18, and 9.22. On the other hand, Marcus also bids himself not to be distracted from his work by what is going on in others' command centers (5.3, 7.55), and not to let himself be infected by others' command centers (8.56).

58. One of the practical consequences of this is outlined at 7.5: others can draw on the ideas generated by your command center and help you put them into effect.

NOTEBOOK 9

[1] Any act of injustice is an impious act, because universal nature has made rational beings to help one another and benefit one another as they deserve, without ever doing harm, and to transgress against the will of universal nature is plainly to sin against the eldest of the gods and goddesses. Lying too is a sin against the same goddess, because universal nature is the nature of existing things, and existing things and the facts are intimately related. Universal nature is also called Truth and is the original source of everything that is true.[1] So anyone who lies intentionally is committing an impious act, insofar as he wrongs

---

1. As many entries show, Marcus was a lover of honesty and truth. "Truth" and "justice" were his two watchwords. His name, before he became emperor, was Marcus Annius Verus. "Verus" means "the true," and the emperor Hadrian was so impressed with the young man's honesty that he dubbed him "Verissimus," "the most true" (Cassius Dio, *Roman History* 69.21.2).

people by deceiving them; but anyone who lies unintentionally is also committing an impious act, insofar as he clashes with universal nature and wields disorder in a fight against the orderly universe. After all, anyone who resists truth is involved in a fight, and one of his own making, because he's been granted the necessary resources by nature, and it's his neglect of these resources that has made him incapable now of distinguishing falsehood from truth.[2]

Moreover, pursuing pleasure in the belief that it's good and avoiding pain in the belief that it's bad[3] are also impious acts, because there are bound to be many occasions when a hedonist finds fault with universal nature for "unfairly" allotting something to bad or good people, in the sense that bad people often find themselves in pleasant circumstances and possess the means to make them happen, while good people meet with pain and things that cause pain. Moreover, there'll be times when anyone who's afraid of pain will be afraid of some future event in the world, which is an outright act of impiety, while anyone who pursues pleasure will be tempted into wrongdoing, which is clearly impious.

---

2. Whereas in jurisprudential terms voluntary and involuntary wrongdoing are treated differently, Marcus here describes involuntary wrongdoing as culpable. Since, for Stoics, all actions are chosen actions, there is really no such thing as involuntary wrongdoing.

3. That is, hedonism. The most famous philosophical hedonists were the Epicureans, but here Marcus is also talking about those we may call "everyday" hedonists—like most of us.

Now, faced with things toward which universal nature is indifferent (because it wouldn't have created both of them if it weren't indifferent toward them both),[4] those who want to be in compliance and conformity with nature should also be indifferent. So anyone who isn't indifferent toward pain and pleasure, death and life, fame and obscurity—things that universal nature treats indifferently—is clearly acting impiously. When I say that universal nature treats these things indifferently, I mean that, thanks to the sequence of cause and effect, they all happen indifferently to every generation and every succeeding generation of existing things, due to an age-old impulse of providence. Following this impulse, universal nature set out from a certain starting point to create the present orderly arrangement of things, once it had conceived certain principles that would govern all that would happen in the future and had separated out powers to generate things with substantial existence, to transform these things, and to create things of the same kind to succeed them.

[2] It takes quite an accomplished man to leave the world without ever having tasted deceit or any kind of dissembling, and without having indulged in luxury and vanity, but a second-best course is to have had enough of these things before you breathe your last. Or do you propose to devote yourself to depravity? Has experience not taught you yet to flee from the plague? After

---

4. This is not a strong argument as it stands. A hedonist could reply that universal nature had created one of the opposites as a goal for us to aim for, and the other as something to avoid.

all, corruption of the mind is far more pestilential than any kind of noxious spoiling of the air we breathe. For the plague affects living creatures in their animal nature, but corruption of the mind affects human beings in their humanity.[5]

[3] Don't belittle death, but welcome it as one of many expressions of nature's will. Disintegration is no different from any other natural process that life's seasons bring: youth and age; growth and maturity; teething, growing a beard, hair turning gray; conception, pregnancy, childbirth. So what's appropriate for a man who has thought things through isn't treating death as something to be dismissed or ignored or despised, but waiting for it on the understanding that it's a natural process. Just as now you wait for the time when a baby will emerge from your wife's womb,[6] so you should await the hour when your soul will shed this shell that encases it.

But if you want an unphilosophical, emotionally satisfying prop, you should think about all the stuff you're going to leave

5. What Marcus says here is perfectly general, but any mention of a plague would resonate with the fact that in the late 160s, Roman armies returning from the east brought back a terrible plague (the "Antonine Plague"), which continued to ravage Rome and Roman armies abroad for the rest of Marcus's reign. See the Introduction, xix–xx. Even on his deathbed in 180, Marcus is reputed to have said: "Why weep for me? Think rather of the plague and the fact that death is the common lot of us all" (*Historia Augusta: Marcus* 28.4).

6. So Faustina was pregnant again, but unfortunately this does not help us date this notebook. The last child of theirs to survive was born c. 170, but a nonsurvivor may have been born later. Faustina died c. 175.

behind and the kinds of characters with which your soul will no longer have to mingle. That will make it easy for you to face death. For although you absolutely shouldn't reject them, but in fact should care for them and treat them gently, it's still worth bearing in mind that the people from whom you'll be parted don't share your principles. I mean, the only thing that could possibly pull you back and make you cling to life would be if you were allowed to go on living with people who had adopted the same principles as yourself. As things are, however, you can see how tedious it is to live with people whose views are out of harmony with yours. It's enough to make you say: "Hurry up, death! I dread the possibility that I too might forget myself."[7]

[4] Any transgression is a transgression against oneself. A wrongdoer harms himself by making himself a worse person.[8]

[5] Wrongdoing is the outcome not just of action but often of inaction as well.

[6] It's enough if one's current belief is true, if one's current action has the common good as its objective, and if one's current

---

7. In this entry Marcus combines two consolations about death— that it is a natural process (see, e.g., 2.12), and that it will bring relief from the crassness of the world and the danger of forgetting who he really is, a splinter of the divine reason and bound to do good.

8. See especially Plato's *Gorgias*. The idea was fully taken over by the Stoics from Plato's Socrates.

state of mind is willing acceptance of every externally caused thing that happens.[9]

[7] Clear your mind; control your impulses; extinguish desire; see that your command center retains its self-mastery.[10]

[8] Irrational animals share one soul, and rational creatures partake of one intelligent soul, just as the earth of all earthy things is single, and the light by which we see is single and the air we breathe is single, if we are creatures endowed with vision and life.

[9] Anything that shares some essential quality with other things seeks its own kind. Everything earthy sinks earthward, everything watery merges with other liquids,[11] and the same goes for airy things. In fact, it takes force to keep these elements apart. Fire moves upward because of the elemental fire,[12] but is so ready to assist in combustion here on earth that any material that is somewhat dry is inflammable because among its ingredients it contains less of anything capable of retarding combustion. And

---

9. The Stoics (and especially Epictetus) divided everything into two categories. Some things were "up to us," "of our own choosing," or "within our power," and in these cases we do the best we can. Things that are not up to us, that are caused by something outside of ourselves, we tolerate or sidestep without resentment.

10. The final clause is the summation of the other three: if you do those three things, your command center will retain its mastery of itself.

11. Plainly not true of oil and water, but we get the point.

12. In Stoic cosmology, fire, as the lightest of the elements, occupies the upper regions of heaven. Since like tends to like, that is why fire on earth tends upward.

so everything that partakes of intelligent nature similarly seeks its own kind. Or rather, it has an even stronger predisposition to do so, because to the extent that it's superior to the other things I've mentioned, it's that much more ready to commingle and blend with what is like it.

At any rate, from the very beginning, among irrational creatures there existed swarms, flocks, the feeding of young, and something like love, because there were, after all, souls involved, and at this higher level there was a tendency to unity of an intensity not to be found in plants or stones or logs. In rational creatures, this same tendency manifests as communities, friendships, households, assemblies, and treaties and truces at times of war. And among still higher beings there exists a kind of unity consisting of discrete things, such as one finds among the heavenly bodies. Thus the higher up the scale one goes, the greater the possibility there is of an interactive connection being forged even among discrete things.

Now compare the world at present. Currently, intelligent creatures are alone in having consigned to oblivion the urge to unity with one another. Only here is the merging of like with like something one never sees. But, run from it as they might, it still catches up with them. Such is the power of nature.[13] If you pay attention, you'll get the point. I mean, you're more likely to find

---

13. It is not just hard to contravene nature, but impossible. Seneca (a Stoic from the early first century CE) quotes a prayer of Cleanthes from the third century BCE, which contains a perfect expression of the idea: "Fate *guides* the willing and *pulls* the unwilling" (*Letters* 107.11).

earthy things separated from one another than a human being who's cut off from other human beings.

[10] A human being bears fruit as well, so does God, and so does the universe. Each of them is productive in its own season. Never mind if convention has reduced the proper usage of the word to vines and so on. Reason too has its fruit, both general and particular, and its issue consists of more things of the same kind as reason itself.

[11] If you can, get them to mend their ways, and if you can't, remember that this is exactly why you've been endowed with kindness. Even the gods are kind to such people and help them achieve some of their objectives—health, wealth, prestige.[14] That's how good they are. You can do it too. Or tell me: who's stopping you?

[12] Labor on, but not as one who's miserable and wants people to feel sorry for him or admire him. You should want one thing only: to act or refrain from action as the social principle requires.[15]

[13] Today I freed myself from all the things that were afflicting me, or it would be more accurate to say that I *ejected* all

---

14. So, as at 3.11, 5.36, and 6.45, Marcus accepts that, as emperor, he has to negotiate his way in a world that treats as important things that are, in strict Stoic terms, indifferent. He justifies this by reference to the goodness of the gods in this respect, and does so again at 9.27. For the goodness of the gods in general, see 1.17, 2.3, 6.44, 7.70.

15. That is, whether or not your action would enhance the common good.

the things that were afflicting me, because they weren't outside me, but inside, inherent in my beliefs.

[14] There's nothing here that isn't experientially familiar, temporally impermanent, and constitutionally squalid. Everything now is just as it was in the time of those we've buried.

[15] The things of this world stand all by themselves outside our gates, with no knowledge of themselves and no way to tell us about themselves. So from where do we get information about them? From the command center.[16]

[16] Good and bad for a rational and social being lie not in passivity but in action, just as virtue and vice for him lie not in passivity but in action.[17]

[17] For a stone tossed into the air, there's nothing bad in descending, and ascending isn't good for it either.[18]

[18] Delve below the surface into their command centers, and you'll see what these people are like whose criticism you're worried about, and how poor they are as critics of themselves.[19]

---

16. As Epictetus said, gold itself does not tell us that it is gold (*Discourses* 1.1.5). It is up to us to identify our experiences and decide what to do about them.

17. So a rational creature is fulfilled if he does good and impaired if he does bad, both in terms of particular actions and overall.

18. This is a metaphor for the human condition (see the very similar 8.20): things change, and that is neither good nor bad, even though every change is a death (9.19, 9.21). For reasons not to fear change or describe it as good or bad, see especially 7.18, but also 2.17 (end) and 8.6.

19. The thought is repeated a few entries later, at 9.27, and again at 9.34. See also 4.38, 6.53, and 7.62.

[**19**] Everything is changing. You yourself are constantly changing and, in a sense, perishing, and so is the universe as a whole.

[**20**] It's best to leave someone else's transgression there with him.[20]

[**21**] The ending of an activity or an impulse or a belief—its cessation and its death, if you will—isn't a bad thing. And then what about the stages of life, such as childhood, adolescence, youth, and old age? In their case too, every change is a death.[21] It's not something they fear, is it? Again, what about your life with your grandfather, then with your mother, then with your father?[22] And as you find many another death and change and ending in your own life, ask yourself: "Was it something to fear?" By the same token, then, the ending, cessation, and transformation of your life as a whole is nothing to fear either.[23]

[**22**] Hurry now to your own command center, to the command center of the universe, and to the command center of the man in question. To your own, to make sure that it's disposed toward justice; to that of the universe, to remind yourself what

---

20. It is his problem, not yours, so do not let it affect you. See 7.29.

21. The death of childhood is the birth of adolescence, and so on.

22. As a young child, Marcus was largely brought up by his grandfather M. Annius Verus; his mother lived with him while he was young (1.17); and then he entered the household of his adopted father, the emperor Antoninus Pius.

23. Change is normal, so the change that we call death is normal too, nothing to get wrought up about. See also 2.17 (end).

it is that you're a part of; and to his, to understand whether what he did was ignorant or planned, and at the same time to appreciate that his command center is kin to your own.

[23] Precisely because you personally are part of the whole that is the body politic, every one of your actions should contribute to a life the purpose of which is to improve society. Any action of yours, then, which doesn't closely or remotely take as its reference point the goal of improving society creates a rupture in your life and prevents it from having integrity, and is just as socially divisive as when a member of a community takes it upon himself to detach himself from the common concord.

[24] Children's tantrums and games, and "spirits sustaining corpses,"[24] make the impact of the "Vision of Hades" more vivid![25]

[25] Consider the cause of any object and what kind of a thing it is. Take it in isolation from the object's matter, and then determine the maximum amount of time that an object with these specific qualities is, given its nature, able to subsist.[26]

---

24. A slight adaptation of a saying of Epictetus: see 4.41.

25. The "Vision of Hades" (Greek *Nekyia*) is the title of a section of Homer's *Odyssey* (our Book 11) in which Odysseus summons from Hades the ghosts of the dead. Perhaps Marcus is taking it to be a fanciful tale—but one that is still to be taken more seriously than passing tantrums and our fleeting lives.

26. See Notebook 4, note 39. Marcus certainly intends the conclusion that things are ephemeral, but it is hard to see how the exercise he is suggesting works, or helps toward that goal. In the course of both 3.11 and 10.9, and at 12.18, he again suggests that if one knows the nature of a thing, it is possible to determine its life span.

[26] You've endured countless troubles by not letting your command center get on with what it was made to do. Enough is enough!

[27] When you're the object of disapproval or loathing, or their words express those kinds of feelings, go to their souls. Go below the surface and see what they're like. You'll see that there's no need for you to derange yourself in order to get them to think of you in a certain way. But you are obliged to be benevolent to them, because by nature they're your friends. And the gods help them in all sorts of ways through dreams and oracles, at least to attain the objectives they prize.[27]

[28] The cycles of the universe never change; around and around they go from age to age.[28] Now, either every single thing that happens is the outcome of an individual impulse by the universal intelligence (in which case every experience must be accepted as willed by it), or it had a single initial impulse and

---

27. Divination through dreams was used chiefly for healing purposes, so that health is one of the indifferents that ordinary people are helped by the gods to gain. Entry 9.11 adds "wealth" and "prestige." Because the Stoics believed that everything was connected, even if the connection was hard to discern, and because they believed in providence and the governance of the world by divine reason, they accepted divination, considering it science rather than superstition, and it was in part as a result of their influence that astrology became influential in the Roman world.

28. On eternal recurrence, see Notebook 2, note 42.

everything else has followed as a consequence.[29] So what is there to worry about? Everything is either atoms or fate. In short, the choice is between divine intervention, in which case everything is as it should be, or mere chance,[30] in which case you must still not be ruled by chance yourself.

Soon earth will cover us all, and then earth too will change, and an endless sequence of changes will take place: first, the changing of the earth, and then the changing of what the earth changed into, and so on ad infinitum. If one bears in mind these successive waves of change and alteration, and their speed, one will come to see everything that is mortal as contemptible.

[29] The universal cause is a torrent; it carries everything with it. So, my friend, what to do? Just do what nature is currently demanding of you. If you have the opportunity, go ahead straight away, without letting your attention be distracted by wondering whether anyone will know what you're doing.

---

29. The same exclusive alternatives at 6.36; see also 7.75. Both are compatible with Stoicism.

30. The usual choice between a Stoic worldview and an Epicurean one: see Notebook 4, note 8. Here Marcus does not even bother to comment on the "purposelessness" option, beyond contrasting it with the Stoic one.

Don't expect to create Plato's ideal state,[31] but be satisfied if you make even the slightest progress, and regard that in itself as no small achievement. How worthless are these little men doing state business while imagining that they're acting like philosophers, stuffed with snot as they are![32] I mean, is someone going to get them to change their minds? Unless or until they do, they're no better than slaves, deploring their circumstances and pretending to do what they're told. Go on, then:[33] now's the time to tell me about Alexander, Philip, and Demetrius of Phalerum.[34] Well, if they realized what nature wanted of them and trained themselves accordingly, I'll follow their lead. But if they were just playing grandiose roles, no one has condemned

---

31. The ideal state of his *Republic*. Plato himself almost certainly did not intend it to be a blueprint for a possible city-state, and so it quickly became proverbial for an unreachable ideal, a city of the kind envisaged by Zeno, the founder of Stoicism, in which everyone is an enlightened sage. Cicero memorably described the idealistic Cato the Younger (see 1.14) as "speaking and voting as though he were in Plato's Republic, rather than the dregs of Romulus" (*Letters to Atticus* 2.1.8).

32. All these men produce is waste matter. Knowing Marcus's devotion to philosophy, people around him pretended to share his interest, in the hope of promotion—or so says the historian Cassius Dio, at *Roman History* 71.35.2.

33. Marcus is addressing one of the "little men" he has been talking about.

34. Demetrius is an example of a politician who imagines that he is thereby acting as a philosopher. Philip and Alexander are mentioned as examples of supposedly great rulers; they fail Marcus's severe and Stoic idea of greatness.

me to imitate them. The work of philosophy requires simplicity and modesty; don't mislead me into pompous affectation.

[30] Take a look from on high and what do you see? Countless herds, countless ceremonies, voyages of every kind being undertaken in storm and calm, the endless variety of people being born, living together, passing away.[35] Think also of the lives lived by others in the past, the lives that will be lived after you, and the lives that are being lived today by barbarian peoples. See how many people there are who don't even know your name, how many of them will very soon forget you, and how many of them may be praising you now but will very soon be denouncing you. Recognize that neither memory nor fame nor anything else at all has any importance.[36]

[31] Imperturbability in the face of things that are externally caused; justice in all activity that is initiated by yourself—that is, impulses and actions the purpose of which is just acting for the common good—because this in accord with your nature.

[32] You can get rid of many superfluous troubles that depend entirely on your beliefs, and you'll immediately provide yourself with plenty of mental space. Encompass the whole universe with your mind, contemplate the everlastingness of time, and consider

---

35. Marcus indulges in some wordplay with these last three verbs, but it is not capturable in English: *ginomenōn, sygginomenōn, apoginomenōn.*

36. Apart from virtue, that is; but in this entry Marcus is trying to counter his tendency to vanity, which is not an attribute of a virtuous person.

the speed with which individual things change. How short the time is between birth and disintegration, how vast the time before your birth, and how similarly infinite the time after your disintegration!

[33] Everything you see will very soon perish, and those who witness the perishing of these things will very soon perish themselves. A man who died in extreme old age and a boy who died early will be made the same.

[34] What are their command centers like? What are they interested in? What do they love and value? Practice seeing their souls naked.[37] How presumptuous of them to imagine that they're hurting you with their criticism or doing you good by singing your praises!

[35] Loss is just change, and change pleases universal nature, which is responsible for everything that comes to pass and for the goodness of everything that comes to pass. Good things have happened from eternity, and there will be more in the infinite future. Why, then, do you say that everything that has happened and will happen is bad, that none of the host of gods has the

---

37. This is a divine perspective: 5.27, 11.13, 12.2. In Plato's *Gorgias* (523c–d), the dead are presented to the underworld judges with their souls naked and displaying all the scars caused by their wrongdoing when alive. But the general suggestion that to understand a person and their motives one has to delve into their command center is familiar from, for example, 4.38 and 9.18.

power to correct the situation,[38] and that the world has been condemned to be unremittingly afflicted by evil?

[36] The matter that makes up each and every thing is rubbish—water, dust, bones, stench. Or again: marble is calcified earth, gold and silver are earth's waste, clothing is animal hair, purple dye is shellfish blood,[39] and so on and so forth.[40] The breath that animates us is much the same, changing from this to that.

[37] No more making your life miserable by grumbling and playing the ape![41] Why disturb your peace of mind? There's nothing new here, is there? What is it that's upsetting you? Its cause? See it for what it is. Its matter, perhaps? See it for what it is.[42] Apart from cause and matter, there's nothing else. By the gods, become a simpler and better person, and do it now! Three years is as good as a hundred for this quest.

---

38. The consolatory thought that the world must be good, because the gods would have corrected it if it was bad, also underlies 2.11 and 12.5, and is an unusual ray of brightness against the background of Marcus's habitual pessimism.

39. See Notebook 4, note 35. Purple dye was extremely expensive and therefore a sign of prestige.

40. Marcus undertakes a similar exercise in objectivity at 6.13.

41. It is not quite clear what Marcus means by "playing the ape." It probably means courting others' good opinions ("flattery" is also combined with "grumbling" at 5.5), but possibly "aping" in our sense of imitation. And then there are the undertones of behaving in a subhuman manner.

42. Again, Marcus urges himself to slow down—here, to take time to see things as they truly are—as a way of calming down.

[38] If he did wrong, it's his problem, but perhaps he didn't.[43]

[39] Either everything is the outcome of a single intelligent source,[44] as in a single body,[45] in which case the part mustn't find fault with things that happen to it in the interest of the whole,[46] or else there are just atoms and everything is a cocktail of ingredients with only dispersal in their future.[47] So why worry? Ask your command center: "Are you dead? Have you been corrupted? Have you sunk to the level of a wild animal? Are you dissembling? Are you running with the herd and sharing their fodder?"

---

43. Actions have consequences, so that what seems wrong now might later turn out to be right: see 11.18 (point 5).

44. There are two versions of this idea: "Either every single thing that happens is the outcome of an individual impulse by the universal intelligence, or it had a single initial impulse and everything else has followed as a consequence" (9.28).

45. Everything the body does follows from an impulse of its governing soul.

46. If the amputation of a limb is necessary to preserve the health of the whole, the limb must not complain.

47. The usual choice between a Stoic and an Epicurean worldview, with the conclusion that, in either case, there is no need to worry. So, rather than worrying about death, Marcus concludes (in terms very reminiscent of 5.11) that one should concern oneself with the state of one's command center.

[40] The gods are either powerless or powerful. If they have no power, what's the point of prayer?[48] And if they do have power, isn't it preferable to pray for them to grant the ability not to fear or desire or be hurt by anything, rather than asking to have this or not have that? I mean, there's no doubt that, if the gods have the power to help human beings, they can help in these respects. You might respond by saying: "The gods have made these things 'up to me,' so isn't it better for you to manage in a self-reliant way the things that are up to you, rather than being concerned in a slavish and submissive way with things that aren't up to you?"[49] But from where did you get the idea that the gods don't also help with things that are up to us? Anyway, start praying for these things, and you'll see for yourself. One man's prayer is "Help me

---

48. On prayer and the gods: 5.7, 6.23, 6.44, 12.14. Marcus's position runs counter to orthodox Stoicism, because he thinks it worthwhile to pray for help in matters that are, strictly, "up to us."

49. That is, rather than praying at all, for anything; the choice the objector is offering is the Stoic one between being self-reliant where things that are up to us are concerned and not worrying about other things. Prayer, therefore, did not play a large role in Stoicism; in effect, you pray only for the ability to be rational and accept what is not up to you. The poetic prayer of Cleanthes, quoted by Epictetus at the end of his *Handbook*, is typical: "Lead me, Zeus, both you and Destiny, whereso'er you have ordained for me, and I shall gladly follow. And if I am unwilling out of wickedness, still I shall follow." Marcus does not deny this, but he adds that, human weakness being what it is, prayer to the gods can do no harm, and may help.

to bed that woman," while yours is "Help me not to desire to bed that woman." Another's is "Help me get rid of that man," while yours is "Help me not to want to get rid of that man." Another's is "Help me not to lose my child," while yours is "Help me not to be afraid of losing my child."[50] In short, turn your prayers around like that and see what happens.

[41] This is from Epicurus:[51] "During my illness, I didn't make my physical suffering a topic of conversation or talk about anything like that to visitors. Instead, I continued to talk as a natural scientist, expounding my principal doctrines, and focusing especially on this very point, how the mind, despite the fact that it shares in such physical disturbances, remains unperturbed and preserves its specific good. Nor," he goes on, "did I let my doctors get all bigheaded as if they were doing something important. I just got on with my life as well and nicely as usual."

---

50. Marcus never directly addresses marriage and children, so it is hard to assess his position, but it was probably in line with other Roman Stoics, for whom they were "preferred indifferents"—that is, things that are not essential to a life of virtue but that can help in that regard. Because marriage was seen as a proper form of relationship, Marcus and other Roman-period Stoics disapproved of adultery and homosexuality.

51. What follows is Epicurus, fragment 191 Usener. Marcus is the only source for the fragment. It was probably extracted from one of Epicurus's letters to disciples. See 7.64 for another example of Marcus's agreeing with the Stoa's great rival; and he often finds the two schools compatible on the subject of not fearing death.

You should do the same as him when you're ill—if you happen to be ill—and in all other circumstances. All the schools agree that one shouldn't abandon philosophy under any circumstances whatsoever, and shouldn't lower the level of one's conversation to that of people who have no background in philosophy or natural science. Focus exclusively on what you're doing at any moment and the instrument with which you're doing it.

[42] Whenever a person's lack of shame offends you, you should immediately ask yourself: "So is it possible for there to be no shameless people in the world?" It isn't, and you should therefore stop demanding the impossible.[52] He's just one of those shameless people who must necessarily exist in the world. You should keep the same thought readily available also for when you're faced with devious and untrustworthy people, and people who are flawed in any way. As soon as you remind yourself that it's impossible for such people not to exist, you'll be kinder toward each and every one of them. It's also helpful immediately to consider what virtue nature has granted us human beings to deal with any given offense—gentleness, for instance,

---

52. The existence of evil posed a problem for Stoics, who believed that the universe was guided by a good God. Mostly, Marcus is concerned to deny the existence of evil, either by arguing that it is all in the mind and you can change your mind, or by claiming that if we saw the big picture, we would see that what seems bad is actually good. Here he adds that it is (logically?) impossible for there not to be bad people.

to counter discourteous people,[53] and other ways to counter others. Generally speaking, you can get someone who's gone astray to mend his ways—and, whatever his wrong, a wrongdoer is missing his mark and has gone astray.[54] Besides, have you been harmed in any way? You'll find that none of the people who make you lose your temper has done anything that might affect your mind for the worse; and outside of the mind there's nothing that is truly detrimental or harmful for you. Moreover, what is unusual or surprising about an uneducated man doing uneducated things? It's worth considering whether you ought rather to blame yourself for failing to foresee that he would transgress in this way. After all, you even had the resources, in the form of your ability to think rationally, to appreciate that he was likely to commit that fault, yet you forgot it and are now surprised that he did exactly that.

But, above all, when you find fault with someone for lack of fidelity or gratitude, turn and look at yourself, because the fault was plainly yours. In the first instance, your mistake was to have trusted a man with such a character not to let you down; in the second, you failed to do the favor for its own sake, on the assumption that you would immediately reap your full reward just from the action itself. If you've done someone good, what more do you want? Aren't you satisfied with having acted in

---

53. Aristotle's account of gentleness, which he calls the opposite of anger, is illuminating: *The Art of Rhetoric* 2.3.

54. On Socratic and Stoic principles, all wrongdoing is "missing the mark"—thinking that something is the right thing to do when it is not.

conformity with your nature? Do you want remuneration as well? It's as if the eyes sought compensation for seeing or the feet for walking. Just as eyes and feet were made for a particular purpose, which fulfills them because the performance of that function is what they were designed to do, so, because human beings were made to do others good, when a man does something that benefits someone else, he's doing what he was made for, and is fulfilled.

NOTEBOOK 10

[1] My soul, will you ever be good, simple, single, and naked,[1] brighter than the body that encases you? Will you ever know what it is to be the kind of man who feels love and affection for his neighbors? Will you ever be fulfilled, wanting nothing, craving nothing, desiring nothing animate or inanimate to satisfy your pleasures—not time in which to enjoy them for longer, nor a place or country or climate, nor congenial people? Won't you instead be content with present circumstances and find pleasure in the company of whoever is present? Won't you convince yourself that everything you're presented with stems from the gods, and that all is well and will continue to be so, all that the gods are glad to give you and that they'll continue to give you, because it contributes

---

1. All these four adjectives come to the same thing. The soul should be unhampered by extraneous needs and focused entirely on doing good to others and perpetuating the divine plan.

to the preservation of the perfect living creature,[2] a creature of goodness, justice, and beauty, which generates everything, sustains and contains everything, and embraces all things that are disintegrated and in their turn give rise to other similar things? Will there ever come a time when you're fit to be a citizen of the community of gods and men without finding fault with them or being condemned by them?

[2] Observe what nature requires of you, as if you were subject only to nature,[3] and then do it, and welcome it as long as your animal nature isn't impaired. Next, observe what your animal nature requires of you, and accept that in full, as long as your nature as a rational being isn't impaired.[4] And a rational being is bound also to be a social being. Rely on these rules and don't trouble yourself further.

[3] Every event that takes place either can or can't be endured by you, given your nature.[5] If an event that takes place is within the natural limits of your endurance, don't complain, but put

---

2. That is, the universe. See also 5.8, the tone of which is similarly devotional and religious.

3. That is, like a plant, which was considered to be capable only of growth. Marcus, as often elsewhere, is going through a progression, here from plant to animal to rational being.

4. It is easy to see how one's animal nature could impair one's rational nature (e.g., getting drunk), but less easy to see what it is about plant nature that might impair one's animal nature. Being rooted, or in other words stubbornly unresponsive?

5. Comparison with 7.33 and 7.64 shows that Marcus is thinking above all of pain.

up with it, since you can, given your nature. If it goes beyond those limits, don't complain, because it will simply finish you off. But remember that nature has made you capable of enduring anything, as long as it is up to your judgment to render it endurable and tolerable by representing to yourself the doing of it as either advantageous or your duty.

[4] If he's making a mistake, instruct him in a kindly fashion and show him what he's overlooking. If you can't do that, blame yourself—or no one, not even yourself.[6]

[5] Whatever happens to you was being created for you from eternity, and from eternity the web of causation was weaving for you not just your existence but this particular event as well.[7]

[6] Whether atoms or nature, the first assumption has to be that I'm a part of the whole that is directed by nature, and then the second, that I'm related by affinity to parts that are of the same kind as myself. If I bear these principles in mind, then (a) insofar as I'm a part, I won't be discontented with anything allotted to me by the whole. For nothing that's beneficial to the whole can

---

6. Compare Epictetus, *Handbook* 5b: "Finding fault with others when things are going badly for him is what an uneducated person does. Finding fault with himself is what a partially educated person does. Finding fault with neither others nor himself is what a fully educated person does."

7. The image of fate as a woven web is common in *Meditations* (3.4, 3.11, 3.16, 4.26, 4.34, 5.8, 7.9, 7.57) and is natural, given that one of the three Fates in Greek mythology was Clotho, the weaver. Entry 5.8 combines the image of the web with the idea of personal predestination, as here.

be detrimental to a part.[8] In fact, the whole contains nothing that doesn't contribute to its own good. Now, although that feature is common to all natures, universal nature has an additional feature, that there's nothing outside it that could compel it to engender something detrimental to itself.[9] Provided, then, that I remember that I'm a part of a whole of this kind, I won't be discontented with anything that happens to me.[10] (b) Insofar as I'm related by affinity to parts that are of the same kind as myself, I'll do nothing that opposes the common good. Rather, my fellow parts will become the object of my endeavors: every impulse of mine will be steered toward the common good or steered away from the opposite. If I succeed in this, my life is bound to flow smoothly and contentedly, just as you'd observe that the life of a citizen of any state flows smoothly and contentedly if he spends his days

---

8. Marcus puts the idea to political use at 5.22 and 10.33; see also 6.54. But is it true? Commonsense suggests that the amputation of a limb is certainly harmful for the limb, even if the whole body is preserved by the operation. Moreover, Marcus claims (in the next sentence) that this is a deduction from the fact that "The whole contains nothing that doesn't contribute to its good." But, strictly, nothing at all about the good of the parts follows from that.

9. In Stoic physics, the universe was bounded, but outside it was nothing—no thing, void. Since the universe "contains nothing that doesn't contribute to its own good," it would have to be something from outside that would do it harm.

10. The argument, if we accept the premises, proves that everything that happens is good.

acting to the advantage of his fellow citizens and welcoming all that the state assigns him.

[7] The parts of the whole, all the natural components of the universe, are bound to perish, where by "perish" I mean "undergo change." Now, if this is bad for them as well as being a naturally inevitable phenomenon, the universe would not be well managed, since the parts are always in the process of changing and by their constitutions are specifically made to perish. Are we to suppose that nature deliberately set out to harm its own parts, by giving them a tendency to be harmed and making them inevitably liable to harm? Or should we think that such things go on without nature having anything to do with it? Neither alternative is convincing.[11]

If one were to dispense with universal nature and rely on the individual natures of things to explain death, even then it's absurd to agree that it's in the nature of the parts of the whole to change, and yet to be surprised or resentful when death happens, as though it were something unnatural for them, especially seeing that the disintegration that's taking place breaks a thing

11. Comparable notebook entries: 4.42, 8.20, 9.17 (change is not bad); 5.29, 9.21 (so death is not bad); 6.1 (the universe does no harm to its parts).

down into its components.[12] After all, disintegration is either the dispersal of a thing's constituent elements, or its solid component turns to earth and its spirit to air, so that they are received back into the seminal principle of the universe.[13] And this remains true whether the universe undergoes periodic conflagration or is renewed by unending changes.[14]

But don't think that either the solid or the airy part date from the time of a person's birth.[15] His entire body was gained

---

12. Since death is the disintegration of a thing into its component elements, it is in its nature, as made up of the elements, to die. The next sentence adds that this is the case whether one believes either the Epicurean or the Stoic teaching on what the constituents of things are and what happens to them at death ("dispersal of atoms" being the Epicurean option). No explanation of death as unnatural will satisfy Marcus.

13. And the seminal principle of the universe reuses them for the next generation of entities. In general, it is the seminal principle of the universe that ensures that the properties of one generation of things are passed on to the next generation of things.

14. Again the contrast between Stoicism and Epicureanism. The Stoics believed in the periodic destruction by fire of each universe in an unending series; each universe was renewed by constant change (e.g., 6.15), but, strictly speaking, those changes were not "unending," because they came to an end with each conflagration. The Epicureans, however, saw the universe as eternal, but consisting all the time of different combinations of atoms.

15. In this final paragraph of the entry, Marcus makes it clear that he is thinking primarily of human beings. He kept the discussion general in the first two paragraphs.

as fresh material just yesterday or the day before as a result of the food he ate and the air he breathed, so it's this that changes, not what his mother bore. You might suppose that a person's body is closely connected with what makes him the specific individual that he is, but this really has no bearing on what I've just been saying, in my opinion.[16]

[8] If you ever get to call yourself good, moral, honest, conscientious, amenable, and dignified,[17] never exchange them for other labels or lose them. And, if you do lose them, recover them quickly. Remember what they were supposed to mean in your case: "conscientious" was discriminating attention to individual objects and "observant"; "amenable" was willing acceptance of whatever is allotted to you by universal nature; and "dignified" was the elevation of your thinking part above the smooth or rough motions of the body, and above fame, death, and so on. So, if you consistently deserve these labels (without longing to hear them applied to you by others), you'll be a changed man and you'll enter upon a changed life. To remain as you've been up to now, to be mangled and defiled in the kind of life you live

---

16. Because Marcus would respond, presumably, by saying that a person can retain her specific identity throughout all the changes she goes through. Plato's *Symposium*, at 207d–208b, is relevant, culminating in: "The continued existence of any mortal creature does not involve its remaining absolutely unchanging for all time. . . . As its attributes pass away and age, they leave behind a new generation of attributes which resemble the old ones."

17. Marcus is indulging in a little wordplay: the last three adjectives in Greek are *emphrōn, symphrōn, hyperphrōn.*

at present, is an extremely stupid form of clinging to life—like those half-eaten animal fighters who, despite being badly injured and covered with blood, still beg to be returned to prison until the next day, so that they can be exposed again, just as they are, to the same claws and teeth.[18] Make these few labels your vessel, then, and if you're able to stay afloat, do so as one who has been transported to the Isles of the Blessed.[19] If you find yourself backsliding and losing control, don't despair, but secrete yourself in a corner where you can recover control.[20] Or you might even choose to take leave of life altogether, not in anger, but in a spirit of simplicity, self-reliance, and modesty; then you'll have achieved at least this one thing in your life, that you left it in this spirit. But you'll find it much easier to hold onto these labels if you remember the gods, and bear in mind that what they want is not to be fawned upon, but that all rational beings should be

---

18. In Marcus's day, it had long been the practice to condemn some criminals to death by fighting animals (usually big cats) in the arena as a form of public entertainment. Since the second half of the first century CE, not a few of these criminals had been Christians, many of whom were sent into the arena without weaponry, or chose to do so. If Marcus's example is a case of clinging to life, perhaps the fighters were supposed to be executed, as criminals, if they were still alive at the end of the bout, but they beg to go on for just one more day (see also 4.47). At 6.46, Marcus claims to find all such games tedious, if not disgusting.

19. The Isles of the Blessed were a mythical paradise reserved for those of especially pure spirit and for the heroes of legend.

20. Such a "corner" is more fully described in 4.3.

assimilated to them,[21] and that a fig tree should do the work of a fig tree, a dog the work of a dog, a bee the work of a bee, and a human being the work of a human being.

[9] Buffoonery, war, excitement, lethargy, servitude: those sacred principles of yours are daily liable to be erased if you conceive of them and put them to work in an unscientific way. The way in which you regard and do anything must be such that you're able to carry out the duties that circumstances impose on you, while at the same time applying your principles and keeping latent, but not buried, the self-assurance you've gained from your understanding of particular doctrines. When will it be simplicity that pleases you? Or dignity? Or the application of your rational mind to each and every event, to determine what it is essentially, what place it has in the world, how long it will last given its nature, what it's made of, who can make it their own, who can give it and take it away?[22]

[10] A spider counts it a great achievement to have caught a fly, as one man does if he catches a small hare, another a sprat in his net, another wild boars, another bears, and another

---

21. The description of the purpose of life as assimilation to the gods goes back to Plato, as, for instance, at *Theaetetus* 176b.

22. For the exercise of penetrating into something by asking many questions about it, see also 3.11 and 8.11.

Sarmatians.[23] The point being that, if you examine their principles, they're all robbers, aren't they?[24]

[11] Make it a systematic practice to consider how all things change into one another, pay constant attention to the changing, and train yourself in this respect. Nothing is more conducive to objectivity. A man who looks at things objectively divests himself of his body.[25] He knows that very shortly he'll have to leave all this behind when he departs from the world, and so he commits himself wholly to justice in his own actions and entrusts himself to universal nature when it comes to events that are beyond his control. It never occurs to him to wonder what people will say or think about him, or what they'll do against him, but he's content, first, if he always does what is right and, second, if he embraces his lot in its entirety. He gives up every distraction and

23. If this is not merely a generalized statement, it may be the only explicit reference in the book to contemporary events, here the Marcomannic Wars. Marcus's war against the Sarmatians ended with their repulsion in 175, and to commemorate his victory, Marcus added "Sarmaticus" to his name. So here Marcus, typically, sneers at his victory as trivial.

24. One of the tales about Alexander the Great has him confronting a pirate he had captured and rebuking him for his piracy. To this the pirate replied that people called him a robber, but Alexander, whose robbery was on a massive scale, an emperor.

25. This is a very Platonic thing to say. For Plato, objectivity about the world was gained by seeing the Forms in themselves, and this was a kind of training for death (as he puts it in *Phaedo*) because it is the soul or mind operating independently of the body, in the immaterial realm of Forms.

diversion, and all he wants is to continue straight on the path of law and thereby to follow God.[26]

[12] Where it's within your power to consider what has to be done, there's no need for guesswork. If you can see the way forward, take it without turning aside, and if you can't, hold back and consult your best advisers.[27] If you meet with obstacles, make use of the resources you have and proceed cautiously, keeping always to the course that seems to you to be just. For there's nothing better than the attainment of justice, since the only real failure is falling short of justice. Anyone who follows reason in all things is immune to external pressures, unencumbered, joyful, and composed.

[13] The moment you wake up, ask yourself: "Is it going to bother me today if matters that are being fairly and properly attended to are criticized by someone else?" No, it isn't. These men who get a kick out of praising or criticizing others—can you have forgotten how they behave as they recline on their couches or while they're eating? Have you failed to notice what they do, the kinds of things they like and dislike,[28] what thieves and

---

26. The fact that the last part of this entry is in the third person is interesting. As elsewhere (e.g., 3.16), it may be an attempt by Marcus not to claim this much enlightenment for himself.

27. See 4.12 and 8.16 for Marcus's justification for taking advice. He felt that justification was needed, because usually a Stoic aimed for self-reliance.

28. This is one of Marcus's most common ways of assessing character: 4.38, 7.34, 7.62, 9.34.

robbers they are? I don't mean that they're literally thieves; they don't make use of their hands and feet, but the most valuable part of themselves, in which there's the potential for fidelity, modesty, honesty, law, and the spirit of goodness.

[14] To nature, which gives all things and takes them back, an educated, modest man says: "Give what you want; take back what you want"—not in an impudent manner, but only as nature's loyal subject.

[15] Short is the time remaining. Live like a highlander.[29] It makes no difference where a man is, here or there, if wherever he finds himself he treats the world as a single nation state.[30] Let men see and observe an honest man living in accord with nature.[31] If they can't bear it, let them kill him, because that's better than living as they do.

[16] No more abstract discussions about what a good man is like: just be one!

[17] Keep all time and all being constantly before your mind, and see that, in terms of being, every individual thing is no more

29. The exact opposite of Marcus's way of life—the simple life of an upland pastoralist.

30. That is, as though all his fellow human beings, as rational creatures, deserved to be treated kindly and justly.

31. Since everywhere else (e.g., in the very next entry) Marcus feels he has not succeeded at living in accord with nature, I think he is not referring to himself here, although that is a possible interpretation of the words. It is more a conditional: "If they were ever to find an honest man and they can't bear it, they can always kill him."

than a fig seed, and in terms of time no more than a twist of a drill.

[18] If you pay close attention to each existing thing, you'll see that it's already in the process of disintegrating—that is, experiencing change and a kind of decay or dispersal—and that by its nature everything is born to die.

[19] Bear in mind what they're like when eating, sleeping, copulating, defecating, and so on. And then what they're like as haughty marshalers of men or as testy deliverers of disproportionate punishments. How many men were they slaves to not long ago, and for what reasons! And before long they'll be among such men again.[32]

[20] Every person and every thing is benefited by the provisions of universal nature and is benefited precisely at the time it provides them.

[21] The earth loves rain, the sublime air is moved by love,[33] and the universe loves to create everything that's due to happen

---

32. Marcus may be talking about some of his officers during the war, who will soon return to Rome and feel obliged to curry favor again with the powers that be there.

33. These two clauses paraphrase famous lines from a play by Euripides (fragment 890 Nauck[2]). They are also paraphrased by Aristotle, at *Nicomachean Ethics* 1155b2–4: "Euripides says that when the earth is parched it loves rain, and the sublime heaven, when full of rain, loves to fall to earth."

or exist. So I say to the universe: "What you love I love too." Isn't this also the meaning of the phrase "This loves to happen"?[34]

[22] Either you continue to live here in your familiar routine, or you withdraw from life by your own choice, or you die if you've completed your service. Those are the only alternatives, so there's no need to worry.

[23] It should always be clear to you that, as the saying has it, "Yonder field is no different," and that everything is the same here as on a hilltop or the seashore or wherever you like.[35] You'll find[36]

---

34. In order to capture Marcus's point, this is a literal translation of a Greek idiom that would normally be translated "This tends to happen."

35. See 4.3. Changing one's location does not change one's mental habits; you carry the same baggage with you. The only secure location is your inner citadel.

36. The paraphrase of Plato that follows is very loose, so the future tense here probably means "You'll find when you refer to the text" (which he currently did not have with him). But Marcus was going to be disappointed, because the passage of Plato that he refers to has nothing to do with the theme of the entry, the sameness of things. See the next note.

that Plato's words are spot on when he talks of being "penned in a highland sheepfold" and "milking bleating flocks."[37]

[24] What is my command center to me? What am I making it at the moment? What am I currently using it for? Is it devoid of intelligence? Is it disengaged and cut off from society? Is it so attached to and implicated with the body that it's being moved by its movements?

[25] Anyone who absconds from a master is a runaway slave.[38] The law is our master, and so anyone who breaks the law is a runaway slave. So is someone who's moved by grief or anger or fear to resent something, past, present, or future, that has been ordained by the power that directs the universe, which is law,

---

37. Marcus plucks a few words from his memory of Plato's *Theaetetus* 174d–e, but their relevance to the entry is dubious. In the course of a lengthy contrast between the philosopher and various men of the world, Plato says: "When the philosopher hears a tyrant or a king being eulogized, to his mind it's a herdsman being congratulated for a high yield, and rulers are just like keepers of pigs, sheep, or cattle, except that the creature they farm and milk is more intractable and treacherous than other animals; and to his mind a ruler is bound to become just as uncivilized and coarse as a herdsman, because he has no time for culture, and the fortifications he's erected around himself are no different from a highland sheepfold." Perhaps Marcus means that, wherever he finds himself and whatever the sameness of things, he will face the same tension between being a ruler and wanting to be a philosopher.

38. As emperor, Marcus implemented stricter laws against runaway slaves.

the law that assigns our due to each of us. So anyone who's being moved by fear or grief or anger is a runaway slave.

[26] A man ejaculates into a womb and withdraws, and then another cause takes over and fashions a finished baby. What incredible causes! What an incredible result! Next, the child releases some food down its throat, and then another cause takes over and creates sensation, motivation—life, in short, and strength, and a whole lot of other incredible results. Think about these processes, which go on quite invisibly, and see the power behind them. It's the same kind of seeing that enables us to see the power that makes things fall or rise; in neither case do we use our eyes, but the powers are no less apparent for that.[39]

[27] Constantly bear in mind how everything that's happening now happened also in the past. Bear in mind too that it will all happen in the future as well—entire plays with the same kinds of scenes, already familiar to you from your experience or from history books. Visualize them: for example, the whole of Hadrian's court, or that of Philip or Alexander or Croesus.[40] The scenes were all the same, though played by different actors.[41]

---

39. On upward and downward movement, see 9.9. We cannot see the force itself, but only its results.

40. A similar group of people are described as actors on a stage at 9.29, a different group at 5.32. For life as a play ("All the world's a stage"), see also 3.8, 11.1, and especially 12.36.

41. Note that this is "same scenes, different actors" within a single cycle of the universe. It does not deny the absolute identity of each recurrence of the universe as a whole (see Notebook 2, note 42).

[28] Think of anyone who's upset or displeased by anything as resembling a piglet kicking and squealing as it's being sacrificed. That's a good image for the man who, alone in his bed, complains to himself about our "bondage."[42] Consider, too, that although mere compliance with events is inevitable for all creatures, only rational creatures have been granted the ability to comply voluntarily.[43]

[29] As you undertake every particular action, stop and ask yourself whether losing the ability to do it would make you fear death.

[30] The moment you find yourself offended by a flaw in someone, you should stop and consider whether you have similar flaws. Are you, for instance, taking money to be a good thing, or pleasure, or fame, or anything of that kind?[44] This idea will quickly make you forget your anger, because you'll realize that he had no choice in the matter. I mean, what's he to do? If you can,

---

42. The moaning man was presumably ill in bed. Moaning is a sign of someone who refuses to accept his lot in life.

43. We are again reminded of the ending of Cleanthes's prayer, quoted by Seneca (*Letters* 107.11): "Fate *guides* the willing and *pulls* the unwilling." For Epictetus's version of the rest of the prayer, see Notebook 9, note 49. Everyone must yield to his destiny anyway, so it is better to do so willingly.

44. All of which are "indifferents" to a Stoic, neither good nor bad.

however, you should get rid of whatever it is that's leaving him no choice.[45]

[31] When you see Satyron or Eutyches or Hymen, think of a member of Socrates's circle; when you see Eutychion or Silvanus, think of Euphrates; when you see Alciphron, think of Tropaeophorus; when you see Severus, think of Crito or Xenophon;[46] when you see yourself, think of one of the Caesars; and do likewise in every instance. Then the following thought should occur to you: "Where are they now? Nowhere, or no place as such."[47] This will enable you to see human life as smoke and nothingness, especially if you remind yourself that, once something has changed, it will never again exist throughout all eternity. So what is there to worry about? Why isn't it enough for you to spend the little time that you have without discomposing yourself? Look at the material and the opportunity you're shunning. What is it all except practice for the intelligence that

---

45. Since mistakes and wrongdoing are the result of the false belief on the part of the wrongdoer that what he is doing is the right thing for him to do, and will be to his advantage, then in theory he can be corrected by showing him the error of his thinking.

46. See "The People and Gods of *Meditations*," though we do not know who some of these men were.

47. Their souls will have survived in some form after death, but "in no place as such."

has surveyed human life with scientific accuracy?[48] Stay where you are, then, until you've appropriated even what life has to offer you, as a strong stomach appropriates everything it takes in, and as a good blaze appropriates everything that's tossed into it and uses it to produce flame and light.

[32] Let no one truthfully call you duplicitous or bad; let him be a liar if he thinks such things about you. This is entirely up to you. I mean, who's going to stop you being good or simple? Only, you must decide to end your life if you don't have these qualities, because in fact reason has no time for a man who doesn't have them.[49]

[33] Given the material at hand, what's the most sound thing that can be done or said? The point is that, whatever answer one gives to this question, it *can* be done or said, and there's no need to make excuses as though you were being prevented from doing so. You'll never stop deploring your circumstances until it's as pleasant for you to act in keeping with your human nature, whatever material you encounter and are presented with at any

---

48. The theme of the ability of the mind to make good use of whatever "materials" it is presented with is continued in the entry after next.

49. At 6.42, however, in a more generous mood, Marcus allows that everyone plays some part in the divine plan. For loss of rationality as a sufficient reason for suicide, compare the neat saying of Diogenes of Sinope, the founder of Cynicism: "Reason or the rope" (Diogenes Laertius, *Lives of the Eminent Philosophers* 6.24).

time, as it is for a voluptuary to revel in luxury.[50] You must come to regard as enjoyable every action you can take that's proper to your own nature, and there are no conditions that make it impossible for you to take such action.[51] There are some conditions under which a roller is unable to move in the way that's proper to it, and the same goes for water, fire, and anything else that's subject to a nature or a soul that lacks reason. After all, there are many ways in which these things might be hindered or impeded. But rational intelligence has the ability to make its way through every obstruction, thanks to its nature and its will.

Visualize the freedom with which reason moves through everything[52]—as fire moves up, as a stone moves down, as a roller rolls down a slope—and look no farther. For all other obstacles are either due to the body, worthless corpse that it is, or else they cause no damage or harm at all unless the mind believes it so or reason itself permits them to. If this were not the case, anyone

---

50. So a rational man does not just find ways around obstacles, turning them to his advantage, but welcomes them, as part of God's plan, because he knows that nothing external to the mind can do him harm. This helps us to understand Marcus's take on determinism: on the one hand, the obstacles, just like all our circumstances, are predetermined, but on the other hand, that does not mean we do not exercise our rationality and will to make the best of them. This is not complete freedom of will, but it is in keeping with Stoic determinism. See further the Introduction, xlvi–xlviii.

51. So a life in accord with nature is also a pleasant life, though the pleasures are not the coarse ones of the body.

52. This is presumably the mysterious movement of 6.17.

who met with obstruction would immediately be harmed. At any rate, that's what obtains for all other created things: if any one of them experiences anything bad, it is thereby impaired. But in our case, one might even say that a person actually becomes better and more admirable by making correct use of his circumstances. And remember, in general, that nothing harms a man, who is by nature a citizen, that does not harm the city,[53] and that nothing harms the city that does not harm the law. And not a single one of what are generally thought of as calamities harms the law. So anything that does no harm to the law does no harm to either city or citizen.

[34] When someone has been bitten by true principles,[54] even a very brief and hackneyed prompt[55] can serve as a reminder to dispel sorrow and fear. For instance: "The wind scatters the leaves on the ground; such is the race of men."[56] Your children too are mere leaves, as are these people who acclaim you with such loyalty and praise you to the skies or, on the contrary, curse

---

53. This rather dubious proposition (see Notebook 10, note 8) is also asserted at 5.22.

54. The metaphor originated with Plato, at *Symposium* 217e–218a.

55. Marcus recommends such concision also at 4.3. The precepts or axioms that he had stored in his memory or in a handbook had to be brief and simply formulated in order to be effective. See the Introduction, xxxi–xxxii.

56. The quotations in this entry are all snatches from Homer, *Iliad* 6.147–149, though Marcus does not quote them in order. The quotations are accurate, so either he had a copy of the *Iliad* with him or he knew the passage by heart.

you and criticize or mock you behind your back, and as are those too who will perpetuate your fame after your death. For all of them "arrive at springtime," and then the wind blows them down and the "trees put forth" others in their place. A short life is the common lot of all men, and yet you constantly avoid some things and strive for others as if they were going to last forever. In a little while you too will close your eyes, and whoever it is who saw to your burial will soon be mourned by others.

[35] A healthy eye must see all that is visible and not say "No bright colors, please!" That would be a symptom of eye disease. A healthy ear or nose must be ready for everything that can be heard or smelled. A healthy stomach must be similarly ready for everything edible, as a mill is ready for everything it's been made to grind. And so a healthy mind must be ready for everything that happens, but a mind that says, "I hope my children are safe," or, "I'd like to be praised by everyone for everything I do," is like an eye that wants only pale colors or teeth that want only soft foods.

[36] No one is so fortunate that there won't be some people standing by his deathbed who welcome the "dire event." Suppose he was serious and wise: there'll be someone there at the end who'll say to himself: "What a relief to be rid of that stickler at last! Not that he was ever openly hard on us, but I could sense his tacit disapproval."[57] That's what they'd say about such a man,

---

57. The "serious and wise" man is the Stoic sage, so Marcus is saying, in an ironic tone of voice, that there would be some people who would be relieved at the death of even a fully enlightened person.

but what about me? How many more reasons there are for being greatly relieved at being shot of me! When you come to die, then, you'll think of this and your departure will be eased by the realization that "The life I'm leaving is one in which even my associates, on whose behalf I labored, prayed, and brooded so much—even they want to see me gone, and are probably hoping that my death will make life easier for them." So why would anyone want to cling to life and prolong his stay here? But take care that this doesn't make you depart thinking less kindly of them. Continue to be yourself: friendly, benevolent, serene. Then again, don't take your leave from them as though you were being forcibly dragged away. In a good death, the soul slips easily out of the body, and that should be how you withdraw from them too. After all, it was nature that bound and joined you to them, and is now breaking the connection. It's true that I'm being separated from people who are, in a sense, my relatives, but I leave without resisting and without needing to be forced, because death too is one of the things that is in accord with nature.[58]

---

58. Death is a natural process, because of the natural law that everything that is born will die and because death is no more than the separation of the elements that made up the person during life. As a natural process, it should not be described as "bad"; if anything, it is good, because it is good for the whole to recycle its elements and nothing that is good for the whole can be bad for any of its parts (6.54, 10.7, 12.23). Hence Seneca occasionally called dying a duty (e.g., *Letters* 77.19).

[37] Do your best to acquire the habit of asking yourself, every time anyone acts: "What's his intention in doing this?" But start with yourself and examine yourself first.[59]

[38] Remember that the puppet master controlling your strings is the power hidden within you.[60] Without it, there's no activity, no life—no person, one might even say. When you think of it, be sure never to confuse it with the vessel that contains it and the organs that have been molded around it. They're tools, like an adze, with the only difference being that they're conjoined with us. After all, the fact of the matter is that none of these parts is any more use to us without the cause that starts and stops it than a shuttle is without a weaver, a pen without a writer, or a whip without a carter.

---

59. Since actions in the external world were, on a strict Stoic view, invariably matters of indifference, the Stoics judged people by their intentions more than by their actions.

60. The command center, your guardian spirit. Usually, Marcus uses the puppet metaphor to illustrate a negative, that we are tugged around by our impulses rather than subjecting them to our will.

NOTEBOOK 11[1]

[1] The properties of the rational soul: it sees itself; it elucidates itself; it makes of itself whatever it wants to be; it gathers its own fruit (whereas the fruit of plants and the equivalent in animals are gathered by others); it achieves its end at whatever point life may come to a close. Unlike a dance or a play or something like that, where if the performance is cut off at any point, the production as a whole is incomplete, the rational soul fully and completely finishes every one of its projects, whatever scene is being played and at whatever point it's overtaken by death, so

---

1. This notebook falls into two parts. The first part, up to 11.21, is the usual mix of mini-essays interspersed with shorter maxims and reflections; the second part consists of extracts from Marcus's commonplace book.

that it can always say: "I am fulfilled."[2] Moreover, the rational soul traverses the whole universe, surveying the surrounding void and the shape of the world,[3] reaches out into the infinity of time, encompasses and comprehends the periodic regeneration of the universe,[4] and contemplates the fact that those who come after us will see nothing new and those who went before us saw nothing that wasn't already familiar; in fact, in a sense a man of forty, if he has even a modicum of awareness, has seen everything that has happened and will happen, because it's all the same in kind.[5] Love of one's neighbor is also proper to the rational soul, as are honesty, modesty, and the recognition that nothing is more valuable than itself. This is also a property of law, and so there's no difference between right reason and the reason embodied in justice.

---

2. The same metaphor of an incomplete stage production occurs at 3.8 and 12.36. The rational soul, left to its own devices, acts virtuously all the time, so that at any instant its integrity is complete. Enlightenment is timeless. If an aspirant has perfected her reason, it is not made more perfect by living longer.

3. It would see the universe as a stationary sphere, according to the Stoics, surrounded by void and made up of concentric layers of fire, air, water, and earth. See also 9.32 for the soul's ability to encompass the entire universe.

4. On the periodic regeneration of the universe by fire, see Notebook 2, note 42.

5. It is typical of Marcus's pessimistic streak that he follows a glorious account of the soul's abilities with the idea that, after all, it can only see the same old things again and again.

[2] You'll think little of the delights of song (or dance or pancratium)[6] if you divide the melody up into its individual notes and ask yourself, in the case of each note, whether you'd be carried away by it[7]—something you'd be reluctant to admit. The same goes for dance too, if by an equivalent process you break it down into its separate movements or postures, and do the same for pancratium as well. In general, then, with the exception of virtue and virtuous action, remember to go straight to the component parts of everything;[8] dividing things up like this will encourage you to think little of them. Then apply this procedure to your whole life as well.

[3] How admirable is the soul that's ready at every moment in case it's time for it to be released from the body—ready, that is to say, for extinction, dispersal, or survival. But this state of

---

6. Pancratium was a kind of violent combination of boxing and wrestling. Its closest equivalent today is mixed martial arts, which is sometimes called "modern pancratium."

7. This is a very poor argument. Obviously, a song is more than the sum of its individual notes, and Marcus comes close to acknowledging that a whole is greater than its parts at 3.2 and 12.30. But, in a sense, that is precisely Marcus's point: the previous entry suggested that only virtue was complete and perfect in itself at every moment. The somewhat silly method of analysis in this entry, then, is designed to show the incompleteness and imperfection of things other than virtue.

8. Virtue is the only thing that is truly good (while all other good things are indifferents), so there is no point in trying to analyze it with a view to disdaining it.

preparedness must stem from a specific decision,[9] not from mere contrariness;[10] it must follow careful and serious thought, and you mustn't make a big production out of it, otherwise you won't be able to convince others too.

[4] Have I done something that contributes to the common good? Then I've been benefited.[11] Always keep this truth readily available for consultation, and under no circumstances stop doing so.

[5] What's your job? Being good. How else can that come about except with the help of the philosophical theories that

---

9. Typical factors that might influence such a decision are clearly laid out in 3.1.

10. At this point, our manuscripts of Marcus's text add "like the Christians," and their "contrariness" is explained by editors as their otherworldliness and their consequent willingness to die as martyrs when they could survive by recanting. Scholars are about evenly divided on whether the reference to the Christians originated with Marcus or a later commentator on the text. In my opinion, it did not originate with Marcus, because it does not fit grammatically into the sentence that Marcus wrote. It reads just like a marginal gloss that has slipped into the text, and its appropriateness here is far from clear. On the whole question, including Marcus's policies as emperor toward Christians, see P. Brunt, "Marcus Aurelius and the Christians," in *Studies in Stoicism* (Oxford University Press, 2013), 407–441.

11. See 5.16 for some argument supporting this proposition. It is also the meaning of the idea that the soul gathers its own fruit (11.1).

explain the nature of the universe and the specific nature of human beings?

[6] Tragedies were originally produced as reminders of what happens in the world—to call attention to the fact that these events are natural and that what you find attractive in the theater should not cause you sorrow on the larger stage of life. You get to see that these things are inevitable and that even those who call out "O Cithaeron!" put up with them.[12] Some of the playwrights' lines are useful as well, this one in particular:[13] "If I and my sons are neglected by the gods, this too has its reason," but not forgetting "It's pointless to let mere things make you angry," and "Lives are harvested like ripe ears of wheat," and so on.

12. The reference is to line 1391 of Sophocles's *King Oedipus*. Oedipus has realized that he was exposed as a child on Mount Cithaeron, and that therefore it must be he who murdered his father and married his mother and brought divine punishment down on Thebes. So tragedy is supposed also to teach us not to complain at our misfortunes.

13. The three quotations that follow also occur at 7.38–41; see the notes there.

After tragedy, productions of Old Comedy were introduced.[14] These plays were marked by an educational freedom of speech, and contained useful reminders, enhanced by their very outspokenness, of the evils of arrogance. (Something like this was also Diogenes's reason for adopting this feature of comedy.)[15] Next consider Middle Comedy[16] and then ask yourself why New

---

14. We still today use the terms "Old Comedy," "Middle Comedy," and "New Comedy." Old Comedy was the first phase of Athenian comic playwriting, down to about 400 BCE, of which we have a number of complete plays from the pen of Aristophanes of Athens and a number of greater or lesser fragments from both him and his contemporaries. The most striking aspect of Old Comedy was its freedom. The playwrights made up their own plots (unlike tragedians, who usually based their plays on familiar myths and legends) and set them in contemporary times or fantasy-land. They also enjoyed considerable freedom of expression: they slandered their contemporaries and made free use of slang, vulgarities, and obscene and lavatorial jokes. Marcus's description of Old Comedy as educational was not only a common view, in general, but also that of the playwrights themselves.

15. Both the speech and behavior of Diogenes of Sinope, the founder of Cynicism, were famously outrageous. Many anecdotes about him are preserved by Diogenes Laertius, in the sixth book of his *Lives of the Eminent Philosophers*. Marcus too likes occasionally to employ Cynic outspokenness: 4.48, 5.12, 5.28, 6.13, 8.24, 8.37, 9.29, 9.36, 10.19.

16. This clause suggests that in this entry Marcus is drafting in note form an essay he wants to write later. The topic interested him because of the moral lessons that dramatists were trying to communicate.

Comedy[17] was introduced, which marked the gradual decline of comedy into clever imitation of life.[18] It's generally recognized that playwrights from these later periods also came up with some useful sentiments,[19] but, taking the enterprise as a whole, what were the authors of poetry and plays of this kind hoping to achieve?

[7] How clearly it strikes you that there's no other role you could play in life that would be as well suited to the practice of philosophy as the one you now find yourself playing![20]

[8] A branch cut off from its neighboring branch is, of course, cut off from the whole tree. In the same way, a human being who's cut off from even one other human being has fallen away from

---

17. Middle Comedy was a somewhat tamer form of Old Comedy. New Comedy was tamer still, consisting largely of soap-operatic, light comedies; the protagonists were recognizable types (clever slaves, grumpy old men, etc.), portrayed with great skill.

18. The work of Menander of Athens, the chief surviving representative of New Comedy, was considered so realistic that one critic, Alexander of Byzantium (third century CE) exclaimed: "O Menander! O Life! Which of you imitated the other?"

19. They, and especially the New Comedians, invented many pithy, gnomic sayings that could be lifted from their context and repeated as a form of popular wisdom. Menander's "one-liners" were especially memorable, such as "He whom the gods love dies young," and "We live not as we wish to, but as we can."

20. The entry shows Marcus in an unusually positive mood about his work (see also 8.9); it gives him plenty of opportunities to practice virtue. It is directly contradicted by what he says at 8.1: "your role militates against your ever becoming a philosopher."

society as a whole. In the case of a branch, it's someone else who does the cutting, but the separation of a man from his neighbor is his own doing, the result of hating him and spurning him, and he fails to realize that he has at the same time severed himself from the community as a whole. But we've been granted a great boon by Zeus, the founder of human society: we can graft ourselves back on to our neighbor and again become component parts of the whole.[21] However, the more often such separation happens, the harder it becomes for the part that withdraws to be reunited and restored to its position. Generally speaking, a branch that has grown along with the tree from the beginning, animated by the same breath[22] and standing fast with it, is quite different from one that has been grafted back on after being cut off, whatever gardeners say.[23] You can share a trunk with them without sharing their principles.

---

21. See also 8.34 for Marcus's awe at this wonderful gift of God. But in this entry he is more pessimistic, or realistic, claiming at the end that once split off, you can never fully reunite again. See also 3.6: "Once you've turned your attention elsewhere and turned aside from your path, it will be impossible for you to give your undivided attention and the highest honor to the good that is peculiarly your own."

22. At least from the time of the philosopher Anaxagoras of Clazomenae in the mid-fifth century BCE, it had been believed that plants breathe. The particular kind of breathing they did was called "transpiration" (see 6.16).

23. This is not true. A few years after being grafted, a grafted tree is as indistinguishably healthy as one that has never been grafted. The gardeners were right.

[9] With right reason as your guide, those who stand in your way will be unable to deflect you from a sound course of action, but you mustn't let them force you to renounce your kindness to them. You must be equally on your guard in both respects. You need to make sure not only that your decisions and actions are unshakable, but also that you continue to be gentle toward those who try to thwart you or cause you grief in some other way. Treating them harshly would be no less a sign of weakness than abandoning a course of action and being cowed into giving up. After all, a man who sets himself at odds with others, when they are by nature relatives and friends, is just as much a deserter as a runaway soldier.

[10] "Under no circumstances is nature inferior to art";[24] in fact, the arts imitate the natures of things. If this is true, human skill and ingenuity can never outdo universal nature, which is the most perfect and comprehensive of all natures. Now, all the arts and crafts create the lower in the interests of the higher,[25] and so, therefore, does universal nature as well. Hence the origin of

---

24. This is probably a quotation because it scans as a line of verse, but the source is unknown.

25. A cobbler, for instance, makes shoes (lower) for a human being (higher).

justice,[26] and justice in its turn is the basis for all the other virtues.[27] For justice is lost if we treat indifferent things as important, or are easily deceived, or are liable to falter and change our minds.[28]

---

26. The suggestion seems to be that justice imitates nature in subordinating the lower to the higher, the inferior to the superior. Marcus might have in mind Plato's idea, as expressed in *Republic*, that a just soul is one in which the superior part, the rational soul, is master of the two inferior parts, the passionate and appetitive souls. But he might only be saying that justice preserves the natural hierarchy of things. This presumably obtains for human society, as well, so that Marcus's conception of justice is not democratic: see also Notebook 1, note 26; Notebook 5, note 51; and Notebook 8, note 9, on Marcus's politics.

27. The Stoics believed in the unity or inter-entailment of virtues, but Zeno, the founder of the school, had made wisdom the primary virtue, not justice. But, if they are inter-entailing, then it does not really matter which virtue one starts with. Marcus gives the honor to justice also at 5.34, 9.1, and 12.24. His emphasis on justice is on a par with, and due to, his emphasis on doing good to others and, as emperor, to the Roman community as a whole. In typical Stoic fashion, there is also a self-regarding aspect: in doing good to others, one is benefited oneself (e.g., 7.74) and gains the tranquility that comes from fulfilling one's human nature (7.28, 8.26).

28. This is Marcus's sketch of how justice relates to the other primary virtues, which are wisdom, modesty, and courage (as at 5.12, whereas the list at 3.6 substitutes honesty for wisdom). Taking indifferents to be important shows a lack of wisdom; being easily led astray shows a lack of modesty, because a modest person should know his place and his mind; and faltering shows a lack of courage.

[11] Your peace of mind is disturbed by the pursuit or avoidance of things, but these things don't force themselves on you; in a sense, you force yourself on them. At any rate, if your faculty of judgment doesn't trouble itself with them, they too will remain inert,[29] and evidently you'll be neither pursuing nor avoiding them.

[12] When the luminous sphere of the soul neither reaches out for anything external nor shrinks back inside itself, it suffers no inflation or collapse, and shines with a light that enables it to see the truth of all things and the truth within itself.[30]

[13] Is someone going to despise me? That's his concern. Mine is to see that I don't do or say anything that deserves to be despised. Is someone going to hate me? That's his concern. I'll remain kind and benevolent to everyone. I'll also be ready to show this particular person what he's overlooking, not harshly and not as a way of flaunting my patience, but genuinely and tactfully, or in the spirit displayed by the famous Phocion, unless

---

29. If you suspend judgment about things, they cannot disturb your peace of mind, because all such disturbances stem from your opinion or judgment about things, not from the things themselves. On the "inertness" of things, see also 4.3 (end) and the further references there.

30. See 8.41 for the soul as a sphere. Marcus places a lot of weight on the metaphor here, almost as if it were more than a metaphor. A sphere was held to be the most perfect solid, and therefore suitable for divine entities.

he was pretending.³¹ That's how one should be on the inside, visible to the gods as a man who isn't the kind to be moved to anger by anything or to voice bitter complaints. After all, how could anything bad happen to you if what you're currently doing is proper to your nature, and if you accept whatever it is that's currently finding favor with universal nature, as one who devotes his energy to the realization of anything, whatever it may be, that contributes to the common good?

[14] Although they despise one another, they behave obsequiously to one another; although they want to overshadow one another, they grovel to one another.³²

[15] How corrupt and devious is a man who says, "I've decided to be straight with you"! What are you up to, man? There's no need for this preamble; the facts will speak for themselves. Your face should be an open book. Honesty is immediately clear from the tone of voice and the look in the eyes, just as a loved one

---

31. Phocion's execution after a mock trial by the Athenian people in 318 became likened to the trial of Socrates, and among his famous last words were the ones Marcus is thinking of. When asked if he had a message for his son, he said: "Tell him not to hold a grudge against the Athenians." It is unclear why Marcus might think he was being insincere.

32. This is probably a snapshot of some of Marcus's courtiers, since the behavior he sketches is found in courts throughout the ages.

immediately knows everything from his lovers' glances.[33] In short, a good, sincere person must resemble a stinking goatherd, in the sense that anyone who comes close to him should, willy-nilly, immediately be aware what he's like. But calculated sincerity is like a concealed blade. There's nothing more shameful than wolf-friendship;[34] there's nothing more important than avoiding it. The eyes of a man who's good, sincere, and kind reveal what he's like, and you can't mistake him.

[16] Make your life the best you can. The ability to do this lies in the soul, provided that it treats indifferents as indifferent. The way to see their unimportance is to examine each of them by dividing it into its parts, as well as seeing it as a whole, and by remembering that none of them forces itself upon us and produces an opinion about itself in us. No, they remain inert,[35] and it's we who generate judgments about them and, so to speak, inscribe these judgments in ourselves, even though it's possible for us not to do so, and it's also possible for us immediately to

---

33. Both "loved one" and "lovers" are masculine, so Marcus is envisaging homosexual love. The terms were familiar from the Greek pederastic tradition: the loved one is a teenager, and his lovers are older, in their twenties or more. At this stage, he would have more than one prospective lover (hence Marcus's plural), but he would eventually honor just one of them with his compliance.

34. The feigned friendship of a wolf, as in one of Aesop's fables, in which a wolf gets a shepherd to trust it so much that he leaves it in charge of his flock.

35. See Notebook 4, note 12.

erase any such judgment that we've inscribed unconsciously. It's worth bearing in mind also that you won't have to pay attention to these indifferents for very long before your life will have come to an end. Besides, can they make life difficult for you? If they're in accord with nature, enjoy them[36] and they won't make any difficulties. If they're not in accord with nature, try to find those that are in accord with your nature and focus on them, even if they strike others as dishonorable. After all, everyone is forgiven for seeking his own good.[37]

[17] Whatever you encounter in life, consider its origin, what it's made of, what it's changing into, what it will be like after it's changed, and that it will come to no harm as a result of changing.

[18] First,[38] remember the various kinds of relationship I have with them: we were born to help one another; from

---

36. Strictly, of course, a Stoic should not enjoy any indifferents; but those that are in accord with nature—such as health and education—are "preferred" indifferents, allowed to play a minor role in a Stoic's life.

37. A rash assertion, even if meant only as a pleasantry, because it threatens to undermine the concept of punishment. Since on Stoic doctrine everyone seeks their own good, even criminals think they are doing what is best for them. Perhaps we can forgive them ourselves, but society, one might think, must still punish them. Perhaps, like Plato in his later years, Marcus would have preferred criminals to be cured rather than punished.

38. In this entry, Marcus runs through nine principles to follow in dealing with his fellow men, and especially when he finds them hard to bear and succumbs to his tendency to lose his temper with them. There is a great deal of overlap with other entries in the book, perhaps especially 9.42.

another point of view, I was born to be their custodian, as a ram is of a flock or a bull of a herd; then again, from a fundamental perspective—that is, starting from the principle that, if we rule out atoms, it's nature that directs the universe—it follows that lower beings exist for the good of higher beings, and that higher beings exist for the good of one another.[39]

Second, remember how they behave while eating, while reclining on their couches, and so on, and most importantly how their principles leave them no choice, and yet how they preen themselves on what they do.

Third, remember that there's no need to complain if what they do is right, and that if it's not right, they're acting involuntarily and out of ignorance. For no soul is voluntarily deprived of the truth,[40] and by the same token no soul is voluntarily deprived of the ability to deal equitably with anything according to its worth. At any rate, people don't like to be called unjust,

---

39. In what sense is the *scala naturae* a deduction or inference from a rationally ordered universe? Probably just because it is, to Marcus's mind, one of the fundamental orderings of the world. Since it is, he claims, the *nature* of the lower to serve the higher (see, e.g., 5.16, 5.30, 7.55), then, in a world ordered by universal nature, this natural phenomenon will be operative. Again, we see Marcus's undemocratic spirit.

40. This idea is attributed to Plato at 7.63.

discourteous, and avaricious, or, in general, to be thought of as likely to wrong their neighbors.[41]

Fourth, remember that you yourself often do wrong and are no better than them. Even if you refrain from certain kinds of transgressions, you still have the capacity to commit them, and it's just cowardice or a concern for your reputation or some other equally bad reason that keeps you from committing the same kind of wrongs as them.

Fifth, remember that you can't be quite sure that they *are* doing wrong, because many actions serve some further purpose.[42] Generally speaking, a great deal of experience is needed before one can confidently express an opinion about what someone else is doing.

Sixth, when you're too angry or impatient, remember that human life is fleeting and before long all of us will have been laid to rest.

Seventh, remember that it's not people's actions that disturb our peace of mind (because their actions are the business of their own command centers), but our own opinions of their actions. At any rate, eliminate the judgment that they're doing something hurtful, and be willing to let go of it, and anger comes to an end. How does this elimination take place? By realizing that what's

---

41. For Marcus, this is evidence of the soul's struggle to be the soul of a good man. Even the fools still know, in their heart of hearts, that justice is better for them than injustice, whatever the evidence to the contrary. This is one of the main themes of Plato's *Gorgias*.

42. So the end might justify the means, in Marcus's view.

hurting you involves no shame for you. For if it were not the case that only shameful things are bad,[43] it would necessarily follow that you too often do wrong, and are a robber and a thoroughly shifty character.

Eighth, remember that we suffer more from getting angry and upset about such things than we do from the things themselves that are making us angry and upset.

Ninth, remember that kindness is irresistible if it's genuine, not phony or feigned. After all, what can even the most abusive person in the world do to you if you keep on being kind to him and, if the opportunity arises, gently offer him advice and take the time to show him the error of his ways right when he's trying to do you harm? "No, my child.[44] This is not what we were born for. It's not I who am harmed, child, but you." Gently, and in general terms, show him that this is how things are—that not even bees act like this, nor any other gregarious creatures. But you must be sure to do this with affection and in a calm state of mind, not insincerely or in a reproachful tone of voice. Don't talk to him like a schoolmaster or with the aim of impressing any bystanders

---

43. The only things that are bad are personal imperfections or vices. These are shameful, because it is entirely up to us not to have imperfections and not to behave viciously.

44. This sounds patronizing, but it is precisely Marcus's point that, rather than responding with anger, one should adopt a kind of avuncular attitude, which affords some detachment and perspective. Besides, it is less patronizing in Greek, as a not uncommon way an older man could address someone much younger.

there might be, but address your words to him as you would if he were alone, even if there happen to be bystanders.

Bear these nine points in mind as though they were gifts you'd been given by the Muses,[45] and begin at last to be a human being, while you still live.

It's not just getting angry with people that you should avoid, but flattering them as well. Neither flattery nor anger contribute to the common good and both have harmful consequences. Every time you lose your temper, make sure you have readily available the thought that anger is not a manly quality[46] and that in fact gentleness and calmness are more manly, qua more human. Fortitude, strength, and courage are attributes of a calm and gentle man, not one who's irascible and easily offended, because the closer a man is to being impassive, the closer he is also to being a man of power.[47] Anger is just as much a sign of

---

45. Marcus does not mean any precise correspondence between the nine Muses and his nine precepts.

46. As it was commonly held to be. The topics of anger and anger management were of great interest to philosophers and essayists throughout antiquity. In addition to this long entry of Marcus's, we have two survivors in Plutarch's essay *On the Avoidance of Anger* and Seneca's lengthy treatise *On Anger*. The Aristotelian school held that anger was a kind of energy that could support the work of the rational mind; Marcus and the Stoics very strongly disagreed.

47. Because he is not distracted and thereby weakened by his feelings. One of the advantages of controlling unnecessary passions is that your energy is not wasted and can be put to better uses.

weakness as suffering is, because both an angry man and a man in pain have surrendered to a wound they've incurred.

If you feel so inclined, you could also accept a tenth gift, from the Leader of the Muses,[48] the proposition that it's insane to expect bad men not to do wrong, because that would be a case of desiring the impossible. But to concede that they wrong others, while expecting them not to wrong you, would be unfeeling and tyrannical.[49]

[19] There are four ways above all in which the command center can take a turn for the worse. You should be on your guard against them at every moment, and whenever you detect them, they must be eradicated by your telling yourself, as appropriate for each case: "This thought is unnecessary," or "This thought tends to dissolve society's bonds," or "What you're about to say does not come from yourself" (which you should regard one of the most monstrous things that can happen). And the fourth aberration for which you need to take yourself to task is when the more divine part of you is overcome by and succumbs to the less worthwhile, mortal part, or in other words the body and the body's rough and smooth motions.[50]

---

48. A title of Apollo, the god of, among other things, culture. The Muses dance, while he plays his lyre.

49. It would be tyrannical, I suppose, because, like a tyrant, Marcus would be setting himself above the law—the law that bad people do wrong.

50. Smooth bodily motions are pleasant; rough ones, unpleasant.

[20] Your spirit and the entirety of the fiery element in you naturally tend upward,[51] but, in obedience to the universal scheme, they're held back down here, confined in the compound of your body. All that is earthy and all that is liquid in you tend downward, but they're raised up and held in a position that's unnatural to them.[52] So even the elements obey the universe and stay in place when they've been assigned a post, until the signal is given authorizing their dissolution from there again. Isn't it terrible, then, that your mind is the only part of you that's disobedient and discontented with its proper place? Yet it's under no constraint; the only influences on it are in keeping with its nature. Nevertheless, it refuses to comply and takes the opposite course, in the sense that any movement toward unjust and self-indulgent behavior or toward anger, sorrow, and fear is precisely a severance of oneself from nature. And every time the command center resents something that happens to it, that too is it abandoning its proper place, because it was made for reverence and piety toward the gods just as much as it was made for justice.[53]

---

51. See also 9.9. Spirit (*pneuma*) is a mixture of fire and air, the two most refined elements, and so moves upward.

52. We walk erect, and the circulation of the blood in the body, for instance, defies gravity. At the macrocosmic level, some Stoics explained that the world remained stable at the center of the universe because of the equilibrium between the two downward-tending elements and the two upward-tending elements.

53. For the impiety of such resentment, see, for example, 5.8 and 9.1. Reverence toward the gods entails accepting every experience that they have allotted you, knowing it to be for the best.

In fact, reverence and piety toward the gods are forms of equity, and are therefore more venerable than justice.[54]

[21] "Unless a man has one and the same aim throughout his life, he cannot be one and the same person throughout his life."[55] This saying is incomplete as it stands, without an addition that specifies the kind of aim he must have. What most people take to be good, in some sense of the word, varies, but they agree in certain cases, those where the common good is concerned, and so a man should aim for the common good of society. Anyone who directs all his impulses toward this goal will act with perfect consistency and hence always be the same man.

---

54. Equity is obedience to unwritten laws—to the principles of natural law and right—and may even therefore sometimes take precedence over written laws, obedience to which is justice. This dilemma lies at the heart of Sophocles's famous play *Antigone*. As Marcus implies here, unwritten law was commonly considered divine in origin—the will of the gods—and to apply universally, whereas man-made law varied from society to society.

55. The source of the quotation is unknown. Could it express one of Marcus's own thoughts? It sounds like the kind of thing he might have thought, and inner and outer consistency were considered important by both Socrates and the Stoics.

[22] Think of the hill-dwelling mouse and the house mouse, and the agitation and trepidation of the latter.[56]

[23] Socrates used to call the opinions of the masses "Lamias"—bogeys to frighten children.[57]

[24] During their festivals, the Spartans would put seats in the shade for their visitors, while they themselves sat anywhere.[58]

[25] Remember the reason Socrates gave Perdiccas for refusing to come to his court: "I want to avoid dying the worst

---

56. One of Aesop's fables. The stuck-up town mouse, appalled by the roughness of his country cousin's life, invites him to town for the good life. But the town has so many dangers—dogs and so on—that the town mouse lives in constant fear and trepidation, and the country mouse realizes that he is better off living a simple life in the mountains. The entry resonates with Marcus's suggestion to himself that he "live like a highlander" (10.15).

57. Lamia was a legendary queen, living in North Africa. After all her children died, she ordered the killing of everyone else's children as well. Hence she became a bogey for children: "If you're naughty, Lamia will come and get you!" At *Crito* 46c, Plato has Socrates say that they should resist the attempt of the Athenian majority to get them to change their minds by frightening them with bogeys such as imprisonment and execution, but that is as close as we get in extant Socratic works to this story (see also Plato, *Phaedo* 77e). Marcus probably got it from Epictetus, *Discourses* 2.1.15, although Epictetus uses Plato's word for "bogey," not "Lamia." Like Socrates in *Crito*, Marcus is thinking primarily of fear of death.

58. The lesson for Marcus is that it is possible to be both tough and courteous.

of deaths"—that is, without having been able to repay a favor he has received.[59]

[26] In the Epicurean writings, it's suggested that one should constantly remind oneself of someone from earlier times who practiced virtue.[60]

[27] The followers of Pythagoras[61] recommend that we should start the day by looking up at the sky to remind ourselves of entities that remain constant and unchanging as they accomplish their work, and of their orderliness and purity, and their nakedness, given that nothing veils a star.

[28] Think of how Socrates behaved, dressed only in his underclothes, when Xanthippe left the house with his cloak,

---

59. It was Archelaus of Macedon (reigned 413–399 BCE), not his predecessor Perdiccas, who invited Socrates to come and tutor his children and be the resident court philosopher. Socrates refused because (he claimed) it would be an unequal bargain: he could never adequately repay Archelaus's kindness. A number of other luminaries, including the Athenian playwright Euripides, did accept Archelaus's invitation. The story first occurs in Aristotle, *The Art of Rhetoric* 1398a, but without the description of dying in debt as "the worst of deaths."

60. This is Epicurus, fragment 210 Usener. Seneca (*Letters* 11.8–9 and 25.5) attributes it specifically to Epicurus, not vaguely to Epicureans. The idea was that an Epicurean should constantly be asking himself: "What would Epicurus think of what I'm doing?" But a Stoic too was expected to have interiorized his teacher's voice; perhaps this in part explains the exercise Marcus undertook in writing Notebook 1.

61. See also 7.47 on the benefits of observing the heavenly bodies.

and of what he said to his friends who retired in embarrassment when they saw how he was dressed.[62]

[29] Where literacy is concerned, you can't be a leader until you've been a follower. The principle is even more relevant to life.[63]

[30] "Born a slave, you have no share in reason."[64]

[31] "And the heart within me laughed."[65]

[32] "They will rail at virtue, addressing it with harsh words."[66]

---

62. Marcus is our only source for this story, so we have no way of knowing what Socrates did and said, though it is likely that he poured scorn on his visitors' conventional attitude. There are a number of stories, all apocryphal, on the theme of Socrates's domestic troubles with his wife, Xanthippe.

63. Solon, the Athenian poet and statesman of the early sixth century BCE, and one of the Seven Sages of Greece, had said: "Learn to obey before you command" (Diogenes Laertius, *Lives of the Eminent Philosophers* 1.60). The saying became proverbial.

64. This is a line from an unknown play. Like many slave-owning societies, the ancient Greeks and Romans stifled their consciences with the thought that slaves were subhuman, though this was the kind of conventional idea that might be challenged by playwrights and philosophers. The lesson Marcus wants us to learn is that to act without reason is to act like a slave, obedient to external commands rather that one's own guardian spirit.

65. This is from Homer, *Odyssey* 9.413 (Odysseus laughing at his triumph over the blinded Cyclops Polyphemus), but Marcus's reasons for quoting it are obscure.

66. An inexact memory—or a deliberate alteration—of Hesiod, *Works and Days* 186, which has "parents" where Marcus has "virtue."

[33] It's crazy to look for figs in winter, and it's no less crazy for someone to look for his child when that's no longer possible.[67]

[34] Epictetus used to say that when you kiss your child you should silently tell it: "Tomorrow you will die." "But that's an inauspicious thing to say." "No," he says, "it's not at all inauspicious, but it expresses a natural process. Otherwise, it would be inauspicious to talk of wheat being harvested."[68]

[35] Green grape, ripe grape, dried grape: every phase a change, not into nonexistence but simply into a state that didn't exist at the time.[69]

[36] No one can rob you of your faculty of volition.[70]

[37] He said that we must discover an art of assent[71] and, in the sphere of impulses, must pay careful attention to make sure

67. A paraphrase of Epictetus, *Discourses* 3.24.86–87. All the following entries, up to 11.38, are paraphrases of Epictetus. The point of this one is that there is no point in mourning a lost child or a childless marriage.

68. Based on Epictetus, *Discourses* 3.24.88–89. For similar expressions (that are bound to appear unfeeling to us), see 8.49, 9.40 (end), 10.34, and 10.35. For death as a natural process, see, for example, 2.12.

69. Based loosely on Epictetus, *Discourses* 3.24.91–92. For the thought, see 4.36, 5.13, and 7.25.

70. A direct quotation of Epictetus, *Discourses* 3.22.105. For the thought, see, for example, 8.48 and 12.14.

71. On the Stoic concept of assent, see the Introduction, xlviii–xlix. This entry is Epictetus, fragment 27 Schenkl.

that every impulse is conditional,[72] contributes to the common good, and is commensurate with the value of what it's an impulse for. He also said that we should avoid desire altogether and bring aversion to bear on nothing unless it's up to us.[73]

[38] "So," he said, "the contest is for no trivial prize; what's at stake is madness or sanity."[74]

[39] Socrates used to say: "What do you want to have? The souls of rational or irrational creatures?" "Rational creatures." "What kind of rational creatures? Sound or corrupt?" "Sound ones." "Then why don't you make that your aim?" "Because we already have them." "Then why are you fighting and quarrelling?"[75]

---

72. See 6.50 and 8.7, and for the Stoic doctrine of proceeding "with reservation," see Notebook 4, note 2.

73. See 8.7 on the opposites, desire and aversion: a rational nature makes good progress when it "restricts its desires and aversions to things that it's possible for human beings to attain or avoid." There is no point in desiring to have or not to have something that it is not within our power to attain or avoid.

74. Epictetus, fragment 28 Schenkl. Presumably, the madman here is one who refuses to accept the life that he has been allotted, while the sane man accepts every experience.

75. The aggressive questioning is typically Socratic, but there is nothing like this entry in the extant Socratic literature (chiefly Plato and the relevant works of Xenophon), and the style is equally reminiscent of Epictetus's *Discourses*, which is probably where Marcus got this from; it is Epictetus, fragment 28a Schenkl. Marcus liked it because of its implication that (as he often puts it) rational beings are made for one another, made to help one another, and made to work together in the community of rational beings.

NOTEBOOK 12

[1] All those things that you pray to get in the due course of time—you can have them now if you don't deny yourself them. What you have to do is leave the past behind, entrust the future to providence, and, focusing on the present alone, direct it toward piety and justice: piety, so that you embrace your lot,[1] seeing that it was nature that brought you to it and it to you; and justice, so that you speak the truth without restriction or equivocation, and act in conformity with law and equity. Don't let anything stand in your way, such as someone else's iniquity, or what people think or say, or, of course, the sensations of your casing, the body

---

1. A good man's duty and pleasure lie in accepting all that is allotted to him: see especially 4.33, 5.8, 6.44, 10.1, 10.6. Since it is the gods who gave him his lot (e.g., 12.11), it is a matter of religious duty too. There is a marked spiritual tone to this concluding notebook, and Marcus seems to be rehearsing many of the fundamental themes of earlier notebooks in preparation for his death.

(they are the concern of the body, which is what experiences them). So, whenever it may be that you find yourself close to departure, if you relinquish everything else and honor only your command center, the god within you, and if what you fear isn't that you're going to stop living, but that you never started living in accord with nature, you'll be a man worthy of the universe that gave you birth and you'll no longer be a stranger in your own country, surprised by what happens day by day as though it were unexpected,[2] and dependent on one person after another.[3]

[2] God sees all command centers stripped of their material vessels, their worthless casings, because he has only his intelligence with which to make contact, and the only contact he has is with what has flowed and been channeled from him to them. If you too get into the habit of doing likewise, you'll rid yourself of many distractions. After all, is it at all likely that a man who's blind to the flesh that encases him will waste his time admiring clothing, houses, or any such trappings and stage sets?

---

2. The image of the stranger recurs at 2.17, 4.29, 4.46, and 12.13. Marcus's frequent reflections on the sameness of things is a way for him to stop being surprised by things. Surprise is a sign of not serenely accepting every experience in your life as assigned to you by the gods and of ignorance about the way things are.

3. The entry is a summary of how to prepare for a peaceful death. Such summaries are even more prominent in this twelfth notebook than in the others, and it is plausible to suggest that it was the last notebook Marcus wrote and that he knew his death was imminent. By the same token, living in the present moment is more a feature of this book than others.

[3] There are three things of which you are composed: body, spirit, mind. Of these, the first two belong to you insofar as it's your job to care for them, but, properly speaking, only the third is really yours. It follows that if you separate from yourself—that is, from your mind—all that other people do or say, all that you yourself have done or said, all that disturbs your peace of mind as looming in the future, all the properties of the body that encases you or of the spirit that is embedded in it that are not subject to your volition, and all that swirls around you, driven by the whirlwind of the external world, until your mind has been released from the bonds of fate, and lives purified, untrammeled, on its own, doing what is right, willingly accepting everything that happens, and speaking the truth—if, I say, you detach your command center from what has become attached to it as a result of its being attracted by bodily feelings, and from all that is to come and all that has gone, and make yourself, in Empedocles's words, "a rounded sphere, rejoicing in encircling solitude," and train yourself to live the only life you have, that is in the present moment,[4] you'll be able to pass what remains of your life, up until your death, with a mind that is tranquil in itself, kind to others, and at peace with your guardian spirit.[5]

[4] I've often found it astonishing how everyone loves himself more than anyone else, and yet attaches less importance to his own opinion of himself than he does to what others think

---

4. The present moment is all one has: 2.14.

5. The long, periodic sentence that occupies most of this entry is something of a tour de force.

of him. At any rate, if a god or a wise mentor came and told him not to entertain any ideas or thoughts without simultaneously also voicing them for others to hear, he wouldn't be able to stand it for even one day. This proves that we place more weight on our neighbors' opinions of us than we do on our own.

[5] How come the gods organized everything so well, and with the good of human beings in mind, and yet overlooked this one thing: that some men—perfectly good men, who did a lot of business, so to speak, with the gods and whose pious behavior and observance of ritual brought them into a particularly close relationship with them—why is it that, once they die, they're not born again, but are completely and utterly extinguished?[6] If this is in fact the case,[7] you can be sure that, if it was meant to be

---

6. The playwright Euripides had one of his characters take the gods to task for precisely this omission: *Heracles* 655–672.

7. Marcus's uncertainty is perhaps due to a divergence in Stoic doctrine. Some held that all humans—good, bad, and indifferent—suffer exactly the same fate at death: that is, the return of their four constituent elements to their natural locations in the universe, while others held that the souls of all humans, but especially of good ones, survive death for a greater or lesser period of time (though they do not seem to have specified quite where or how the soul continued—but see Notebook 12, note 30). This latter view might have dovetailed with a belief in reincarnation, but no Stoic took that route. Nevertheless, Marcus was tempted by a belief in reincarnation or some form of personal survival: see Notebook 5, note 48, and Notebook 8, note 56.

otherwise, the gods would have made it otherwise.[8] I mean, if it was right for them to survive, the possibility would have existed for them to survive, and if it was in accord with nature, nature would have seen to it. So from the fact that it isn't so (assuming it is a fact), you can rest assured that it wasn't meant to be so. Even you can see that just by raising the question you're asking God to justify the way he has arranged things. But we wouldn't be asking the gods to explain themselves if they weren't perfectly good and just, and it follows from this that, in their organization of the universe, they wouldn't have allowed anything to be unjustly and unreasonably neglected.

[6] Keep practicing even when there seems no hope of success. The left hand is useless for most things because of lack of practice, but it grips a horse's reins more firmly than the right hand because it's had plenty of practice.[9]

[7] Think about what kind of person you must be, in body and soul, when overtaken by death.[10] Contemplate the shortness of life, the yawning gulf of time behind and before you, the frailty of all matter.

---

8. A common form of argument for Marcus: given that the gods are good and benevolent, then the way things are is the way they ought to be. In logic, this is called the "is-ought fallacy."

9. Left-handedness was rare and discouraged in ancient Rome (the Latin for "left" is *sinister*). When riding, the right hand was needed for a switch or for weaponry.

10. The idea that philosophy is a "preparation for death" was powerfully argued by Plato in *Phaedo*.

[8] Observe the causes of things stripped of their casing:[11] the purpose of every action; what pain is; what pleasure is; what death is; what fame is; who's responsible for a person's distraction; how no one is obstructed by anyone else; that "Everything is as you take it to be."[12]

[9] In applying your principles, you must be a pancratiast rather than a gladiator.[13] A gladiator lays his sword aside and takes it up, but a pancratiast is never without his hands and all he has to do is make fists of them.

[10] See things as they truly are by dividing them into matter, cause, and purpose.

[11] Look how much freedom a man has not to do anything except what will meet with God's approval, and to accept everything that God allots to him as being in accordance with his nature!

[12] The gods are not to be blamed, because they do no wrong, either deliberately or involuntarily. Nor are men to be blamed, because they do no wrong that isn't involuntary. So don't blame anyone.[14]

---

11. Everything consists of cause and matter (e.g., 7.29), so to strip a cause of its "casing" is to focus on it in itself, without the matter.

12. See 2.15 for the quotation.

13. See Notebook 11, note 6, on pancratium.

14. Compare 8.17 and 10.4. See also Notebook 11, note 37, for a possible downside to Marcus's thinking.

[13] How ridiculous—and how profoundly a stranger to the world—is someone who's surprised by anything that happens to him in the course of his life![15]

[14] Either the necessity of fate and an unalterable arrangement, or a propitiable providence, or an anarchic, random jumble.[16] If an unalterable necessity, what's the point of resistance? If a providence that's open to propitiation, make yourself worthy of help from the gods.[17] If an undirected jumble, be thankful that in such a maelstrom you have within yourself a mind that provides direction. If the flood should carry you off, it can take only your body and your spirit; it won't carry off your mind.

[15] The light of a lamp shines and continues to shed light until it's extinguished. Will the truth, justice, and moderation in you be extinguished before their time?[18]

---

15. On surprise, see Notebook 12, note 2.

16. The first alternative is the Stoic one; the second is popular belief; the third is the Epicurean position.

17. On propitiation and prayer, see 5.7, 6.23, 6.44, and especially 9.40. As a Stoic, Marcus did not believe that one's destiny could be altered by propitiation of the powers that be. He seems rather to think that prayer should be used to bolster one's own efforts; that is the kind of help from the gods that a Stoic might want.

18. That is, before death, but the entry is ambiguous. Marcus might either be encouraging himself to keep going right up to the moment of his death, or he might be reflecting on the awful fact, acknowledged in 3.1, that senility might rob him of his powers before death. On balance, the former seems more likely.

[16] When you get the impression that someone has done wrong, ask yourself: "How can I actually know that it was a wrong?"[19] And if it really was a wrong, remember that he was thereby passing sentence on himself,[20] and that his wrongdoing was therefore the equivalent of poking himself in the eye. Remember that anyone who wants a bad man not to do wrong is like someone wanting a fig tree not to produce sap, or babies not to cry, or horses not to neigh, or anything else not to do what it's bound to do. I mean, if that's his disposition, what else can he do? So, if you feel strongly about it, change his disposition for the better.[21]

[17] If it's not right, don't do it; if it's not the truth, don't say it. Your impulses should be under your control.

[18] Always try to see what prompts a thought in you, and expose it for what it is by identifying separately its cause, its matter, its purpose, and the span of time within which it will necessarily cease to exist.[22]

[19] It's time to appreciate that you have within yourself something that's stronger and more divine than the things that

---

19. See 11.18, point 5 (and also 9.38), for this charitable view of wrongdoing, a marked blunting of Marcus's attitude elsewhere.

20. See 9.4: he condemned himself to be punished, because in doing wrong he wronged himself.

21. "Either instruct them or put up with them" (8.59).

22. See Notebook 4, note 39, and Notebook 9, note 26: Marcus thinks that this extra insight can somehow be gained by seeing a thing for what it is.

generate the passions in you and in general tug you around like a puppet. What's in my mind right now? Might it be fear? Mistrust? Desire? Something else like that?

[20] First, never act without plan and purpose. Second, set your sights on no other goal but the common good.

[21] Remember that in a short while you won't exist at all, and the same goes for everything that you now see and all the people now alive. It's a fact of nature that everything changes, deteriorates, and perishes, so that the next generation of things can come into existence.

[22] Remember that "Everything is as you take it to be"[23]—and that what you take things to be is up to you. Anytime you want to, then, you can eliminate the belief and, like a sailor after rounding a headland, you'll find calm water, perfect stillness, and an unruffled bay.[24]

[23] Nothing bad happens to any action at all that comes to an end at the appropriate time, just because it has come to an end, and nothing bad happens either to the person who performed the action, just because it has come to an end. By the same token, then, the totality of all actions, which is a life, suffers nothing

---

23. The famous saying of Monimus of Syracuse: see Notebook 2, note 43.

24. This has been an important thread in the book (see, e.g., 7.14). Marcus consoles himself with the thought that what he thinks is up to him and that he can therefore eliminate negativity by refusing to entertain thoughts that have negative consequences. Entry 12.25 repeats the point.

bad, provided that it comes to a timely end, just because it has come to an end, and nothing bad happens either to the person who brings this sequence of actions to a timely end.[25] The time and the cutoff point of a life are given by nature, sometimes by one's own nature, as when one dies of old age, but in general by universal nature, which by the changing of its parts keeps the whole universe forever young and fresh.[26] Now, anything that benefits the universe is bound to be altogether fine and timely, and it therefore follows that the ending of life isn't bad for the individual (nor is it shameful, because it's not a matter that's subject to his volition and it doesn't have a negative effect on the common good), but actually good, because it's timely for the universe, benefits it, and is compatible with it. And so it's the

---

25. The argument is similar to those of 2.17 (end) and 9.21, with the new addition of the "timely end" factor. The concept of an appropriate time to die allows suicide (under extreme circumstances), while accommodating the timing considered appropriate by the gods. See Notebook 3, note 3, for the Stoic view of suicide.

26. See, for example, 6.15, 7.25. Because in the previous sentence Marcus seems to accommodate suicide, and because the only alternative offered in this sentence is a natural death (e.g., of old age), he must be counting suicide as a death caused by universal nature. The argument would perhaps go something like this: circumstances beyond my control have made it impossible for me to "live in accord with nature"; these circumstances were allotted me by universal nature; therefore, my death was wanted by universal nature, and I really have no choice in the matter.

man who takes the same path as God and takes God's objectives as his own who is "taken" by God.[27]

[24] You must always have the following three points of doctrine readily available. First, as regards your actions, that you should never act without purpose or do anything that differs from what Justice itself would have done; and as regards external events,[28] that they occur either by chance or by providential design, and that you shouldn't find fault with chance or censure providence. Second, what kind of creature each of us is from embryo formation until soul formation,[29] and from soul formation until soul surrender: what we're made of and what we're dissolved into. Third, that if you were suddenly in a position to look down from on high on human life in all its chaotic diversity, you'd find it singularly unimpressive, because you'd simultaneously be seeing

---

27. Or "possessed," as we would say.

28. All events are either one's own doing or externally caused (see, e.g., 12.32), so this is an exhaustive division and Marcus is talking about how to think of anything that happens in one's life.

29. Since soul was regarded as airy, its formation was considered to start when a baby drew its first breath. The soul is thus the animating factor in animate creatures, as well as the mind of rational creatures. While in the womb, an embryo was considered by the Stoics to have a plant-like existence; the shock of leaving the warmth of the womb and entering the world was what caused a baby to take its first breath and draw air in to permeate every fiber of its body and form its soul. In human animals, this soul eventually becomes a rational soul, the "command center." Only humans have rationality and are rationally motivated; they share the other basic soul functions (the five senses, speech, and reproduction) with animals.

all around yourself the great company of beings who populate the air and the aether;[30] and that however many times you were raised aloft what you'd see would never change; it would just be the same old ephemeral things. And these are what we deluded beings consider important!

[25] Rid your mind of the thought and you're safe and sound. Is anyone stopping you from getting rid of it?

[26] When you find something hard to bear, there are things you're forgetting.[31] First, that everything happens in compliance with universal nature. Second, that the wrong being done to you is someone else's concern. Third, that everything that happens has always happened and will always happen, and is happening right now all over the world. Fourth, that the relationship between any one person and the rest of the human race is particularly close, not in the sense that they share blood and seed, but because they have intelligence in common. Fifth, that every person's mind is a god and is an emanation of the divine. Sixth, that nothing really

---

30. The "aether," the fiery highest region of the heavens, was considered to be the location of the stars, which embodied the orderliness of the universe, as opposed to the "diversity" of human life. It is not clear what Marcus means by the beings who populate the air; if he does not simply mean the sun, moon, and planets, he might be nodding toward the popular belief (followed by some Stoics) that this is where good and bad spirits live and/or the disembodied souls of the recently dead (see 4.21).

31. What follows is a compressed aide-mémoire, summarizing many of the main points of the book and especially of Notebook 2. See also 4.3 for another such summary.

belongs to anyone, but his child, his body, and his very soul have come from heaven. Seventh, that "Everything is as you take it to be."[32] Eighth, that the present moment is all the life that anyone has, and all the life that he loses.[33]

[27] Continually remind yourself of all those highly dissatisfied men who pushed the boundaries of fortune in one way or another—in terms of fame, perhaps, or catastrophes met with, or enemies made. And then ask yourself: where is it all now? Smoke and ashes, the stuff of stories or not even that. Then all cases of the following kind are to be considered: Fabius Catullinus on his country estate, Lusius Lupus in his gardens, Stertinius at Baiae, Tiberius on Capri, Velius Rufus, and in short the combination of an *idée fixe* and presumption.[34] How worthless was all that expenditure of effort! How much more philosophical it is for someone to use the materials he's been given to make himself a man of justice and moderation, a follower of the gods—and to do so in an unaffected way, because there's no one more unbearable than a man who, in his delusion, boasts about his lack of vanity.

---

32. Monimus's famous saying again: see Notebook 2, note 43.

33. This idea is spelled out in 2.14.

34. We know of all or most of these people but lack detail, except in the case of Tiberius. Somehow, to Marcus's mind, they are all examples of men who retired from public life (Baiae was a seaside resort town in Campania) to pursue an obsession. What seems most likely to me is that they were obsessed with redesigning their estates, including the erection of magnificent buildings (as we know Tiberius did on Capri): they had retired, but still wanted to draw attention to themselves.

[28] When people ask, "But have you ever seen the gods? What makes you so certain of their existence that you revere them like this?" I reply, first, that they are in fact visible[35] and, second, that I haven't seen my soul either, but I'm still in awe of it. So that's how it is with the gods as well: every time I experience their power, I ascertain that they exist[36] and I revere them.

[29] Salvation in life comes from always seeing everything as it really is, by distinguishing its matter and its cause, and from wholeheartedly doing right and speaking truth. Then all that's left is to enjoy a life of linking one good deed with another, leaving not the slightest gap between them.[37]

[30] Sunlight is single, even if it's divided by walls, hills, and countless other things. The substance created things share is single, even if it's divided among countless bodies, each with

----

35. The sun and the moon were regarded as gods, as were the "fixed" stars, and they are all visible. But Marcus may also mean "visible in dreams and in epiphanies" and "visible in their effects" (as Socrates had urged in Xenophon, *Memorabilia* 4.3).

36. See 10.26: "In neither case do we use our eyes, but the powers are no less apparent for that." Marcus is implying an argument from design, pioneered by Socrates: the universe appears to show intelligent design in that it has been made in ways that seem deliberately to favor human beings; therefore, there must be a designer.

37. See 6.7: "Find joy and rest in one thing alone: in moving from one socially useful act to another, while remaining mindful of God." This is the kind of pleasure Marcus could allow himself; see Notebook 5, note 17. But, in general, Marcus hardly touches on the question of whether the good life is pleasant.

its own individual properties. Soul is single, even if it's divided among countless natures and individual entities. Intelligent soul is single, even if it seems to be disunited. Now, even though all the parts of the things I've mentioned—their airy and their material parts, for instance—are insensate and have no feeling of kinship, nevertheless they are held together by the principle of unity and the attraction of like to like. But mind has the property of tending of its own accord toward what is like it and uniting with it, keeping the feeling of community intact.[38]

[31] What is that you want? To stay alive—which is to say, to be conscious, to be moved by impulses, to wax and then to wane, to use your voice, to think? Do any of these things really strike you as desirable? But if none of them is worth taking seriously, make it your goal to follow reason and God. However, valuing the things I mentioned militates against doing this, and so does resenting the fact that death will deprive you of them.

[32] What a tiny fraction of the infinite gulf of time has been allotted to each of us! It's very quickly swallowed up by eternity. What a tiny fraction of the entirety of substance! What a tiny fraction of the entirety of soul! What a tiny clod of earth you crawl on, compared to the earth as a whole! Bear all this in mind and think nothing important except acting in compliance with

---

38. As rational beings, we are aware of our kinship with other rational beings—other human beings and the gods. We are all the inhabitants of the Great City of the universe, where we share a common life.

your nature and being acted upon by whatever universal nature brings your way.[39]

[33] What use is your command center making of itself? This is the absolutely critical issue. Everything else, whether or not it's subject to your volition, is just carcasses and smoke.

[34] The best way to wake up to the insignificance of death is to realize that even hedonists belittle it.[40]

[35] A man for whom only what is appropriate is good, to whom it is irrelevant whether the number of actions he carries out as dictated by right reason is greater or smaller, and to whom it makes no difference whether the time he has to see the world is longer or shorter—to such a man even death is nothing to fear.

[36] My friend, you were a citizen of this great city.[41] Does it really matter to you whether it was for five years or a hundred? The laws of the city[42] apply equally to all. What is there to fear, then, since it's not a tyrant or a corrupt judge who's banishing you from the city, but the same nature that brought you into it in

---

39. Marcus seems to be preparing himself for death in this and the following entries, culminating in the very last entry of the book.

40. Marcus is thinking of the Epicureans, but his dismissal of them as "hedonists" does not do justice to their nuanced teachings about pleasure. Epicurus famously said, "Death is nothing to us," on the grounds that nothing can be called good or bad unless sense experience is involved, and death is the absence of sense experience (*Letter to Menoeceus* 124).

41. The Great City that is the universe.

42. That is, natural law, including the law that everyone will die, sooner or later.

the first place? It's as though a praetor,[43] after engaging an actor for a comedy,[44] were to dismiss him mid-show.[45] "But I haven't played all five acts, only three!" Quite so, but in life the play might be over after three acts. The ending is decided by the one who was formerly responsible for your constitution and is now responsible for your disintegration. You have no responsibility for either. Go serenely, then, matching the serenity of the god who is dismissing you.[46]

---

43. In Marcus's Rome, it was one of the praetors' jobs to provide theatrical amusements for the public.

44. In 3.8, the actor is a tragic actor.

45. Marcus returns to the idea that life is a play (3.8, 9.29, 10.27, 11.1, 12.2). On the unimportance of the length of a life, see especially 2.14.

46. On dying with serenity, see also 2.3, 2.17, 4.48. This is a moving and fitting final entry, prefaced by the thoughts on death in the immediately preceding entries. It is hard not to think that, at the time of writing, Marcus knew that he was dying.

THE PEOPLE AND GODS
OF *MEDITATIONS*

Further information about the most eminent of the people and gods mentioned by Marcus can be found in either *The Oxford Classical Dictionary* or *The Cambridge Dictionary of Classical Civilization*.

AGRIPPA (8.31) Marcus Vipsanius Agrippa (late 60s–12 BCE) was the emperor Augustus's most trusted friend and virtually his co-emperor at certain points. He was instrumental in many of Augustus's military victories both before and after he became emperor.

ALCIPHRON (10.31) Otherwise unknown.

ALEXANDER (king of Macedon) (3.3, 6.24, 8.3, 9.29, 10.27) Alexander III of Macedon (reigned 336–323 BCE), known as "the Great," is most famous for conquering the Persian empire between

334 and his death in 323 BCE. He became a very important figure in Roman cultural history.

ALEXANDER (language teacher) (1.10) A Homeric scholar from Phrygia (Asia Minor), very famous in his day. Aelius Aristides, who was also taught by Alexander, gives us a sketch of the man in *Oration 32, Funeral Address in Honor of Alexander*.

ALEXANDER (Platonist) (1.12) A philosopher and rhetorician from Cilicia and Marcus's Greek-language secretary while he was based in Pannonia during the Marcomannic Wars.

ANTONINUS PIUS (1.16, 4.33, 6.30, 8.25) The emperor before Marcus (reigned 138–161) and the subject of the eulogies at 1.16 and 6.30. He became the adopted son of the emperor Hadrian in 138 and, at Hadrian's behest, adopted both Marcus and Lucius Verus as his sons, who were therefore marked out as future co-emperors.

APOLLONIUS (1.8, 1.17) A Stoic philosopher from Chalcedon (in Asia Minor, close to Byzantium). Antoninus Pius arranged for him to be one of Marcus's teachers and brought him to Rome. The belletrist Lucian of Samosata says that Apollonius set out for Rome like Jason setting out on his quest for the Golden Fleece (*Demonax* 31)—like the cat that got the cream, as we would say.

ARCHIMEDES (6.47) The mathematician and inventor Archimedes of Syracuse (third century BCE) is still a household name today.

ARIUS DIDYMUS (8.31) A Stoic, originally from Alexandria in Egypt; Augustus's court philosopher.

ASCLEPIUS (5.8, 6.43) The god of healing.

ATHENODOTUS (1.13) One of the teachers of Fronto.

AUGUSTUS (4.33, 8.5, 8.31) The first emperor of Rome, ruling from 27 BCE until 14 CE.

BACCHEIUS (1.6) Possibly a Platonist.

BENEDICTA (1.17) Probably a slave of Marcus's household.

BRUTUS (1.14) Marcus Junius Brutus was the son-in-law of Marcus Porcius Cato, and, famously, one of the assassins of Julius Caesar. Brutus killed himself after his forces had been defeated (in the civil war that followed the assassination) by Octavian, the future emperor Augustus.

CAEDICIANUS (4.50) Unknown.

CAESAR, JULIUS (8.3) Marcus mentions him for his military exploits, which included the conquest of almost all France and winning the civil war against Pompey. He then became the virtual sole ruler of Rome, until his assassination by Brutus and others in 44 BCE.

CAESO (4.33) A hero of the early Roman Republic.

CAMILLUS (4.33) Marcus Furius Camillus saved Rome after the Celtic sack of the city in 390 BCE and was considered the Second Founder of the City.

CATO (grandfather) (4.33) Marcus Porcius Cato (234–149 BCE) was a famously principled statesman.

CATO (grandson) (1.14) The Stoic Marcus Porcius Cato killed himself rather than accept the rule of Julius Caesar. His biography was written by Thrasea.

CATULUS (1.13) Cinna Catulus was a Stoic philosopher, but little is known of him apart from the fact that Marcus attended his lectures.

CECROPS (4.33) A legendary early king of Athens who rivaled Theseus in Athenian legend as the founder of the city.

CELER (8.25) Probably Caninius Celer, one of young Marcus's rhetoric teachers and previously the secretary of the emperor Hadrian.

CHABRIAS (8.37) Unknown freedman.

CHARAX (8.25) Unknown.

CHRYSIPPUS (6.42, 7.19) Born in Cilicia but lived and worked in Athens, where he became head of the Stoa in 232 BCE and died in 207. He was chiefly responsible for developing the theoretical aspects of Stoicism: "If there had been no Chrysippus, there would have been no Stoa" (Diogenes Laertius, *Lives of the Eminent Philosophers* 7.183). He is the only one of the early Stoics that Marcus mentions. Zeno of Citium was the first head of the school, and then Cleanthes of Assos.

CLOTHO (4.34) One of the three Fates. See Notebook 3, note 15, and Notebook 10, note 7.

CRATES (6.13) A Cynic philosopher (360s–280s BCE), originally from Thebes but resident in Athens; he was one of the teachers of Zeno of Citium, the founder of the Stoic school.

CRITO (10.31) An Athenian friend of Socrates after whom Plato named one of his dialogues.

CROESUS (10.27) King of Lydia in Asia Minor in the mid-sixth century BCE. Despite his legendary wealth and power, he was overthrown by Cyrus the Great, who was in the process of creating the mighty Persian empire, which was eventually overthrown two hundred years later by Alexander the Great.

DEMETRIUS (Platonist) (8.25) Possibly Demetrius of Alexandria, who flourished in the second century.

DEMETRIUS OF PHALERUM (9.29) An Aristotelian philosopher who was the sole ruler of Athens, under Macedonian protection, from 317 to 307 BCE.

DEMOCRITUS (3.3) Late fifth / early fourth century BCE, originally from Abdera. He was a prolific writer, famous especially as a scientist (he co-invented atomic theory) and moral philosopher. Many fragments of and testimonia to his work survive, and although Marcus refers to him only once by name, he is quoted at 4.24 and 7.31 as well.

DENTATUS (4.33) Manius Curius Dentatus defeated the Greek king Pyrrhus in 275 BCE and prevented him from sacking Rome and establishing a Greek kingdom in southern Italy.

DIOGENES (8.3, 11.6) From Sinope on the Black Sea, the famously ascetic and outrageously independent founder of Cynicism. The contrast in 8.3 between him and Alexander was traditional, because they were contemporaries, and there is a famous anecdote about their meeting, contrasting the worldly power of Alexander with the noble detachment of Diogenes (Plutarch, *Life of Alexander* 14).

DIOGNETUS (1.6) Marcus's art teacher, but clearly also his mentor more generally.

DION (1.14) Marcus was probably thinking of Dion of Syracuse, who died as an opponent of the tyranny of Dionysius II—but because he was aiming to set himself up as a tyrant, he is not a very good example of what Marcus is trying to illustrate.

DIOTIMUS (8.25, 8.37) Unknown freedman.

DOMITIUS AFER (1.13) A teacher of Athenodotus.

EMPEDOCLES (12.3) From Acragas in Sicily, a philosopher-mystic of the fifth century BCE.

EPICTETUS (1.7, 4.41, 7.19, 11.34, 11.36) Although these are the only explicit mentions of Epictetus, Marcus often draws on his work without mentioning his name. Epictetus was born into slavery around the middle of the first century CE and became the personal assistant of a man called Epaphroditus, who worked as a secretary in the imperial court in Rome. When he was freed, he set himself up as a teacher of Stoicism (his teacher had been Musonius Rufus) first in Rome, and then in Nicopolis on the west coast of Greece. He died c. 135. He wrote nothing himself, but a pupil, Arrian, compiled from lecture notes his *Discourses*, of which we have four complete books and some fragments.

EPICURUS (7.64, 9.41) Epicurus was born on the Aegean island of Samos, but toward the end of the fourth century BCE he started a philosophical school in Athens, a few years before Zeno of Citium instigated Stoicism there. Both Epicureanism and Stoicism became very influential throughout the Hellenistic and Roman periods, and a great rivalry existed between them.

EPITYNCHANUS (8.25) A freedman of Marcus, whose name fortuitously occurs in a surviving inscription (*Corpus Inscriptionum Latinarum* VI 166), but otherwise unknown.

EUDAEMON (8.25) Possibly Gaius Valerius Eudaemon, a distinguished governor of Egypt under Antoninus Pius.

EUDOXUS (6.47) A polymath of the fourth century BCE who revolutionized Greek astronomy.

EUPHRATES (10.31) A Stoic philosopher of the first and early second century CE.

EUTYCHES (10.31) Unknown, but apparently a contemporary of Marcus, and a Platonist.

EUTYCHION (10.31) Unknown, but apparently a Stoic philosopher contemporary with Marcus.

FABIUS (4.50) Unknown, but possibly the same man as the next entry.

FABIUS CATULLINUS (12.27) Unknown.

FAUSTINA (8.25) Marcus's aunt and the wife of Antoninus Pius, the emperor before Marcus and his father by adoption (1.16). Marcus's wife, mentioned but not named in 1.17 and elsewhere, was also called Faustina; she was one of the daughters of Antoninus Pius.

FRONTO (1.11) Marcus Cornelius Fronto, from Numidia (in Roman North Africa), was appointed by Antoninus Pius as one of Marcus's teachers in rhetoric, and they remained friends even after Marcus deserted rhetoric for philosophy. Fronto was the most famous orator in Latin in the world. Some of the letters written between him and Marcus have survived and reveal a warm and close relationship. These letters are available in English translation in C. Haines, *Fronto: Correspondence*, 2 vols. (Harvard University Press, 1919, 1920).

HADRIAN (4.33, 8.5, 8.25, 8.37, 10.27) Publius Aelius Hadrianus, emperor of Rome from 117 to 138.

HELVIDIUS PRISCUS (1.14) Thrasea's son-in-law, executed under Vespasian, and whose same-named son was executed under Domitian.

HERACLITUS (3.3, 4.46, 6.42, 6.47, 8.3) The famously obscure philosopher from Ephesus (western Asia Minor), c. 500 BCE. See Notebook 2, note 49, and Notebook 4, notes 15 and 68, for summaries of his influence on Stoicism.

HIPPARCHUS (6.47) From Nicaea in Bithynia, but spent most of his life on Rhodes; an astronomer of the second century BCE.

HIPPOCRATES (3.3) From the island of Cos, lived in the fifth century BCE and was the most famous doctor from the ancient world, until Galen. He was thought to have initiated the more scientific study of medicine (though of course scarcely scientific by our standards), but the great majority of the works ascribed to him in what we call the Hippocratic Corpus became attached to his name as the founder of the school rather than because they were actually written by him.

HYMEN (10.31) Unknown, but apparently a contemporary of Marcus, and a Platonist.

JULIANUS (4.50) Unknown.

LEPIDUS (4.50) Unknown.

LUCILLA (8.25) Marcus's mother, Domitia Lucilla (died late 150s), also mentioned, though not by name, at 1.3. She was one of the wealthiest women in Rome, and her salon was a center for the appreciation of Greek culture.

LUSIUS LUPUS (12.27) Unknown.

MAECENAS (8.31) Gaius Maecenas was a trusted friend of the emperor Augustus who wielded power by means of his immense wealth and his known closeness to the emperor rather than by holding political office. He was Augustus's lieutenant for civic work, Agrippa's for military work.

MARCIANUS (1.6) An otherwise unknown philosophy lecturer.

MAXIMUS (1.15, 1.16, 1.17, 8.25) Claudius Maximus, a senator and proconsular governor of the province of Africa, active under Antoninus Pius. Marcus presents him as a possessor of all the fundamental Stoic virtues.

MENIPPUS (6.47) From Gadara in Syria, a Cynic philosopher of the third century BCE. He specialized in satirical, moralizing tracts.

MONIMUS (2.15) Monimus of Syracuse (fourth century BCE), primarily a Cynic philosopher. The saying attributed to him at 2.15 recurs at 12.8, 12.22, and 12.26.

MUSES (11.18) The nine Muses were the patron goddesses of the arts, sciences, and culture in general; hence a "museum" in our day is a place to admire and learn about culture.

NERO (3.16) Nero Claudius Caesar, emperor of Rome from 54 to 68 CE; he had already, by Marcus's time, become a byword for self-indulgence and cruelty, after an initial period as a good ruler.

NESTOR (4.50) Nestor of Pylos was the wise and famously long-lived elder who accompanied the Greek forces at the legendary siege of Troy, as told by Homer in his *Iliad*.

ORIGANION (6.47) Unknown freedman.

PANTHEA (8.37) From Smyrna in western Asia Minor, she was the mistress of Lucius Verus, Marcus's brother (by adoption) and co-emperor. She was the subject of a flattering written portrait by the belletrist Lucian of Samosata in his *Imagines*.

PERDICCAS (11.25) Perdiccas II, king of Macedon c. 450–413. Marcus is mistaken in thinking that it was he who invited Socrates to take up residence in the Macedonian court.

PERGAMUS (8.37) Unknown freedman.

PHALARIS (3.16) Tyrant of Acragas (Agrigento) in Sicily in the first half of the sixth century BCE; his cruelty was legendary.

PHILIP (9.29, 10.27) King of Macedon 360–336 BCE, the second of his name, who was responsible for the rise of Macedon to superpower status; his son, Alexander the Great, continued his work in this respect.

PHILISTION (6.47) Unknown freedman.

PHOCION (11.13) An Athenian general and politician in the fourth century BCE. Not much is known about his life, except its famous ending, alluded to by Marcus, but he became known, especially in Roman times, as Phocion the Good for his integrity, or at least his consistency in championing the rights of the wealthy over the common people.

PHOEBUS (6.47) Unknown freedman.

PLATO (7.48, 9.29, 10.23) Athenian philosopher, c. 429–347 BCE. Along with Xenophon, Plato is chiefly responsible, through his writings, for our knowledge of the work and character of Socrates.

POMPEY (3.3, 8.3, 8.31) In an astonishing career, Pompey the Great (106–48 BCE) annexed much of the Near East for Rome and cleared the Mediterranean of pirates, but his ambitions led him into civil war with Julius Caesar, in the course of which he died and his family was eliminated.

PYTHAGORAS (6.47, 11.27) Originally from the island of Samos, a thinker of the sixth century BCE. His work seems to have centered on arithmology, the effect of music on the emotions, the doctrine of reincarnation, and special dietary rules; but as a result of the systematizing efforts of his later followers he was credited with more or less the entirety of the complex of hard science, pure and applied mathematics, and mysticism that is the Pythagorean tradition.

RUSTICUS (1.7, 1.17) Quintus Junius Rusticus, a statesman who lived by Stoic principles, was instrumental in encouraging Marcus to take philosophy seriously. Marcus awarded him his second consulate in 162, and he was Prefect of the City from 163 until his death in 168.

SATYRON (10.31) Unknown, but apparently a contemporary of Marcus, and a Platonist.

SCIPIO (4.33) Publius Cornelius Scipio Africanus (236–183 BCE) defeated Hannibal in the Second Punic War and was therefore considered one of the saviors of Rome.

SECUNDA (8.25) Wife of Maximus (1.15).

SEVERUS (1.14, 10.31) Gnaeus Claudius Severus Arabianus, father of the husband of Marcus's eldest daughter (name unknown), an Aristotelian and evidently a political philosopher as well as being active in Roman politics.

SEXTUS (1.9) The Stoic philosopher Sextus of Chaeronea was the nephew of the famous essayist and biographer Plutarch of Chaeronea (who was himself a Platonist and wrote treatises against Stoicism). Sextus taught in Rome, and Marcus attended his lectures even while he was emperor (Philostratus, *Lives of the Sophists* 557).

SILVANUS (10.31) Unknown, but apparently a Stoic philosopher contemporary with Marcus.

SOCRATES (1.16, 3.3, 3.6, 6.47, 7.19, 7.66, 8.3, 11.23, 11.25, 11.28, 11.39) Marcus's philosophical ideal and considered by the Stoics to be a sage, such as they all aspired to be. Socrates was an Athenian philosopher of the fifth century BCE, famously the teacher of (among many others) Plato and Xenophon. He is credited with having drawn a line under the kind of proto-scientific philosophy that preceded him and having initiated what we think of as modern philosophy, especially with his interest in rational inquiry, ethics, and metaphysics. Marcus's Socrates is a Stoicized version, with his interests limited to virtue and care of oneself.

STERTINIUS (12.27) The Stertinii were a fairly eminent family in Rome; it is not certain which of them Marcus is referring to, but it is probably Quintus Stertinius, an exceedingly wealthy doctor from the first century CE, who spent some of his wealth embellishing the city of Naples and, apparently, nearby Baiae.

TANDASIS (1.6) A philosophy teacher, otherwise unknown.

TELAUGES (7.66) Possibly the Telauges who was the only son of the philosopher-mystic Pythagoras, if the fictional dialogue referred to at 7.66 featured an aged Telauges and a young Socrates.

THEODOTUS (1.17) Probably a slave of Marcus's imperial household.

THEOPHRASTUS (2.10) From Eresus on the island of Lesbos, he succeeded Aristotle as head of the Lyceum in 322 and died in the early 280s. Few of his many works survive, but he continued and developed Aristotle's polymathic enterprise in every sphere, from logic to botany.

THRASEA (1.14) Publius Clodius Thrasea Paetus, a Stoic, was forced to commit suicide by the emperor Nero.

TIBERIUS (12.27) Tiberius Julius Caesar Augustus was the second emperor of Rome (reigned 14–37) but spent the last decade of his life in semiretirement on the island of Capri. There are substantial remains on the island of his magnificent villa.

TRAJAN (4.32) Marcus Ulpius Traianus, emperor 98–117.

TROPAEOPHORUS (10.31) Otherwise unknown.

VELIUS RUFUS (12.27) Unknown, but a correspondent of Fronto (Haines II.87).

VERUS (brother of Marcus) (8.37; see also 1.17) Lucius Aelius Aurelius Commodus was Marcus's brother by adoption and his junior co-ruler from 161 until his death in 169. On becoming joint emperor, he dropped "Commodus" from his name in favor of Marcus's "Verus." He had a reputation as a libertine, but has probably suffered by being contrasted with sober and serious Marcus.

VERUS (father of Marcus) (8.25; see also 1.2) Marcus's father, Marcus Annius Verus, died too young (c. 130) to achieve the eminence for which he seemed destined by his family's close connections to the imperial throne and by his marriage to the wealthy Domitia Lucilla.

VERUS (grandfather of Marcus) (1.1) Marcus Annius Verus was so favored by successive emperors, especially Hadrian, that he held the consulate three times and was Prefect of the City from 121 to 137. He adopted Marcus c. 130 on the death of his son, Marcus's father.

VESPASIAN (4.32) Titus Flavius Vespasianus, emperor 69–79, and founder of the Flavian dynasty, which was succeeded by the Nerva–Antonine dynasty, of which Marcus was the penultimate emperor.

VOLESUS (4.33) We cannot precisely identify him, but from the context he must have been a hero of the early Roman Republic.

XANTHIPPE (11.28) Wife of Socrates.

XENOCRATES (6.13) From Chalcedon, the third head of the Platonic Academy, from 339 until 314.

XENOPHON (10.31) Athenian historian and polymath whose works featuring Socrates are, along with Plato's, our most important source of information about the Athenian philosopher.

ZEUS (4.23, 5.6, 5.7, 5.8, 11.8) Zeus was the Greek sky god—and hence the all-encompassing king of gods and men. As chief deity of the Greek pantheon, the Stoics naturally identified him with the divine principle in the universe as they saw it.

TEXTUAL NOTES

I have translated the second edition (1987) of the Teubner text of J. Dalfen, *Marcus Aurelius Antoninus: Ad Se Ipsum Libri XII*, except where indicated below. Marcus's Greek is often very crabbed and difficult—he was, after all, just writing notes to himself—and he uses a lot of abstract terms and compound verbs, the meanings of which are not always clear, especially when a word occurs nowhere else in extant literature. It is worth remembering that Greek was not Marcus's first or primary language; it was the language of philosophy, and that is why he chose to use it for his philosophical soliloquies.

As a consequence of all this, the medieval scribes who copied the book introduced many errors and further infelicities. But the book seems to have been scarcely transcribed in any case; our texts of *Meditations* are based very largely on only two manuscripts, and one of those is no longer available for consultation. This is a very thin manuscript tradition. Compare, for instance, the fifty-nine manuscripts for the *Handbook* of Marcus's predecessor, Epictetus.

As a result of all these factors, there is hardly a single entry in the book that does not still—long after all the easily spotted scribal mistakes have been eliminated—contain at least one or two contested words or phrases. It is the job of an editor such as Dalfen to try to pierce through the received text back to what Marcus originally wrote, but I am not alone in thinking that his judgment was not always sound. The Budé text, when it is published, will probably be better, but at the moment only the first notebook has been edited, with an extensive and excellent introduction to the whole of *Meditations*: P. Hadot and C. Luna (eds.), *Marc Aurèle: Écrits pour lui-même*, Vol. 1 (Les Belles Lettres, 1998). We have been promised the completion of the work for a long time.

1.3.1: Reading ἐφεκτικὸν with MS T.

1.12: Reading διὰ τοιούτου τρόπου with MS T and the Suda.

1.14.3: Retaining the phrase bracketed by Dalfen.

1.14.3: Reading ὁμαλὲς with Corais.

1.15.4: Retaining the MSS σχετλίως.

1.16.9: Retaining the clause bracketed by Dalfen.

1.16.20: Deleting ἐκτός with Rendall.

1.16.25: Reading μεμετρημένον with MSS AT.

1.16.25: Reading ἀνθρώπου . . . δεδορκότος with Casaubon and MS AT.

1.16.29: Retaining the MSS reading λελογίσθαι.

1.17.5: Omitting τοιῶνδέ τινων with Morus.

1.17.11: Retaining ἐπινοίαις with the MSS.

1.17.21: Reading ὥσπερ χρήσῃ with Lofft.

1.17.22: Reading συγγραφὰς with Farquharson.

2.1.1: Retaining τοῦτο with the MSS.

2.2.2: Reading κροκύφαντον with MS T, and retaining πλεγμάτιον.

2.3.3: Reading ἀεὶ δόγματα ἔστω with MSS TC.

2.10.3: Retaining the MSS reading φιλοσοφίας ἀξίως.

2.12.1-2: Punctuating with a full stop after νεκρά and no punctuation after ἐφιστάναι (Zuntz).

2.16.2: Reading, with Farquharson, <ὑφ'> ἧς ἐν μέρει ἕκασται τῶν etc.

3.1.1: Retaining the genitives τῆς θεωρίας etc., with the MSS.

3.2.12: Retaining the MSS reading διασυνίστασθαι.

3.3.6: Ignoring Dalfen's addition and reading, with Farquharson, ὅσῳ περίεστι τὸ ὑπερετοῦν.

3.4.5: Retaining μόνα γὰρ τὰ ἑαυτοῦ πρὸς ἐνέργειαν ἔχει with MS T.

3.6.3: Retaining MS T's καὶ τὸ σόν.

4.3.1: Retaining the text bracketed by Dalfen.

4.3.6: Deleting ἔτι with Stich.

4.5: Reading κατασκευῆς with Rendall.

4.18: Omitting the μὴ before περιβλέπεσθαι with MSS AT.

4.27.1: Retaining the MSS reading ἀλλὰ κόσμος.

4.30: Reading ἔχω καὶ οὐκ ἐμμένω with Trannoy.

4.46.3: Keeping μάλιστα in its received position.

4.51.1: I delete Ἐπὶ with Zuntz.

5.1.12: Keeping the MSS ὑπὲρ τὰ μέτρα.

5.6.4: Keeping the words in the order given by the MSS.

5.8.5: Reading γοῦν with MS A.

5.8.8: Reading γὰρ instead of γοῦν.

5.8.12: Retaining the words bracketed by Dalfen.

5.12.2: Reading δυνηθείη τὸ "ὑπὸ τῶν ἀγαθῶν"· οὐ ... with Nauck.

5.15.2: Retaining the MSS τὸ ἀγαθόν.

5.16.3: Retaining the words bracketed by Dalfen.

5.23.2: Omitting Dalfen's added words.

5.23.3: Retaining the words bracketed by Dalfen.

5.26.2: Reading κατὰ τὴν τῶν μερῶν συμπάθειαν with Rendall.

5.28.2: Reading φύσει with MSS AD.

5.31.1: There is probably no need to mark a lacuna here.

5.34: Reading δικαϊκῇ with MS T.

6.10.3: Retaining the reading of MS AT αἷα γίνεσθαι.

6.14.1: With Farquharson, I transfer the clause translated "or merely the ownership of a large number of slaves" to this point from a few lines later (after "some other expertise").

6.15.2: Reading ἐφ᾽ οὗ στῆναι οὐκ ἔξεστιν with the MSS, and transferring the clause with Farquharson.

6.20.1: Retaining the MSS reading ἐρραγεὶς and the words bracketed by Dalfen.

6.23.1: With MS T, I omit the καὶ before κοινωνικῶς.

6.25: I retain the MSS ὁμοῦ.

6.26: I do not follow Dalfen in his transposition of τί οὖν . . . ἀντοργιῇ.

6.30.11: Reading μένειν ἐν τόπῳ with Theiler.

6.31: Retaining the words bracketed by Dalfen.

6.35.1: Reading πῶς οἱ with the MSS.

6.38: Reading ἄλλῳ ἄλλα (with Corais) . . . ταῦτα (Schenkl).

6.40.3: Retaining τὰ ἑαυτοῦ with the MSS.

6.44.3: Retaining συμβαίνοντα with the MSS.

6.45.2: There is probably no reason to obelize the text, though one could add a συμφέρει if the ellipsis was felt to be too harsh.

7.14.2: Retaining τὰ παθόντα with the MSS.

7.16.1: The text of this paragraph is badly corrupt in several respects. In this first sentence, one cannot be sure of Dalfen's addition, but it makes reasonable sense.

7.16.3: Reading, with Farquharson, εἰ δύναται· καὶ λεγέτω ... πάσχει τὸ ψυχάριον ... τὸ λυπούμενον· τὸ δὲ περὶ ...

7.17.1: Reading ἢ ἡγεμονικὸν ἀγαθὸν with Gataker.

7.24.1: A very difficult passage. With the help of several editorial suggestions, I read ὅταν πολλάκις ἐνῇ, ἐναποθνήσκει τὸ εὔσχημον καὶ τὸ τελευταῖον ...

7.31.4: Reading πάντα νομιστί, ἐτεῇ δὲ λίαν ὀλίγα.

7.32-34: I retain the captions bracketed by Dalfen.

7.48: Retaining the epigraph found in the two best MSS.

7.49.1: Adding καὶ with Trannoy.

7.55.6: Reading ἕξει with Richards.

7.56: With Theiler, I read δὴ instead of δεῖ, and with Farquharson I add μὴ before βεβιωκότα.

7.58.3: Reading ὅτι καὶ διάφορον <ὃ πράσσεις καὶ ἀδιάφορον> ἐφ' οὗ ἡ πρᾶξις with Marchant.

7.65: Reading ἀπάνθρωποι with Casaubon.

7.66.3: Reading ἐκείνων after a conjecture of Schenkl's.

7.68.3: Retaining ἢ θεοῦ with the MSS.

7.68.4: Retaining the MSS's datives.

7.75.1: Retaining ἀλόγιστα with the MSS.

8.1.6: Reading ἐλεύθερον with MS T.

8.3.2: Reading ἐκείνων with Farquharson.

8.5.2: Retaining ἴδε αὐτὸ with the MSS.

8.18: Retaining the words bracketed by Dalfen.

8.25.1: Reading Ἁδριανόν with most editors.

8.29.2: Retaining κατὰ φύσιν as the last words of this paragraph.

8.30: I read καὶ περιτράνως.

8.31.2: There is a gap of indeterminate length in the Greek, but the general sense of the missing words is plain.

8.34.5: Not that it affects the translation, but I retain ἐποίησεν with the MSS.

8.35.1: Reading ἔδωκεν (Schultz) ἡ τῶν ὅλων φύσις (Gataker).

8.36.1: Reading ἐπιγεγενῆσθαι καὶ ἐπιγενήσεσθαι with Marchant.

8.38-39: I make κρίνων, φησί, σοφωτάτοις the end of §38, not the beginning of §39.

8.41.5: Reading ἔξωθεν ἐμποδίζει after a suggestion of Dalfen's.

8.45.2: Retaining the MSS's ὀρεγομένη.

8.48.1: Not that it affects the translation, but I read ποιοῦν τι rather than the ποιοῦντι of the major MSS.

8.48.2: Retaining the words bracketed by Dalfen.

8.52.1-2: Removing the changes introduced by Dalfen.

8.52.3: I read ἔπαινον ἢ ψόφον διώκων.

9.1.10: Reading πάντα (Schenkl) instead of κατὰ τὸ.

9.3.5: Retaining ἠθῶν with the MSS.

9.8-9: With Casaubon, I move πάντα from the end of §8 to the beginning of §9.

9.9.10: Retaining νῦν with the MSS.

9.22.2: Retaining νοῦν with the MSS.

9.23.2: Retaining the words bracketed by Dalfen.

9.28.1: Reading ταὐτά with Gataker.

9.28.3: I punctuate on the understanding that τὸ ὅλον is adverbial.

9.29.2: Following Farquarson, I transfer the sentence ὡς ... μεστά to after διανοοῦ.

9.29.5: Reading οὐ μικρόν τί with MS T.

9.29.7: Reading ἕψομαι with Wilamowitz.

9.35.1: Retaining καλῶς with the MSS.

9.35.2: I punctuate without the question mark, and I delete ὃ with Casaubon, but otherwise retain the words bracketed by Dalfen.

9.37.3: Reading πρὸς τῶν θεῶν with Casaubon.

9.39.2: Reading λέγειν with Farquharson.

9.41.2: Retaining ἐὰν νοσῇς with the MSS.

9.42.8: Reading καινὸν instead of κακὸν with Kronenberg.

10.7.1-2: Reading φύσει for φημί, twice (Corais).

10.7.5: Comparison with the wording of 4.14, 4.21.2, and 6.24 suggests that we should read σπερματικὸν λόγον.

10.7.9: Reading τῷ ὄντι with Farquharson.

10.8.6: Reading μένειν ἐπὶ for the first μεμνῆσθαι, following a suggestion by Trannoy.

10.12.1: I suggest ἀπὸ ἑαυτοῦ.

10.13.2: Retaining the MSS's ᾧ γίνεται.

10.15.2: Retaining the MSS's ἐν ὄρει.

10.18: Reading ὥστε θνῄσκειν with Morus.

10.19.3: Not including Dalfen's added ἄλλοις.

10.30.1: Retaining ἀργύριον with the MSS and adding ἢ after κρίνων with Reiske.

10.31.1: Swapping the places of "Severus" and "Xenophon," with Leopold.

10.36.1: Retaining κακόν with the MSS.

10.38.1: Reading ἐνέργεια with Marchant.

11.6.5: Retaining ἐπίστησον with the MSS.

11.9.1: Retaining the words bracketed by Dalfen.

11.16.2: Retaining the words bracketed by Dalfen.

11.18.9: Reading παθεῖν with MS A.

11.18.17: Retaining the MSS's εὐαφῶς.

11.18.18: Reading ἤ τοι with Marchant.

11.19.2: Reading τραχείαις ἢ λείαις <κινήσεσιν> with Fournier. Brilliant.

11.20.2: Retaining φυσικὴν with the MSS.

11.21.3: Retaining ὁμοία with the MSS.

12.3.4: Reading περιηγέι with Rendall.

12.4.1: Reading περὶ αὑτοῦ with Gataker.

12.11: Reading Ἡλίκην (MS T, from the end of §10) ἐξουσίαν.

12.11: Retaining the words bracketed by Dalfen, but prefaced with ὡς (Farquharson).

12.14.1: Reading ἀνάγκη εἱμαρμένης with some MSS.

12.15: Deleting ἤ with Reiske.

12.16.1: Reading οὐ κατέκρινεν with Corais.

12.16.2: I delete ἐν τοῖς σύκοις. See 4.6: Marcus knew perfectly well that the fruit does not produce the familiar acidic sap of fig trees.

12.17: Reading ἐπὶ σοί (Haines).

12.24.3: Reading ἄφνω with MS A.

RECOMMENDED READING

Since Marcus's focus is almost entirely ethical, so is the focus of the bibliography. I have kept it short and Anglophone, on the assumption that many readers of this book are likely to be students and other members of the intelligent general public. As for those who are professional ancient philosophers, they already know where to go to expand my list in a more scholarly direction. However, some publications that illuminate narrower themes are mentioned as appropriate in the notes.

Marcus's Historical Environment: The two best recent general histories of Rome are M. Beard, *SPQR: A History of Ancient Rome* (Profile, 2015), and G. Woolf, *Rome: An Empire's Story* (Oxford University Press, 2012). Both are very readable, as is D. Potter, *The Emperors of Rome: The Story of Imperial Rome from Julius Caesar to the Last Emperor* (Quercus, 2007).

Three books on Marcus focus more on history than philosophy: the classic study (first published in 1966) is A. Birley, *Marcus Aurelius: A Life*, Rev. ed. (Routledge, 1987); then there are G. Adams, *Marcus Aurelius in the Historia Augusta and Beyond* (Lexington, 2013), and P. Kovács, *Marcus Aurelius' Rain Miracle and the Marcomannic Wars* (Brill, 2009).

Marcus's Philosophical Environment: Stoicism arose early in the Hellenistic period (323–30 BCE), along with other schools and trends, of which Marcus was clearly aware. They can all be studied with the help of K. Algra, J. Barnes, J. Mansfeld, and M. Schofield (eds.), *The Cambridge History of Hellenistic Philosophy* (Cambridge University Press, 1999); A. A. Long, *Hellenistic Philosophy: Stoics, Epicureans, Sceptics*, 2nd ed. with updated bibliography (Bristol Classical Press, 1986); and J. Sellars, *Hellenistic Philosophy* (Oxford University Press, 2018). The last mentioned is particularly readable. There is also a brilliant short introduction: R. Sharples, "Philosophy for Life," in *The Cambridge Companion to the Hellenistic World*, ed. G. Bugh (Cambridge University Press, 2006), 223–240.

The most thorough sourcebook, containing translations of ancient sources for Hellenistic philosophy, is A. A. Long and D. Sedley, *The Hellenistic Philosophers*, 2 vols. (Cambridge University Press, 1987). This book is indispensable for every serious student; the first volume contains translations and commentary, the second the Greek and Latin texts. More handy is the excellent shorter collection by B. Inwood and L. Gerson, *Hellenistic Philosophy: Introductory Readings*, 2nd ed. (Hackett, 1997).

For philosophy during the principate in particular, three outstanding studies are P. Brunt, "Stoicism and the Principate," in *Studies in Stoicism*, ed. by M. Griffin and A. Samuels, with M. Crawford (Oxford University Press, 2013), 275–309; G. Reydams-Schils, *The Roman Stoics: Self, Responsibility, and Affection* (University of Chicago Press, 2005); and M. Trapp, *Philosophy in the Roman Empire: Ethics, Politics and Society* (Ashgate, 2007). A couple of short articles are also worth mentioning: C. Gill, "Stoic Writers of the Imperial Era," in *The Cambridge History of Greek and Roman Political Thought*, ed. C. Rowe and M. Schofield (Cambridge University Press, 2000), 597–615; and J. Sellars, "Stoic Practical Philosophy in the Imperial Period," in *Greek and Roman Philosophy, 100 BC–200 AD*, Vol. 1, ed. R. Sorabji and R. Sharples (Institute of Classical Studies, 2007), 115–140.

Marcus was attracted to the therapeutic aspect of philosophy. For this the essential books are P. Hadot, *What Is Ancient Philosophy?* trans. M. Chase (Harvard University Press, 2002); and M. Nussbaum, *The Therapy of Desire: Theory and Practice in Hellenistic Ethics* (Princeton University Press, 1994; reprint, 2009, with new introduction).

Stoicism: A short but learned introduction to Stoicism is readily available on the web: D. Baltzly, "Stoicism," in *The Stanford Encyclopedia of Philosophy*, https://plato.stanford.edu/entries/stoicism. B. Inwood's *Stoicism: A Very Short Introduction* (Oxford University Press, 2018) is exemplary. Somewhat longer is the eminently readable and informative J. Sellars, *Stoicism* (Acumen/

University of California Press, 2006). All three are highly recommended, and the early chapters of Brennan's book (listed just below) also serve as a very accessible introduction. Then there is an invaluable collection of essays by various hands: B. Inwood (ed.), *The Cambridge Companion to the Stoics* (Cambridge University Press, 2003).

Some books on Stoicism with narrower focuses have been mentioned in the notes to the Introduction or translation, but I list four here for their excellence and because I found them particularly illuminating for reading Marcus: T. Brennan, *The Stoic Life: Emotions, Duties, and Fate* (Oxford University Press, 2005); M. Graver, *Stoicism and Emotion* (University of Chicago Press, 2007); B. Inwood, *Ethics and Human Action in Early Stoicism* (Oxford University Press, 1985); and J. Sellars, *The Art of Living: The Stoics on the Nature and Function of Philosophy*, 2nd ed. (Bristol Classical Press, 2009).

Marcus Aurelius's Stoicism: Nearly all questions about Marcus can be answered by consulting M. van Ackeren (ed.), *A Companion to Marcus Aurelius* (Wiley-Blackwell, 2012). Shorter general accounts are R. Kamtekar, "Marcus Aurelius," in *The Stanford Encyclopedia of Philosophy*, https://plato.stanford.edu/entries/marcus-aurelius; and P. Brunt, "Marcus Aurelius in His *Meditations*," in *Studies in Stoicism*, ed. M. Griffin and A. Samuels, with M. Crawford (Oxford University Press, 2013), 360–393. By far the best book-length account is J. Sellars, *Marcus Aurelius* (Routledge, 2020).

A. S. L. Farquharson, *The Meditations of Marcus Aurelius Antoninus*, 2 vols. (Oxford University Press, 1944) still holds the field as the only detailed scholarly edition of the book; in some respects, it is rather dated now. C. Gill, *Marcus Aurelius: Meditations, Books 1–6* (Oxford University Press, 2013) is a translation and philosophical commentary. P. Hadot, *The Inner Citadel: The* Meditations *of Marcus Aurelius*, trans. M. Chase (Harvard University Press, 1998) is an idiosyncratic work, though filled with insights, that reads *Meditations* as a series of "spiritual exercises." R. B. Rutherford, *The* Meditations *of Marcus Aurelius: A Study* (Oxford University Press, 1989) is the only book that treats Marcus's work as literature as well as philosophy.

Anyone interested in the scholarly question of the degree to which Marcus was not a pure Stoic should consult the following papers: J. Rist, "Are You a Stoic? The Case of Marcus Aurelius," in *Jewish and Christian Self-Definition*, ed. B. Meyer and E. Sanders (Fortress, 1982), 23–45; E. Asmis, "The Stoicism of Marcus Aurelius," in *Aufstieg und Niedergang der römischen Welt* II. 36.3, ed. W. Haase (de Gruyter, 1989), 2228–2252; J. Annas, "Marcus Aurelius: Ethics and Its Background," *Rhizai* 2 (2004): 103–119; J. Cooper, "Moral Theory and Moral Improvement: Marcus Aurelius," in *Knowledge, Nature, and the Good: Essays on Ancient Philosophy* (Princeton University Press, 2004), 335–368; C. Gill, "Marcus Aurelius' *Meditations*: How Stoic and How Platonic?" in *Platonic Stoicism/Stoic Platonism: The Dialogue Between Platonism and Stoicism in Antiquity*, ed. M. Bonazzi and C. Helmig (Leuven University Press, 2007), 189–207; B. Inwood, "What Kind of Stoic Are You? The Case of Marcus Aurelius," in *The Passionate Mind: Essays in Honor of John M. Rist*, ed. B. David (Academia, 2020), 155–180.

ROBIN WATERFIELD is a British classical scholar, translator, and editor, specializing in ancient Greek philosophy and history. He lives in Greece.